ATRIA
BOOKS

Dear reader,

When I first read the proposal for *NERD: Adventures in Fandom from This Universe to the Multiverse*, I knew I'd found a kindred spirit in Maya.

Maya Phillips is a *New York Times* critic at large who has covered everything from theater to the latest Marvel release. But her love of art, of storytelling, started with an all-too-familiar opening scrawl and a fandom that has transcended its core audience to become part of the larger cultural canon.

From a galaxy far, far away to the streets of Gotham, the Hogwarts School of Witchcraft and Wizardy, Sunnydale High School, the Doctor's TARDIS, and the Upside Down and beyond, fandom has been a quintessential part of Maya's life, helping to shape her identity and view of the world from a young age. And she's not alone.

Over the last few decades, a cultural shift has occurred. Being a geek or a nerd isn't so niche anymore thanks to the widespread popularity of some of pop culture's biggest blockbusters and cult favorites. And sharing your favorite world or characters has become shorthand for giving someone else a peek into your soul, an idea of who you are—or wish you were.

In *NERD*, Maya is going back to the beginning and exploring what her favorite fandoms have meant to her and the larger impact they've had on those consumed by them. What do they teach audiences about themselves and the world, about who gets to be the hero—and why, so often, does it end up being kids who need to save the day? Maya sheds new light on some of my own favorites, interweaving personal anecdotes that drive home why we're so drawn to these stories and their universes. I hope you enjoy the nostalgic ride and Maya's incisive critiques and observations as much as I have.

Happy reading!

Mlglesias

Melanie Iglesias Pérez
Editor

Atria Books | 1230 Avenue of the Americas | New York, NY 10020

NERD

Adventures in Fandom
from This Universe
to the Multiverse

Maya Phillips

ATRIA BOOKS

New York · London · Toronto · Sydney · New Delhi

An Imprint of Simon & Schuster, Inc.
1230 Avenue of the Americas
New York, NY 10020

Copyright © 2022 by Maya Phillips

First Atria Books hardcover edition July 2022

ATRIA BOOKS and colophon are trademarks of Simon & Schuster, Inc.

For information about special discounts for bulk purchases, please
contact Simon & Schuster Special Sales at 1-866-506-1949 or
business@simonandschuster.com.

The Simon & Schuster Speakers Bureau can bring authors to your live event. For
more information or to book an event, contact the Simon & Schuster Speakers
Bureau at 1-866-248-3049 or visit our website at www.simonspeakers.com.

Interior design by Kyoko Watanabe

Manufactured in the United States of America

1 3 5 7 9 10 8 6 4 2

Library of Congress Cataloging-in-Publication Data is available.

ISBN 978-1-9821-6577-2
ISBN 978-1-9821-6579-6 (ebook)

For all my favorite stories
And for all the fans who love them

*"We're all stories in the end.
Just make it a good one, eh?"*

—The Doctor

CONTENTS

NERD

NERD

Introduction

A long time ago in a galaxy far, far away . . .

Let's begin there. It's as good a place as any—I've never been a big fan of beginnings. Give me a good ending any day: the grand wake and procession for Morpheus, the king of dreams; Gandalf, Frodo, and Bilbo cruising off to the afterlife.

But if we must begin, let's begin here, at a distance, some time in the past, and not so far, far away as a galaxy but maybe the next borough or state, or the opposite coast, or even, reader, maybe across some other large expanse of land or body of water. If you're not nearby, sorry to make you travel, but we're going to start in New York.

It's 1996, more or less, so let's say 1996, and let's say it's summer, because who can resist the soft warmth of a mid-June or early July day?

Early summer, 1996, late morning in my parents' bedroom. It's bright outside with some cover, though we can see only little whispers of light through the half-opened blinds. The bedspread is untidy, which my mother hates, but this bit of lived-in mess is a small comfort on a weekend. These kinds of mornings I pluck from memory, they're always on a Saturday, when there's no school and, sure, there are weekend chores to be done to a soundtrack of kid-pop hits on Radio Disney, but before then is a lineup of superhero cartoons and maybe even a movie.

If you look to my right, upon a cocoa-brown shag carpet (as I said, we're in the '90s), my parents have a stack of movies lined up by the TV set, the Leaning Tower of Pisa, if Long Island at all resembled Italy and if the tower were made up of miscellaneous VHS tapes.

But somewhere in that stack of workout-tape-and-birthday-video Jenga is a boxed set of three videos. When I say I learned early the beauty of a three-movie boxed set—before Peter Jackson could even dream of the farthest reaches of Mordor—I mean to say that I believed in the holy power of a trinity. I believed in the ceremony of sliding each video out of the box, then out of its individual cardboard sleeve, an image of Darth Vader's helmet blazing on the front of the collection.

I'm watching *The Empire Strikes Back*, the early scenes on the arctic planet Hoth, on this summer day, and I'm unbothered, unworried, as I watch Luke in the cave of an Abominable (space) Snowman. Though I'm only six, I'm not scared, because this all feels familiar, in this echo chamber of memory—I've already witnessed this scene countless times before.

If this wasn't my earliest brush with fandom, it was certainly one of the first. Luke Skywalker, with his floppy hair and doofy, lackadaisical strut, was my first crush. I also envied him. I wanted to be someone meant for adventures beyond the home where she was raised, someone meant for the stars and tests of courage and integrity. I wanted to have the universe crack open and reveal to me all its impossibilities, which would look something like magic. Luke Skywalker wasn't the roguish Han Solo, stylishly cynical and nonplussed, or the headstrong Leia, spirited and worldly, already a leader in the resistance, but a farm boy about to have his world broadened to a story so much larger than his own.

I won't say that all fandoms are connected, that flipping open one comic book will then initiate you into everything from *Akira* to *Batman Beyond*. And perhaps it wasn't quite that way for me. But I do see my fandoms as linked, like stars in a constellation, Tatooine to the Moon Kingdom in the Silver Millennium to Gallifrey to the secret planet Miranda, creating a map of a culture that helped define the way I perceive and interact with the world.

Years after I watched my first *Star Wars* film, I'm grateful for the mainstream, even as it has bloated to ingest nerd culture in the past few years. No longer is *Star Wars* just the campy personal treasure that we had in our boxed set. Superheroes rule the box office. Anime is omnipresent. I've caught Captain America shields and Konohagakure headbands and green Survey Corps hoodies on my subway commute; Goku has casually flown through the streets of Midtown during the Macy's Thanksgiving Day Parade. For all the ways the visibility of nerd culture has removed the air of cultlike exclusivity around fandoms, it has also made what I do as a culture critic so much easier.

Before the superhero boom in the last decade or so, I would never have been able to imagine that comic books—and graphic novels and anime and sci-fi and fantasy and everything else in the ever-expanding realm of nerdy pop culture—could be something I could write about for major prestige publications.

Still, I've gotten the occasional quizzical glance from editors confused by my beat—theater and books, okay, but anime, sci-fi, and comics? "You're all over the place," an editor once remarked, with some amusement, my résumé in hand. And in my worst moments, I'd agree, conceding that I'm erratic in my interests, that the highbrow has no place next to the lowbrow of popular culture.

But here, in this book, I hope you won't find me at my worst. Instead, I hope you'll find me at the same spot where I was back in 1996—glued to the TV screen as a farm boy uses his newly awakened powers to summon a laser sword into his hand.

To think that the elaborate sets and costumes and puppets and exchanges between princesses and rogues isn't a kind of theater is narrow-minded. To think that dual suns rising in a sky isn't a kind of poetry is absurd. To think that highbrow auteurism, whether it's "serious" cinema, prestige television, opera, ballet, theater, poetry, or fiction, is threatened by or so far elevated from the vision of a USS Enterprise or the battles of a millennial loafer named Scott Pilgrim is to reject the idea that *anything* furiously loved by a group of people can be called a fandom, and that anyone who submits to that love and owns it with a passion can be called a nerd. I'm not saying my fandoms are unimpeachable—we also survived George Lucas's cheesiest dialogue and lived to critique them ad infinitum on the internet—but that they are worthy of my love and critical attention not despite but because of their flaws.

Critics are faced with an unfair task: to take an art form they love and break it apart, meticulously examining its pieces. And there's the vision of the critic as a judge of the highest order—a fearsome creature perched on a pedestal—but that person, of course, is a contrivance.

It's the job of the critic to be subjective and to love, at least respect, the art form she is examining. She sits in the center of a Venn diagram of fan and critic, with her personal and professional investment being the point of juncture. Before I was a critic, I was a fan. My childhood—and now, my adulthood—has been shaped by my relationship to nerd culture.

I expect you, reading this, have your own story about your fandoms. Your own thoughts. Perhaps your fandoms intersect with mine. Perhaps they don't. Perhaps you don't define yourself as a nerd at all, hate pop culture, and firmly declare yourself a velvet-waistcoated connoisseur of *Culture*, italicized with a capital *C*, and you've picked up this book only on a whim.

If so, nevertheless, welcome. Sit down for a while. Hang up your coat in the blue police call box you'll find down the hall; a bright corgi named Ein can show you the way. I have something to share with you—the most I can offer, as a critic, to something I love: my time and attention, my reflections and observations, and, finally, myself, my personal accounts and memories.

Here you'll find my thoughts on ever-growing franchises, anime, convention culture, '90s animated cartoons, Black heroes, time travel narratives, the politics of fantasy and space

Westerns, Afro-surrealism, boundary-expanding shows about anxiety and mental illness, and gods and multiple worlds. You'll encounter a motley crew of Avengers, Sailor Scouts, Saiyans, bounty hunters, Wakandans, samurai, space cowboys, mutants, wizards, psychics, vampire hunters, and Jedi knights. And you'll see me, through my years of fandoms, cons, and being the best scruffy-looking nerf-herder I can be.

So now that you're settled in, let's finally begin—for real this time.

Again, it's 1996, and I'm watching a story from a long time ago in a galaxy far, far away. My own story isn't from that long ago and it's much closer, so I won't mind if you sidle up beside me to see the words angling up on the screen and disappearing out into space. I'm at home here, and I hope you'll be too. May you browse, cull it over, and keep what you like. May you find exciting, fantastic new ways to be a fan.

Oh, and . . .

May the Force be with you.

I.
Gotham City, Star City, Metropolis, USA

On building up and breaking down superhero mythologies

I found Gotham City one night when I was about seven years old. I remember the stern, menacing geometry of the skyscrapers. Crisp lines in the perfectly square and rectangular windows, the sharp angles of the buildings. Everything dark—the windows a steely, frosted gray or a muted, impersonal beige, the sky behind it all a hellish red clotted with black, a sky recalling a violent wound. But though the aesthetic hinted at violence and wrongdoing, the foreboding vibe of a suspenseful scene in the horror movie before the attack, the architecture was unimpeachably clean and glossy, every surface unblemished and aggressively modern in design. This was the Gotham from the 1993 film *Batman: Mask of the Phantasm*, which I watched one night when I went with my parents on a trip to Manhattan.

This trip was unremarkable except for the fact that we didn't venture much to the city, despite our proximity to it, just a roughly fifty-minute train ride from the suburbs into the beating heart of the metropolis, with its frenzied action and lights. My parents hated the city, were wearied by all its fuss as though it was a petulant child they were forced to babysit on occasion. My father, Brooklyn-born and Queens-raised, worked for the MTA, but saw Manhattan as a necessary evil. Queens was home and Brooklyn was the borough that was unimpeachably cool, where his family would meet up at his grandfather's brownstone in Bed-Stuy for generations of gossip and laughter and food. Long Island was where we settled. My mother, born in the Caribbean and raised in Queens, walking distance from my father's house, disparaged the city—Brooklyn, the Bronx, Manhattan—as too noisy, too busy, too dirty, too much of a bother. She sat stiffly on subway trains, careful not to touch anything with her leather-gloved hands, eyed the train tracks and sidewalks for rats, skittishly maneuvered around the inevitable homeless person or angry passerby yelling to nothing but the air in front of their face. I, on the other hand, loved the action and excitement; every second in the city felt like I was living in a frame of a film. I felt the energy of New York as though it lived under my skin, a constant buzz of anticipation—of what exactly, I didn't know. The city was a place of endless opportunities and chance encounters. I loved the mystery, imagined the city like a magician, ready to pull something out of its hat.

When we went to Midtown for Broadway, those special occasions when we trooped through the crowds, my parents were both miserable. My father walking too quickly up ahead because we were late; my mother walking behind in her heels, eyes alert and skeptical; and me, at her side, grinning like it was my birthday. And it was, in a sense. Born in Queens, I was a citizen of the city as though it was its own country, and I celebrated it for all its brilliance and ugliness. The city worked hard and was honest but knew how to have fun. It knew danger, and so I feared it a bit, whenever I considered it without my parents at my side. But in those short trips, it never showed me anything that would make me scoff or recoil or sigh like my parents did. I wrapped my arms around it and embraced it in all its magnitude.

My parents' friends—who wore the honorary titles of "uncle" and "aunt"—lived in the Lower East Side. I don't remember how we got there—it could have been via Aladdin's magic carpet or Falkor, for all I know—but I recall simply arriving, and walking downtown, which was so much more demure than the Times Square I knew. I mostly recall it in terms of colors: the brown fortress that was the apartment complex, which seemed to stretch up and out infinitely and seemed to watch the streets around it with its many windows like myriad eyes, and the concrete gray of the inside, startling in its anonymity. Inside, their apartment was compact yet welcoming. I loved the utility of city apartment living. (Fifteen years later, as I tried to squeeze a full-size bed and dresser into my bedroom in a similarly compact Brooklyn apartment that was nevertheless home to two cats, one dog, and three humans, I would come to question this so-called love.) And then there was the proximity to everything: neighbors down the hall, bodegas on the corner, taxis passing on the streets below. While the adults busied themselves with adult conversations about things hopelessly boring to a child my age (probably taxes? Gas prices? Discount furniture?), I plopped in front of the TV, which was playing *Batman: Mask of the Phantasm.*

I didn't discover until later that Gotham City was a kind of alternative New York City; the name itself an explicit allusion to the fact. After all, that night, as I looked at an animated Gotham from the living room of a real Gotham City apartment, I recognized the heights and the shadows but missed the classic skyline and the various landmarks. Batman's city was like a cosplay of my own; reminiscent of the real thing but still wearing a mask. But there's a sense of the pathetic fallacy at work here: this was the city as owned by, and reflective of, its tortured hero. This was the city as Batcave: the buildings rising like stalagmites, a rust-red darkness behind them. There was light, but only the faintest beams, rising up from the ground, angled up toward the highest buildings front and center, creating shadows on the streets below, where the less fortunate denizens lived and worked.

Gotham was also strangely timeless, its classic art deco style touched with a bit of futurism.

Gotham is able to contain the contradictions that come with it being a fiction. In the opening to the film, any approximation of the size of the landscape eludes the eye. The city seems confined in a kind of bubble and yet also seems to extend to infinity, the last rows of buildings fading into the sky until they, too, are just shadows, faint outlines being swallowed by the darkness lurking behind them.

Throughout the film, Batman appears in silhouette, only the white triangles of his eyes in the mask visible. He is styled like the buildings, his body's architecture sharp and pointed, from his triangular bat ears and square jaw to his broad shoulders. The final shot of the movie is of Batman standing sentinel on a rooftop, looking up at the Bat-Signal, then spreading out his cape and flying offscreen; the rest of the city is swallowed by the blackness of his costume.

Batman's New York appealed to my love for drama and darkness, but it was not the only New York I encountered in comic book fiction, nor was it the most relatable depiction of my beloved hometown. For that, there was Peter Parker's city, which was explicitly my New York, just relocated into the Marvel universe.

In those years of Batman and Gotham, I also watched *Spider-Man: The Animated Series* on Saturday mornings, and my dad loved to remind me that Peter Parker was a New York City boy—from Queens, in fact. Forest Hills. That was a real neighborhood, he'd tell me, as though he could point out the house Peter lived in with his aunt May on a map. Peter Parker was *that* close to us, just a short drive away.

It was, after all, a drive he did on the regular. My father worked in Forest Hills, at the Forest Hills–71st Avenue Station. Despite my love for Manhattan and my father's job, I was late to the wonder that is the New York City subway system and wasn't a fan of the expensive Long Island Rail Road, although the Hempstead hub was just a twenty-minute walk from my house. So in college, when I was on break from school, I'd catch a ride with my dad to Forest Hills in the afternoon, when his shift started, so I could hop on the F train from Queens to poetry readings downtown, or hangouts with friends at coffee shops. Sometimes I would head straight into Manhattan, especially during summer break, and I'd loiter on the steps of Union Square, watching the chess players and the skateboarders and the rest of the city walking by. Other times, I'd loaf around Forest Hills, which felt cozy, down to the brick houses and red shingled roofs. I'd walk down Austin Street, staring at the picturesque dessert displays at Martha's Country Bakery, and camp out in the Barnes & Noble that used to be on 70th. I'd stay there for hours, sitting in a discreet corner on the second floor after I'd picked up something from the comics section. By the end of one summer, I had read all of *Scott Pilgrim* and a big chunk of *Sandman.*

When Sam Raimi's *Spider-Man*, starring Tobey Maguire, premiered in 2002, long before the Big Bang that would be *Iron Man* kicking off the Marvel Cinematic Universe (MCU) in 2008, my dad and I went to the movie theater, both thrilled at the prospect of one of our favorites—a hometown favorite—swinging onto the big screen. More than most heroes, Spider-Man has always been defined by his hometown. That small-town tag—*your friendly neighborhood Spider-Man*—and his signature smart-ass dialogue in the comics are what grounded Peter Parker in something more real and recognizable than a faceless city of masks and capes.

In the movie, Peter's superhero origin story starts in a lab at Columbia University during a class trip. Before his untimely death, Uncle Ben lectures Peter while they sit outside the central branch of the New York Public Library at 42nd Street, the iconic stone lions Patience and Fortitude immediately recognizable in the background. Peter runs into Mary Jane outside her waitressing job at the historic Moondance Diner in SoHo. One of the climactic scenes involves the Roosevelt Island Tramway. The city is a character in the story, illuminating our hero, and the cinematography invites us into Peter's worldview. In one scene, the camera angles up, around, and down to capture Peter scaling a brick wall, and that moment of re-direction takes us away from the distant omniscient view and brings us closer to Peter's experience of wonder at his newfound powers. The camera almost "crawls" along with Peter as he makes his way up higher. In another brief shot, after Peter figures out his chic new costume design, we swoop down low as Spider-Man swings in the direction of traffic on a Manhattan street, nearing the cars before arcing back up toward the sky. Nowadays, when I see these kinds of shots of the city, I check the landmarks and street names, trying to see if I can catch something familiar. I know there's a good chance that what I'm seeing is some street corner in Toronto or Chicago masquerading as my New York. But back then, the specifics didn't matter to me at all. All I knew was that this Manhattan towered overhead even more so than the one I'd seen myself. And yet it was easily scaled by heroes; the heroes both elevated my city and brought it down to earth.

Though Tobey Maguire's Spider-Man had New York City all to himself, the Spider-Man of the comics had a lot more company. Marvel heroes were everywhere—in the third annual issue of *The Amazing Spider-Man*, the Avengers aim to recruit Peter to their team, and in one panel, Goliath and the Wasp parade through Manhattan as a policeman declares, "Move along, Avenger! You've got traffic stalled from here to Times Square!"* In the pages of the comics, Spider-Man visits Corona Park, the Washington Square arch, the Plaza Hotel, Mount Sinai Hospital, Empire City in Yonkers, and various other landmark locations, all while encountering Thor flying through the sky in Midtown, Black Panther visiting from Wakanda, and Doctor Strange strolling, in his astral form, down the street. All these heroes, we're meant to believe, nonchalantly populate the city.

The Defenders, like Spider-Man, and more so than the Avengers, are also prominently identified as local neighborhood heroes. The

---

* Stan Lee, *The Amazing Spider-Man* (New York: Marvel, 1966), 5.

devil of Hell's Kitchen, Daredevil, keeps tabs on the streets just west of Times Square but also ventures out to Greenwich Village and the Queensboro Bridge, and makes stops at Port Authority and JFK Airport.

One may wonder at the ratio of heroes to normal citizens in this version of New York, where it seems as though every block has someone flying or swinging overhead; every rooftop, someone perched, peering over the ledge watchfully until a cry for help rings out. One may consider the question of real estate and how these heroes have divvied up their jurisdictions. Perhaps, like a game of Monopoly: the Village to Doctor Strange for $200, Midtown to the Avengers for $400, Harlem to Power Man for $800. These heroes all fight their supervillain foes, apparently just as omnipresent, in a city that embodies the ideals of fortitude and justice while also representing the crooked and criminal. The everyday citizens—commuting to work, trying to pay their rent, going to school, or living on a park bench— seem invisible, because any real-world problems they may face, like gentrification or homelessness, cannot simply be punched out of the sky by the nearest hero around. So the New Yorkers live their lives in the background as the heroes and villains play their games on the rooftops at night.

In one *Daredevil* panel, a man in a button-down and tie peeks out of the window, finger pointed upward, mouth gaping, and says, "Look! There's Daredevil . . . swinging from the rooftops above us!!" A suited man next to him responds, "What with him . . . and Spider-Man . . . and Thor . . . and the Human Torch . . . and all the other costumed cats around here . . . we'll have to keep the shades down to get any work done in this town!"* (I can empathize; more than once I've stopped working mid-task to check out the new *Star Wars* or Marvel movie trailer. With nerd culture thriving, how can we get any work done in this town?)

---

* Stan Lee, *Daredevil: The Man Without Fear!* (New York: Marvel, 1976), 15.

Though in the DC universe, Batman broods in Gotham and Superman flies through Metropolis, it's the Marvel superheroes who seem to have the comic book equivalent of New York City block parties in their issues, with so many "costumed cats" so near at hand. Stan Lee, the godfather of Marvel Comics and one of the most legendary comic book creators of all time, loved New York City, and the city loved him back. At a 2008 convention, Lee recalled one of his favorite Marvel New York crossover moments: "There was one I loved, I think it was the Fantastic Four, and they were at a ball game at Yankee Stadium and there were a lot of press photographers there. So I told Jack Kirby to draw Peter Parker in the background with a camera. And we made no mention of it, he was just in the panel, and we got about a million letters saying, 'We saw Peter Parker at the game. That's terrific.' And it made it seem like these were real characters who live in the same world and occasionally they get together. And that was something I got a big kick out of."[*]

Lee, who was born in Manhattan and raised in the Bronx, emphasized his stories' settings more than many of his peers did. In *How to Write Comics*, he writes, "The setting is vital . . . I set so many of my stories in New York City because I know it well and don't have to think too hard about it. But setting is important since it can influence how your characters think and interact with one another."[†] And in *Stan Lee's Master Class*, he advises comic book writers, "Your job is to make each setting feel believable to the reader . . . If there's anything that drives me crazy looking at today's comics, it's how often the artist barely establishes a location, then skimps on backgrounds for the rest of the scene or the whole story."[‡]

Lee's juxtaposition of costumed heroes and real New York City locations not only made these fantastical figures more realistic but el-

---

[*] Beth Accomando, "A Marvel of a Man: Stan Lee Dead at 95," *NPR*, November 12, 2018.

[†] Stan Lee, *Stan Lee's How to Write Comics* (New York: Watson-Guptill, 2011), 120.

[‡] Stan Lee, *Stan Lee's Master Class* (New York: Watson-Guptill, 2019), 119.

evated the city itself to the status of Mount Olympus, a home of gods. By the mere presence of the heroes in these stories, every detail of the city—a hot dog vendor, a bridge, a subway line—becomes something mythological and important. Whether or not you believe in divine order in real life, in the world of comics, there is undeniably a grand design that places a hero here, a newspaper stand there, a taxi over there; there is some significance to everything.

The fantasy cities of Gotham and Metropolis may remain, to an extent, static, fixed, as they are, in the bubble of their fiction. New York, however, has never been content to remain set, so the same is true of the New York that appears in comics. When I walk through the Lower East Side now, I don't recall the Lower East Side of my youth. The Bed-Stuy I knew when I was young, the one I saw when I visited my great-grandfather, is no longer there, replaced by a more gentrified version. And even Times Square, which I marveled at as a kid, though still a noxious juncture of commercial advertising, has since opened itself up, like an invitation. Walkways were expanded, creating open public spaces where tourists gather to watch buskers or take pictures or sit and rest; and the red TKTS steps to nowhere, sitting right below the Jumbotron, seemed to pop up from the concrete one day when I wasn't looking.

That happens in the comics too—suddenly the city has changed when you weren't looking. Over the years, Marvel's New York City has become more and more detailed. Despite the explicit nods to the city in the early days, the backgrounds were more generic, with plain square and rectangular buildings, vague shops and skyscrapers, and the occasional recognizable landmark. It was a function of the aesthetic, too, a more simplified approach to the illustration design of the characters and scenes on the page. But comics have always been reflections of our times, and different decades brought different fashions (e.g., Peter Parker wearing Greg Brady–style bell bottoms in the '70s), color palettes, and visual approaches. The worlds of Spider-Man and Daredevil, for example, got darker and more detailed, the panels showing off a polished design that exhibited a New York City not as bright and cheery as the one behind the smiling heroes of the '60s but more reflective of a modern world very much awake to its myriad problems.

One of the most defining moments—if not *the* most defining moment—for New York City in recent history was 9/11. All I remember of that time was a reigning sense of confusion, as the kids in my elementary school classroom seemed to halo me in a nervous frenzy of misinformation. (*A building was hit? Two? Where? Here on Long Island? In Manhattan?*) That afternoon, at home, I stood in my parents' bedroom, my mom sitting on the bed watching the news, and the image of the towers crumbling seemed like something out of a movie. Though I saw the cloud and the debris, I didn't fully comprehend it. At eleven years old, I didn't believe that I lived in a world where a human could intentionally kill thousands and forever change my city's attitude, atmosphere, and skyline. That kind of act of villainy could only be reserved for fiction—comic books, perhaps? Right?

But the event was unfathomable even in the New York City of Marvel comics. *The Amazing Spider-Man* No. 36, published that December after the attacks, had an all-black cover. An inside page, also in black, sports just two word bubbles underneath a blunt heading ("We interrupt our regularly scheduled program to bring you the following Special Bulletin."): "Longitude: 74 Degrees, 0 Minutes, 23 Seconds West. Latitude: 40 Degrees, 42 Minutes, 51 Seconds North" and "Follow the sound of sirens . . ."* The next page shows us where we are when we follow the sirens, in an aerial view of downtown Manhattan, where the foundations of what remains of the two towers are still ignited in flame, the smoke billowing out in every direction, mingling among the buildings and snaking along the streets. In the left-hand corner, Spider-Man stands looking ahead, his back to us.

---

* J. Michael Straczynski, *The Amazing Spider-Man 36* (New York: Marvel, 2001), 1.

We've so often seen the hero—Spider-Man, of course, but so many others as well—standing on some rooftop, as stoic and watchful as a statue, ready to save the day. Here we're presented with a perverse alternative: the hero in his usual spot up high, godlike, but his body language is tortured, distressed, helpless. His legs and back are tensed, his shoulders rolled in, his hands desperately clasping the sides of his head. "... God ..." is all he says, looking at the day he couldn't save. As people race the streets in search of shelter, a couple, running and grasping each other, ask Spider-Man, "Where were you?!" and "How could you let this happen?"* It's in this moment that the comic confronts the fragile nature of its own mythology and, by extension, the mythology of the city it depicts.

In comics, we may believe in justice—in clear-cut definitions of right and wrong, good and bad—and in heroes, some of whom are just normal people who were thrown into abnormal circumstances and rose to the occasion. These heroes are immortal, unstoppable. Even in the instances in which heroes have died, the very nature of the comic book genre contradicts any permanent death. The heroes come back, sometimes the same, sometimes in different forms or in a different universe; sometimes it's just the mask that's passed on to another, and yet that hero lives on. Perhaps there's no medium more stubborn than the comic book, which refuses to give up on its heroes—and, even more, will never fail to subscribe to the idea of the hero. I consider myself a cynical New Yorker, and yet I also want to believe that those stories of heroes—everyday good Samaritans, people who will stop and help you if you need it on the subway or in the street—are more common than the stories about the opposite. Even if the heroes are limitless in their worlds, they are not limitless when extracted from the fiction and held up to the reality that their fantasy is meant to mimic. There lies the problem of the uncanny valley of Marvel's New York versus New York, NY: as adaptable as the former

---

* Straczynski, *The Amazing Spider-Man* 36, 3.

can be to the changing times, the latter will always assert itself, particularly in those real moments of tragedy, like 9/11, in the minds of New Yorkers. How could Spider-Man stop the damage wrought by Hurricane Sandy? How could the Fantastic Four help disadvantaged children in poor neighborhoods? Though these heroes might be New Yorkers, their mythos never measure up to the real thing; they're swallowed by the enormity of the genuine article.

The confusion and dismay that Spider-Man encounters in No. 36—the fear of the fictional citizens paired with the hero's realization of his powerlessness, atop the comic's meta understanding of the relative powerlessness of fiction in a time of real-life catastrophe—is also the confusion and dismay of a city that for so long seemed similarly unbreakable. Though Stan Lee decided to make his heroes live in New York because it was the city he knew and loved, such a move wouldn't make sense in any old city. New York had a mythology well before it had heroes, but in New York, Lee's heroes found a landscape that could match their extraordinary stature. The events of 9/11 shook New York. Even now, its citizens—even ones who weren't personally affected by the tragedy—still hold on to some trauma. I think of it sometimes when I'm on the subway and the train stalls for one reason or another—a "police investigation," and I wonder what's being investigated. I look around the car and through the windows into the darkness of the tunnel thinking, with a dull sense of alarm, how I could escape if something were to happen. When I was at the *New Yorker*, my first week working in One World Trade, where Condé Nast keeps its offices, I felt uneasy with the history of the site; it felt like we were in the architectural equivalent of a middle finger. I walked by the memorial fountains quickly, past the tourists, as though if I lingered for too long the dead would reach their hands up from the water to grab me.

But I also remember what happened to New York afterward. The city was shaken, but there was also an aggressive kickback, with declarations of the city's strength. There is, after all, a practical point to every myth: New Yorkers mythologize the city because how else would we process its enormity, its occasional callousness, not to mention its high rents? New York City is great, but we dream it greater just to carry us through the days when it tests our mettle. And that's what we also find in the New York City in comic books. Though Spider-Man couldn't prevent the Twin Towers from falling, he and his fellow heroes (Thor, Captain America, the Thing, Cyclops, Daredevil, Scarlet Witch) and even some villains (Magneto, Doc Ock, Kingpin, Juggernaut, Doctor Doom) are there in solidarity, to help. "We are here" is the insistent refrain in several panels, and it's hard not to believe them, these fantastical characters with the power to fly, shoot lasers, and sling webs, because fans know that their fandoms exist for this very reason: to be there, to provide something extra and extraordinary when reality is bleak and lacking.

When my dad and I saw *Spider-Man* in the movie theater, it was just a few months after 9/11. Sony had needed to adjust their promotional materials by pulling a teaser trailer for the film in which Spider-Man catches a helicopter full of bank robbers by casting a giant web between the Twin Towers.* Though production of the movie was well underway way before the attacks even happened, the tone *Spider-Man* took felt, at times, preternaturally aware of the tragedy that would occur and how fans would need to see scenes of New Yorkers remaining strong and heroic in their own right.

As Green Goblin prepares to attack Spider-Man, suspended in the air, trying to save both a group of children on the Roosevelt Island tram and his love, Mary Jane Watson, he's temporarily distracted by a sudden barrage of food and trash as he flies through the sky. New Yorkers have gathered on the Queensboro Bridge; they use whatever makeshift weapons they can against the Green Goblin, shouting their support to the struggling hero. "You mess with

---

* Josh Weiss, "Watch: 'Lost' Twin Towers Teaser for Sam Raimi's *Spider-Man* Remastered from Original Print," *Syfy.com*, 2019.

Spidey, you mess with New York!" one man yells. "You mess with one of us, you mess with all of us!" declares another.* The moment is heartwarming because the random bystanders on the bridge are a synecdochical representation of the city Spider-Man protects; he's as much a part of New York as New York is part of him, and New York will never let him down. Even when it's in trouble, New York will fight back. The city has the advantage of embodying a convenient paradox: New York contains multitudes, with brilliantly diverse neighborhoods and residents, but New York is also mono-lithic, as though the city's heights and history swallow everything in its shadow. When the people on the bridge cheer on Spider-Man, they're not meant to be individuals but something more, a unified vision of a city. The same sentiment cropped up in the aftermath of 9/11, with the prevalence of phrases like "New York Strong"—all of us, one New York, recovering.

But when I think about New York City post-9/11 and our new-found sense of communal strength and everyday heroics, I think of a scene from Sam Raimi's follow-up, *Spider-Man 2*, from 2004. During a fight with Doctor Octopus, Spider-Man has to stop a runaway sub-way train on elevated tracks. He uses his webs and brute strength to force the train to a stop just before it's about to topple over the end of the tracks, but he's left so exhausted that he slumps forward and nearly falls himself. But hands catch him—the hands of passengers reaching out through the windows to pull him into the car—and raise him over their heads, passing him along until they can rest him on the floor. The passengers' awe as they look at Peter Parker's un-masked face and their promise that they'll keep his secret is affecting, sure, but the part that stays with me is the laying on of hands. There's religion in this moment: the hero symbolically martyrs himself, his body pressed to the front of the train as though on a cross, and is then delivered by the hands of the faithful, handled tenderly as though he

---

* Sam Raimi, director. *Spider-Man* (Sony Pictures, 2002).

himself is an offering. In these fictional moments, there doesn't need to be any mention of our city's resilience through a time of shared trauma; it is there in subtext.

New York is destroyed on the regular—and London and San Francisco sometimes, for a shot of the Eye falling or the Golden Gate Bridge crumbling; and, yes, Tokyo, with many decades of a giant lizard tromping through its metropolis. But New York holds such a unique appeal to your basic, run-of-the-mill chronicler of the apocalypse: disaster is so much more triggering when it finds a home in the places we keep fixed in our memory. What's more iconic and memorable than the New York City skyline, the Empire State Building, and the Statue of Liberty? After years and years of weathering various fictional ends to my city—*Cloverfield*, *The Day After Tomorrow*, *I Am Legend*, etc., etc.—I began avoiding the New York City apocalypse stories. There are only so many shots of crumbled skyscrapers that a New Yorker can take. But the sting I felt while watching these movies was caused by my shared memory of the real disaster that changed the city.

At the climax of the first *Avengers* movie, writer-director Joss Whedon lets loose on Manhattan, showing an army of aliens crashing into buildings and facing off against our heroes in front of Grand Central Terminal, the streets surrounding it covered in rubble and crashed cars. In one of the film's final scenes, we watch TV footage capturing the aftermath and the responses of New Yorkers, politicians, and newscasters. THANK YOU AVENGERS is spray-painted on a wall, a woman puts an OPEN sign on her shop, and a young man dressed as Captain America, wearing the finest that, one can assume, Party City had to offer, skateboards along. Stan Lee himself makes his usual cheeky cameo, turning from his chess match in the park to scoff at the camera, "Superheroes in New York? *Give me a break.*"*

---

* Joss Whedon, *The Avengers* (Marvel Studios, 2012).

The tone of the *Avengers*—the indefatigable optimism of comic book heroism matched with Whedon's signature flourishes of humor and quippy dialogue—thankfully waters down the impact of the movie's images of destruction. The pedestrians are absent, so there is no sense of death or injury, and a team of superpowered (or impressively able) humans—and an actual god—are on the streets and in the skies with a fighting chance at victory. It's not a one-sided attack but a battle, and the villains aren't humans acting on a plot of mass terror, but indistinguishable alien henchmen ordered to invade. Even at the end of the day, despite the city being newly transformed by an extraterrestrial catastrophe, there's no sorrow, just hope and that New York City attitude—and shawarma.

But even if it wasn't the movie's prerogative to make its central battle a bold-faced allusion to real-life disasters (and thank Odin for that), other properties in the Marvel universe did adopt the event as part of the franchise's collective history.

The television series *Agents of S.H.I.E.L.D.* lined up its narrative so as to coincide with and reference the developments in *Avengers* at the time the movie was released. The Marvel TV shows, which generally took a graver, more mature approach to their stories, referenced the battle of New York—the "incident"—with a degree of shock and solemnity that felt reminiscent of the ways real New Yorkers talked about the attacks, especially in those first few years.

But even in the worst scenarios, fictional or otherwise, New York City is always still standing. Ask any born-and-bred New Yorker, and they'll tell you that living in this city, in itself, can be a heroic act. It's crowded, it's loud, it's prohibitively expensive, and sometimes dangerous. Sometimes it's a target.

In 2018 we were treated to another New York, that of Miles Morales, a Spider-Man not from Queens but Brooklyn, and who stumbles through the neighborhood trying to grow into his new superhero identity. I had seen an early preview at Comic Con, surrounded by whooping nerds, giddy with excitement, then saw the movie proper in a packed theater in Brooklyn. The girl sitting next to me was squirrelly in her enthusiasm; she literally sat on the edge of her seat throughout the whole movie and gasped and laughed and applauded unreservedly. And she wasn't the only one.

Like anyone else who has ever seen a single movie or TV show or even glanced at a comic book, I've seen countless visions of my city, either dressed up in fiction or rendered with realism. Each one feels different—Gotham's mean mug is perfectly suited for the exploits of a tortured man who runs around in a bat costume, but it's less the New York of my taste than, say, the Manhattan and Queens traversed by a nerdy boy-spider with goblins, octopuses, and rhinos to bag. And in Miles Morales's New York City in *Into the Spider-Verse*, I encountered my city anew, in a way I hadn't since I was a kid gawking at the bright lights of Times Square.

Late in the movie, after having repeatedly tried and failed to master his new abilities, Miles resolves himself to become the hero—the Spider-Man—that his city needs, restyling the classic Spider-Man threads with a younger-looking, sleeker color scheme and pairing them with his sneakers and a hoodie. Kicking off from the side of a skyscraper, glass shattering in his wake, Miles leans into his fall, arching his back and tossing back his head, spreading out his arms with the gracefulness of a dancer.

Every nerd has a fan moment that sparks off the circuits in your brain like a train of firecrackers. Like Christmas morning, it brings you back to a sense of unadulterated awe and joy that you knew when you were a child. When the frame flips to show Miles, still falling, but now seemingly flying up toward the sky, which is no longer the sky but rather the skyline—the buildings touched with an electric palette of iridescent blues and greens and pinks—I had that moment. It was Miles, in his hoodie and unlaced shoes, a young Black Latino daring to be great. The city was no longer positioned below him, ready to break his fall, but above, as though it comprised the ground floor of heaven. It was a city ready to birth a new hero. I'd say this is the version of the city that I imagined as a kid, but that'd be wrong, because it is so much more.

Every year I go to New York Comic Con (NYCC) with a friend and drink in one of my favorite sights: thousands upon thousands of nerds, cosplaying as heroes, walking the streets of Midtown en masse. On the train ride there, we see maybe the occasional Iron Man or Black Panther, one or two others in cosplay among the puzzled and amused commuters. A smile or nod of acknowledgment, perhaps a shout-out or compliment. But the closer we get to Manhattan, the more we see, until we emerge from Penn Station and head west toward the Javits Center, among X-Men and Defenders and Avengers and Justice Leaguers and Teen Titans.

One year, a teen Spider-Man, admiring our cosplay, stopped me and my friend on our way to the Javits and asked for a picture. The three of us posed, Manhattan towering behind us. New York City looks best when dressed in heroes—but, then again, the city's always had style.

Though I didn't consider myself a resident of Gotham, I did like to imagine that I had a temporary home there—a sublet, perhaps, in one of those sleek, modern high-rises. I enjoyed dropping in on the world of Batman; for as long as I can remember, he had always been my favorite hero. He was the world's greatest detective, an orphan who'd had to overcome the tragedy of his parents' murder, and the fact that he didn't have any superpowers gave him a degree of pulling-oneself-up-by-the-bootstraps superiority. (Curiously, the fact that he was also a white billionaire never seemed to figure in my mind; Jeff Bezos running around in a batsuit doesn't sound as valiant.)

So I dismissed the all-American favorites—Superman, Captain

America, Wonder Woman—as too wholesome, positive, and pure, tossing off those icons without a fair and proper glance. I instead opted for the X-Men, who lived in a world that hated them and treated them as outsiders. I went for tragedy and darkness from the onset and, beyond that, heroes who had a moral breaking point. I remember my father excitedly telling me about Jean-Paul Valley, aka Azrael, and his brief, very violent tenure as Batman: "One time Batman gets hurt, and he gets this other guy to take over, but this guy starts killing people left and right, and Batman goes, 'This guy's *crazy*; we gotta get him outta here.'" And the time Batman "just gets sick of the Joker" and kills him.

Of course, Batman would eventually reach the end of his Bat-rope; Gotham is so relentlessly crime-ridden that it's a wonder anyone opts to live there at all. Batman was born from Gotham's worst: his parents were murdered in front of him when he was just a child. He became a billionaire, and despite any philanthropic pursuits Wayne Enterprises may undertake, he is still in the one percent in an economy that clearly has vast disparities in wealth. Gotham made Bruce Wayne. And when Bruce Wayne donned his bat costume, he could only do so—and continue to do so—because of the mobsters and creeps who lurked in the city. Like in the opening credits to *Batman: The Animated Series*, Batman matches the city's shade and architecture, blending seamlessly into the background; he makes the city, but the city also makes him.

That's one way into the antihero mythology. Batman was always toeing the line between being an enforcer of justice, guardian of the innocent, and just another crazy vigilante with lots of money and gadgets—not too different from the Arkham Asylum patients that he thwarted. This was never as clear to me as it was in Alan Moore's graphic novel *Batman: The Killing Joke*.

In *The Killing Joke*, the Joker decides to prove that one bad day can be all it takes to push a man into insanity, using Commissioner Gordon as his guinea pig. In one of the most dastardly moves in comics, the Joker unceremoniously shoots the commissioner's daughter, Barbara, paralyzing her, and ushers the commissioner through a twisted amusement park ride where he's forced to look at blown-up pictures of his daughter, shown shot and naked. That horrifying spread of panels, which combined literal violence (the shooting), an implied sexual violence (the unfortunate "women in refrigerators" trope, of using female characters to illustrate pornographic horrors), and the bait of an incestuous gaze (a father forced to gaze at his disrobed daughter), was unforgettable in the worst way. Even the shooting itself, mercilessly aimed just under the waist of her skirt, just above her groin, seemed to target her womanhood, as though this was the cost of being a female written in the world of comics: a violent shooting and an exploitative gaze, and the visceral horror of a man unbuttoning the blouse of a woman who is at his mercy.

As much as I recoiled at those pages, so did I marvel at the last one in the book, when Batman faces the Joker, who offers him a joke about two madmen escaping from an asylum, and the two of them laugh hysterically, Batman's arms reaching out to the Joker, their silhouettes styled as matching shadows. Whether Batman is bracing his body against the Joker's as he laughs or strangling him is unclear, with some fans claiming that the ending implies Batman being pushed to his limit and forced to break his no-kill rule (a rule that, for the record, the character had already broken plenty of times in the early comics and various times in between). My preferred reading of this scene is that Batman doesn't kill the Joker. Though the Joker wasn't able to break Commissioner Gordon and welcome him into his sphere of madness, the Joker was able to prove that Batman is just as mad as him. In the interpretation I prefer, Batman chooses to simply coexist with the Joker for even longer, not because it's the right thing to do but because they are the same. This strips him of his moral high ground and even puts his status as hero into question. But beyond their typically more fashionable threads, that's what marks the appeal of antiheroes—how they push back against the conventions and very definitions of the comic book genre to provide something more complex.

The mythology of comic book heroes has evolved to make space for and—in the case of movies and TV shows in particular in the last two decades—adopt as a matter of course the antihero. The antihero has combated the idea that these stories may exist purely as escapist fiction, with perfectly idealized representations of right and wrong. And the antihero is a product of the world around him, perverted by the very acts of wrongdoing he aims to quash. In 2004, while we were still in the infant years of the superhero surge, Frank Castle came to the big screen. *The Punisher*, a joyless action movie with a grisly revenge plot and high body count, was one of the early superhero films with a protagonist who lived in a moral gray area, along with 1997's *Spawn*, whose hero was contracted by the forces of hell, and 1998's *Blade*, whose vampire-hunter hero was half man and half vampire.

But it's Christopher Nolan's *Batman* trilogy that officially set a template for the contemporary superhero film and introduced, in *The Dark Knight*, not simply a "dark" comic book adaptation but one artful enough to garner recognition as a great film overall. Nolan's takes were influenced by Alan Moore's *The Killing Joke* and Frank Miller's *The Dark Knight Returns*; both writers were significant in heralding a grittier aesthetic and more daring content to the world of comics. Though Nolan's Batman was not the morally questionable, hyper-violent Batman that has sometimes cropped up in the comics, the question of how heroism may be defined, and how a hero can even exist in a world of moral gray areas, was still at the heart of Nolan's project. In *The Dark Knight*, the clean-cut hero-politician Harvey Dent says, "You either die the hero or you live long enough to see yourself become the villain,"* which we see come into fruition. Heath Ledger's mold-breaking Joker had his roots in Moore's, bear-

---

* Christopher Nolan, *The Dark Knight* (Warner Bros., 2008).

ing an obsession with chaos and a fascination with what it takes to break down a person's sense of human decency. Though the Joker in *The Killing Joke* fails to break the straitlaced good guy, this Joker does succeed in breaking down the just would-be hero of Gotham, Harvey Dent, who is transformed by his grief into Two-Face. Ultimately Batman must play the role of the villain so that Harvey can still be seen by the city as the hero, despite his final turn into darkness. That's the Shakespearean-style tragedy at the end of *The Dark Knight*, that by the end of the movie, any clear-cut representative of heroism is destroyed; the true hero is hated by the city, and the hero heralded by the city is a lie.

Where we arrive at the ending of *The Dark Knight*—an unsatisfying place of dramatic irony—is a dark role reversal and thematic reversal that contorts one of the simplest, most reliable tropes in comic books, about who gets to save the day, who is celebrated, and who is in the right. It's not unfamiliar: consider how much of the way we view our real-life heroes shifts depending on circumstances, politics, the media. One politician, meant to be a representative of the people and an envoy of American democracy, may be seen as a hero or a villain depending on what side of the aisle you stand with. As the Black Lives Matter movement reminded citizens, police officers may be seen as trustworthy public defenders or people complicit with the systemic oppression that still plagues marginalized groups. White supremacists may be positioned as defenders of an American identity and conservative values or racist vigilantes. And peaceful protestors may be righteous activists or wild insurgents.

In recent years, many shows have incorporated more complex turns along these lines in their antihero characters' arcs, giving them their own come-to-Jesus moments of moral reckoning where, after some soul-searching and many rounds of fisticuffs, they're forced to reconsider their personal codes of ethics. In Netflix's *Jessica Jones*, the titular character struggles to contend with what her powers can do and questions how accountable she is for the things that happened in her past. The Punisher tries to mete out his sense of justice but must come to terms with the personal cost. Likewise, the CW's Green Arrow defines and redefines his limits as he confronts who has "failed" his city. In *Daredevil*, Matt Murdock's moral dilemma is central to the character; raised Catholic, and friends with a priest, Matt is constantly thinking of his faith and considering the question of redemption—who is he to call himself the savior, what right does he have to do what he does, what are his boundaries, and when can he stop? His moniker as "the devil of Hell's Kitchen" calls back to his position on the line between justified action and self-serving retribution. In the series' third season, he's brought back from his selfless sacrifice at the end of *The Defenders*, the Netflix team-up series that ran for one season between *Daredevil* seasons one and two, and considers giving up his hero identity as he recovers in a church. Each of these heroes experience moments when they are vilified and unwanted by the very city they aim to protect, moments when they are cornered and hunted down. The antihero acts like a vaccine to the sickness in the city: wearing the costume of what ails the metropolis (vigilante action, violence, theft, trespassing, etc.), he fights back with good intention, and yet the body may reject him. In that case, as Harvey Dent observed, the hero has stuck around long enough to see himself become the villain.

Hence the trend of grittier superhero films, especially from the DC Extended Universe (DCEU). Choosing a markedly more muted visual palette compared to the MCU films, DC chased the concept of the antihero with Henry Cavill's Superman, a gruff, steely-faced hero, far-flung from Christopher Reeve's charming all-American model; and with Ben Affleck's Batman, more downtrodden than Christian Bale's. DC placed the heroes at odds, in the self-serious, wearisome slog that was Zack Snyder's *Batman v Superman: Dawn of Justice*, which had each of its titular characters question the other's power and methods, but less so in service of character building and strengthening the narrative than as a means to a superficial smackdown rife with scowling faces, destroyed buildings, and lots of costly special effects. We were treated to the same in the mirthless *Suicide Squad*, which aimed to have more fun than some of the DCEU's earlier efforts and also humanize its protagonists, true-blue antiheroes in the sense that they're villains who, by the end, willingly rise to the task of saving the day. But ultimately, despite their service, they too are betrayed by the city they're protecting: Gotham itself manufactures its heroes and villains and decides who is sacrificed for the sake of public good or public opinion. Sony, too, has been drawn into the allure of the dark antihero film, using its catalog of secondary Spider-Man characters, like Venom and Morbius, to mine a macabre aesthetic.

And then there was the pièce de résistance in the form of Todd Phillips's *Joker* in 2019. *Joker* had already garnered plenty of attention weeks before its actual release, so by the time I saw it, with my friend and convention co-conspirator after our first day of NYCC, the movie theater was packed. My friend, already skeptical about the gritty film, and insistent in her opinion that this very kind of tonal prerogative had been the cause of the DCEU's relative failure in comparison to Marvel—the brooding less interesting than the MCU's laughs—mostly went to humor me, though she was vaguely curious. Even in the darkness of the theater I could see her eyebrow pop up again and again at each unbelievable or gross detail; once or twice, during scenes when the Joker, Arthur Fleck, is interacting with his neighbor who he has a crush on, my friend tossed out a quick, agitated gesture of the arm, a flick of a hand, or tilted her head to the side and tented her forehead with her fingertips in a show of frustration. We both glanced down and away as Arthur brutally murdered an ex-colleague. Throughout the rest of Comic Con, even as we took in other trailers, interviews, panels, and more, we still kept coming back to a discussion of *Joker*. We agreed that our takes on the film were a mix of contradictory visceral responses: disgust and awe.

Inspired by Martin Scorsese films like *Taxi Driver* and *The King of*

Comedy, *Joker* is tackled like a school assignment: try to find a way to make a comic book movie without *actually* making it a comic book movie. *Joker*'s solution is to mostly divorce itself from its context, the rest of its universe (though a young Bruce Wayne makes an appearance, he is not yet Batman, if the Batman we know even exists in this version). It instead tethers itself to a presentation of realism—there are no caped crusaders shooting grappling hooks at roof ledges in this city—and mimics the balletic cinematography of prestige Hollywood filmmaking. It's hard to forget the staircase scene, depicting Arthur Fleck, fully costumed as the Joker, dancing carelessly down the steps as the sun streams down upon him. The shot itself is dazzling, as is Joaquin Phoenix's dance, with its quick twists and chorus-line kicks.

Central to *Joker*'s cynical take is another contradiction: a film that aims to be apolitical while also mining political context. Here the concept of the antihero gets confused by the fact that our antihero is, we already know, a murderous villain, and the film struggles to portray him as a complex, sympathetic character without subscribing to his perspective or absolving him of his actions in the name of a vaguely defined political revolution. Arthur, a clown-worker with a disorder that makes him cackle like an evil witch in an old Disney movie, appears as an underdog. He's bullied, beaten, scolded, and then mocked by his idol on national television. Society is broken, Arthur says, and the film seems to agree, showing us Gotham City's grit and corruption, which burdens its protagonist—who also presumably has some unnamed mental illness—and crowns him with what seems to be rightful, unimpeachable victimhood.

Though the Joker becomes a symbol in the city, Arthur himself announces that he isn't interested in the politics behind his revolution. The film isn't interested either, though it, more often than not, glorifies rather than challenges this Joker, who represents a class movement, but one that's alarmingly white and male. But the film is missing more nuance regarding class and race because *Joker* uses Arthur's white male identity to indulge in narrative privilege;

he exists in a space above racial politics. And yet the scenes looked familiar; they reminded me of the white supremacists who have mobilized in the streets countless times in the last several years, and in the January 2021 storming of the US Capitol. Arthur, feeling wronged, wants to incite chaos and succeeds, but the movement is already larger than him; it has absorbed the politics (and radical actions) of a group of people who look like Arthur. It's one of the city's ills suddenly come to life.

Though *Joker* would seem to bring a more realistic character to its story, grounded as it is in the Scorsese-est Gotham City ever, it is also ironically trapped in a central way. *Joker* revels in the gaze of its character and lets the rest of the world fall behind. But that's what makes *Joker* so terrifying and troublesome: the film locks the audience within the perspective of a white man with the power to incite a mass movement without reckoning with how this vision—even one born of injustice and marginalization—obscures other, actually marginalized people.

Years before *Joker*, I encountered a graphic novel that imagined what it would look like if heroes—not idealized heroes, but flawed, sometimes selfish and sometimes immoral individuals in capes and masks—lived in our world. Alan Moore and Dave Gibbons's *Watchmen* satirized comic book heroes and tropes and questioned what would happen if these flawed heroes took a look at the world around them and decided that it was broken and perhaps not even worth saving. It's a conclusion even Batman doesn't come to, even as Gotham City turns against him at the end of *The Dark Knight*.

Discovering the world of *Watchmen* as a teen wasn't like discovering Gotham as a kid; though seedy, Gotham was never irredeemable, if only for the presence of Batman. The world was still gripped by the mythos of the hero—it was a bleak Old Testament–style landscape of injustice and vice that nevertheless had hope because of its god—but the world of *Watchmen* was devastatingly agnostic, most of its gods resolved to a plan of abandonment or destruction.

Watchmen ends with an epigraph: "Quis custodiet ipsos custodes. Who watches the watchmen?," attributed to Juvenal, from *Satires*. This question, from which the graphic novel gets its title, presents the moral quandary at the heart of the book—the same one posed, albeit much less elegantly, by *Batman v Superman* and *Captain America: Civil War*—about how accountability and justice may be redefined in a world where there are gods and vigilantes acting each according to his or her own code. But even so, in the world that *Watchmen* imagines, one wonders if it makes much difference, if everything is already too far gone, just a wink of an eye until the Doomsday Clock strikes midnight.

In the iconic opening panels of the novel, a drop of blood drips down on a happy-face button lying on the street by a gutter, and a man hoses the rest of the blood off the sidewalk as pedestrians stroll by, indifferent. One of them, a red-haired man carrying a THE END IS NIGH sign, walks right through the puddle without stopping, leaving a trail of red footprints in his wake. The words of a masked vigilante named Rorschach hover over the images:

> This city is afraid of me. I have seen its true face. The streets are extended gutters and the gutters are full of blood and when the drains finally scab over, all the vermin will drown. The accumulated filth of all their sex and murder will foam up about their waists and all the whores and politicians will look up and shout "Save us!" . . . And I'll look down, and whisper "No."*

In Moore's world of *Watchmen*, masked vigilantes have been banned and costumed heroes are in the employ of the federal government. A hero has been killed—the Comedian—and Rorschach, our narrator and one of the last remaining vigilantes, suspects a plot to take him and his fellow superhero friends down. During his investi-

---

* Alan Moore, *Watchmen* (New York: DC Comics, 1986), 1.

gation, he reaches out to his peers—Dr. Manhattan, a former scientist turned blue god with a nudist streak; Ozymandias, the smartest man in the world; Silk Spectre, sharp-tongued and with a superhero-sized chip on her shoulder; and the earnest but dweeby Nite Owl. Meanwhile, amid scenes of everyday violence in the streets of the city, the Cold War heats up in the background, and the Doomsday Clock continues ticking, as the world is brought to the precipice of nuclear destruction.

But the threat turns out to be not a nuclear holocaust or some chin-stroking villain but one of the heroes—Ozymandias. His scheme is to save the world from a nuclear catastrophe by manufacturing his own act of destruction, which will force warring nations to cooperate. The other remaining heroes find him just as he's accomplished this feat—he's set a gigantic squid creature upon New York City, causing the deaths of millions—and while Nite Owl, Silk Spectre, and Dr. Manhattan decide to go along with the plan, Rorschach refuses, and is killed by Dr. Manhattan.

M. Night Shyamalan could only dream of such a third-act twist, in which the brilliant, successful golden-boy hero, who takes his name and hero inspiration from a great legendary figure, takes the role of the bad guy. But of course, it isn't as simple as that. News reports suggest that Ozymandias has succeeded in his plan: world leaders hastily make declarations of peace. Like Bruce Wayne and Arthur Fleck, Ozymandias is a hero and villain made by the world around him. The other heroes in the story make their own moral calculations, figuring whether they believe the human cost the city paid was worth this peace, and whether they can knowingly let a massacre and a lie determine the shape of a new world. But the comic itself doesn't necessarily agree with that outcome; it leaves it open for the reader to determine whether the seemingly utopian end justifies the horrific means. There's some gray area: though the comic includes gruesome full-page spreads showing Ozymandias's massacre, and contextual clues that bespeak the immorality of his actions, it also seems to validate his promise of peace. (The incident knowingly evokes the horrific acts of war that countries—including America, as in our nuclear attacks against Japan in the Second World War—justify as being for the greater good.)

The only hero who seems capable of stopping Ozymandias, Dr. Manhattan, the most powerful being on the planet, is, ironically, so emotionally impotent that he has lost his grasp on his humanity. Though he knows in advance that people will die, he must have the Silk Spectre convince him that human life is precious, when he considers it "brief and mundane."* Dr. Manhattan is *Watchmen*'s spoof on the concept of ultimate power. Not only does he question the point of human life and ultimately go along with Ozymandias's plan, but Dr. Manhattan also does some questionable things in service of the government. (Not to mention the fact that he gets into a relationship with a girl inappropriately young for him.) He is used as a lethal weapon by the US in the Vietnam War, and when he reflects on a visit he took to a criminal hideout, he says that "the sighs turn to screams of terror" and that "the morality of my activities escapes me."† Spider-Man taught us that "with great power comes great responsibility," but in this story, Moore asks, who watches those with great power? And what if those with great power don't care to shoulder any responsibility?

Only Rorschach judges Ozymandias; in the end, Rorschach, the one who has seen the city's "true face," is perhaps the closest thing we're offered to a hero. But even that is a meager consolation, because he too is a broken hero—violent, neurotic, and mentally unstable, likely sociopathic, with daubs of misogyny and homophobia. He has been broken by a case he investigated involving a young girl who was murdered and fed to the murderer's dogs. In that episode, Rorschach brutally murders the guilty man and his dogs, sets the house on fire,

---

* Moore, *Watchmen*, Ch 9, 17.
† Moore, *Watchmen*, Ch 4, 14.

and watches it burn as he recounts his thoughts on oblivion. Fittingly, the nihilistic chapter concludes with a quote by Nietzsche: "Battle not with monsters, lest ye become a monster, and if you gaze into the abyss, the abyss gazes also into you."*

Here Moore truly gets at the heart of the antihero trope. The question is how can a hero who truly exists in the world, who sees evil and fights against it, stay pure, stay just? Humans are infinitely susceptible to influences; we adjust to what we encounter, so to say that there is a hero, even fictional, who remains steady and stalwart and just while looking into the abyss—to say that he does not also contain within him the abyss of which Nietzsche spoke, is to say such a hero is a lesser fiction. He is a dream.

Even though he's a flawed hero, Rorschach believes in a black-and-white view of right and wrong, and for sticking to that, he's ultimately punished. We find a worthy, though utterly depressing, metaphor for the inevitably fruitless act of trying to save the world in the subplot of *Tales of the Black Freighter*, a fictional comic book that a character reads while the larger superhero narrative rolls on. In the story, a man survives a massacre and endures unspeakable horrors to return home and save his family from coming danger, but in his fervor and madness and desperate need to save his world, he ironically destroys it. He himself becomes the monster he fears, and declares, in a sentiment that echoes the Nietzsche quote, "The world I'd tried to save was lost beyond recall. I was a horror: amongst horrors must I dwell."†

Though Rorschach—unhinged and unstoppable, until the very end, when he decides he'd rather die than betray his morals—was my favorite as a teen, from his twisted origin story to his ever-shifting black-and-white inkblot mask, I donned the blood-spattered smiley face, as a button on my high school backpack, and carried a minia-

---

* Moore, *Watchmen*, Ch 6, 28.
† Moore, *Watchmen*, Ch 11, 23.

ture rubber Doomsday Clock on my key ring. Both symbols were instantly recognizable, but it's the smile that adorns the front cover of my edition, stares from the first panel on the first page, and glances out innocently from the last panel. Though Rorschach remains my favorite, now it's the Comedian who catches my interest more than before.

In high school, I dismissed the Comedian as the patent bad guy, more villain than antihero—a rapist and a murderer. That hasn't changed, of course, but now I read the Comedian as a tragic figure, not tragic in the sense that he's worthy of our sympathy but rather in the theatrical sense. The Comedian is the fool of the play, who laughs because he sees the loathsome truths of the world. His is a mirthless laugh, which is what I hadn't fully understood before, the depths to his cynicism. Thinking about their time in Vietnam, Dr. Manhattan says that the Comedian's personality "suits the climate" there during the war, with "the madness, the pointless butchery":

> As I come to understand Vietnam and what it implies about the human condition, I also realize that few humans will permit themselves such an understanding. Blake's different. He understands perfectly . . . and he doesn't care.*

Once again, Moore presents us with a hero who has dared to look into the abyss where many wouldn't, but the Comedian represents the cost of indulging in such a sight. It's not just the corruption of the city that he catches, like Rorschach does, but the depravity of a country and a whole world. In fact, the ultimate tragedy of *Watchmen* is that Moore's world explicitly mirrors ours: Vietnam, the Cold War, the constant pointless conflicts. Seeing all this, the Comedian discovers that even he has his limits. When he uncovers Ozymandias's plan, even his deep well of cynicism and understanding of the darkest parts

---

* Moore, *Watchmen*, Ch 4, 19.

of the human condition cannot prepare him for what he can only call a joke—something comical only because of its absolute absurdity, something disconnected from our understanding of what is normal, mundane, human. But even though the Comedian is detestable, he is perhaps still enough of a hero that he wrestles with what to do once he figures out Ozymandias's plan, and is killed for that. Rorschach sums up the Comedian's character in a way that will also recall his own, as he is killed in the end:

> Of us all, he understood most. About world. About people. About society and what's happening to it. Things everyone knows in gut. Things everyone too scared to face, too polite to talk about. He understood. Understood man's capacity for horrors and never quit. Saw the world's black underbelly and never surrendered. Once a man has seen, he can never turn his back on it. Never pretend it doesn't exist.[*]

"Who watches the watchmen?," Alan Moore offered, and years later Garth Ennis responded, "The Boys." Not unlike Moore, Ennis imagined a world in which the superheroes are flawed, but Ennis took it further, creating an oppressively bleak landscape where the superheroes are downright villainous, even sociopathic. Sponsored by a big corporation called Vought-American, these heroes are drug addicts and rapists and murderers. The G-Men, a superhero group that's a transparent spoof of the X-Men, gets not the wise and judicious Charles Xavier as its leader, but a man who abducts, drugs, and sexually abuses children. A German superhero named Stormfront is a neo-Nazi. A Jesus-styled hero named Oh Father, who has twelve underage sidekicks, is casually mentioned to be a pedophile. And a hero named Tek Knight, who surfaces in a subplot about a murder, struggles with a compulsive need to have sex with everything—inanimate

---

[*] Moore, *Watchmen*, Ch 6, 15.

objects, animals—until his unfortunate demise. But that's just the tip of the superheroic iceberg. These great heroes, we also find out, could have stopped 9/11 in this version, or at least helped save some lives, but end up leaving the people to die. At the beginning of the story, our protagonist, a young man named Hughie, is grieving the traumatic death of his girlfriend due to a hero's careless action. Hughie soon meets Billy Butcher, a former CIA agent who keeps the heroes in check through blackmail and violence, together with his band of weirdos, the eponymous "Boys." Hughie is the sympathetic everyman character and becomes the moral compass of the group, but even he gets roped into the bloodshed and brutality.

And so it's hard to figure who to root for in the story. I found both sides detestable; Ennis's world is so dark that we're caught between a moral rock and a hard place. The Boys are our heroic antiheroes who manipulate, lie, torture, and kill. Still, that's better than what we're served on the other side: depravity with a side of untouchable power. Standing between the Boys and the heroes are Hughie and his new girlfriend, Annie, aka Starlight, the newest member of the top hero group the Seven; Hughie and Annie each represent opposite sides of the war but mostly aim to just do the right thing, whatever that means in the circumstances.

But Butcher, like Moore's Comedian, is an extreme example of the antihero who occasionally crosses over to the realm of villainy. Charismatic and intelligent and dedicated to making sure the heroes don't step out of line, Butcher is also cruel and manipulative and driven by an obsessive quest for revenge. Near the end of the series, Hughie finally discovers Butcher's plan—to set loose a bioweapon that would indiscriminately massacre the supers, and he has no qualms about the collateral damage it will cause. Before Butcher sets into action the last part of his plan, he does the unthinkable and murders the rest of the Boys, leaving just Hughie to stop him. But even when it seems like Butcher has completely gone to the dark side, having killed his team and banked on a home-brewed holocaust to fix the world, he reveals that he also wants Hughie to stop him and perhaps even recruited Hughie knowing that he would eventually try to stop him. This is the best we're offered in terms of heroes. But creating another Captain America or Superman in the Homelander and another Aquaman in the Deep and another Wonder Woman in Queen Maeve wasn't Ennis's intention; nor would it be useful or interesting to anyone. What *The Boys* does want to do is to be a critique of celebrity and hero worship, comic book tropes and fantasy, the gross immorality of corporatization and commercialization, and the things American society erroneously values. Unfortunately, all of that is buried under layers of gratuitous violence, pornographic depictions of sexuality and abuse, and offensive language, making the final product more a juvenile exercise in shock value than a story aiming to make a statement.

And yet I did keep reading all the way until the end. Part of it was the engrossing narrative and fascinating cast of characters. But part of it was also how the comic tore down the fantasy of these super-hero characters and the larger mythology of a world of selflessness and justice. There's the New York mythology, but more importantly, there's the American one, and our very Constitution represents an ideal that historically has never matched reality. Of course these heroes are unscrupulous—just look at the world around them.

No matter how these creators approach the execution of their stories, it's easy to see why they made the more adventurous choices, to pursue a realist approach or to really challenge the concept of the antihero. Because there's the temptation to simply replicate the mythology that is the bright and hopeful superhero story, or perhaps expand on it, or, as Moore and Ennis did, break it down and build an alternative mythology.

I have done the same as a fan, and I continue to do so. I have mythologized my city, my home, my own experience with these stories. I subscribe to my fandoms—the world of Batman's Gotham City, Spider-Man's New York, even the New York of *Watchmen* or

The Boys—to engage with a different kind of reality. It doesn't always measure up to the world as we know it; in fact, most times it doesn't, but it also doesn't need to. We may build new stories from the architecture of what came before or we may raze the old and start fresh, and that, too, becomes part of the story, our own personal mythology. Every time I open a comic, I know I'm ready for something, old or new; I'm ready for another myth to believe in.

II.
The Animation Domination, Toonami, and Hellmouth High

TV toons, tropes and trends of the '90s and beyond

More than twenty-five hundred years ago, the Greek poet Hesiod wrote about the ages of man: Golden, Silver, Bronze, the Age of Heroes, and, finally, the Iron Age. If I could be so bold as to borrow Hesiod's framework and apply it to my formative years of TV fandom, perhaps I'd name my ages like so: the Adamantium Age, the Crude Iron(y) Age, the Gundanium Age, and the Age of Silver Bullets. That's how it went for me—the age of superhero cartoons on Saturday mornings; the age of wacky, crass cartoons; the age of after-school and late-night anime; and the age of teen horror.

The Adamantium Age of Heroes

Let me start by saying that I've never been a morning person. My mother has always woken up before the sun, brimming with energy, while my father, who suffered from sleep apnea and for years worked the night shift, was often out cold until the afternoon. I was somewhere in the middle; I could wake up in the morning but would be sloth-like and confused, shuffling from room to room, dozing on the toilet. And yet, Saturday mornings I voluntarily got myself out of bed to make sure I didn't miss my cartoons.

Saturday morning: even now, in my adulthood, when it usually means catching an early class at the gym or getting a jump on errands, still comes with the nostalgic tinge of excitement meaning the beginning of the weekend.

I'm not the only one who grew up with a fondness for Saturday morning cartoons; there's a whole history behind the genre. For many people who grew up in the '60s through the mid-'90s, Saturday morning cartoons were a childhood staple. These programming blocks were born from the idea that animated series were exclusively for kids, and not accessible to adults; cartoons then became their own separate, marginalized category in TV schedules. Since fewer adults were reported to watch TV on Saturday mornings, that time became rebranded and marketed solely toward kids, with sponsors also advertising to children on commercial breaks. Saturday morning cartoons were appealing to children because the programming was marketed as something uniquely for them, beyond the attention or interest of adults. And for adults, here was a block of time during the week that reliably held children's attention and kept them occupied.

Saturday morning cartoons have changed over time though. My mom would tell me of her favorites in the '70s, when she was growing up: *Josie and the Pussycats*, *The Flintstones*, *Scooby-Doo, Where Are You!*—all shows I watched in my own childhood, when they came back around. I'd inherited the classics, like so many other kids I knew, who watched reruns of oldies like *Looney Tunes* with a level of almost reverence. There was something special about watching, at age seven or eight, the same cartoons your parents had watched at that age.

My Saturday mornings were full of shows from a variety of channels, featuring zany '90s kid staples like *Animaniacs*, *Pinky and the Brain*, and *Tiny Toon Adventures*, and a smattering of anime series like *Cardcaptors* and *The Vision of Escaflowne*. But those Saturday mornings were, most importantly, when I was first schooled in superhero fandom. I loved watching Buster and Babs and Yakko, Wakko, and Dot, but what really defined Saturday mornings for me were the comic book stories that were, at the time, mostly exclusive to that time slot. Alongside kookier, playful heroes like the ones of *Freakazoid!*, *Static Shock*, and *The Tick*, I also found the ones that formed my own personal canon. For me, and for a whole generation, they first defined what comic book heroes looked like and what their stories could do, setting the template for the big movie and TV franchises we know today: *Superman: The Animated Series*, *Batman: The Animated Series*, *Spider-Man*, and *X-Men*.

I wonder if I hadn't watched those Saturday morning cartoons, would I be as hyped to see the next *Avengers* film or Spider-Man movie or DC animated show? I imagine I would have still raced through crowds at Comic Con to try to get into the Netflix *Defenders* panel, and I'd still have bought tickets to see *Avengers: Endgame* on opening weekend. But the familiarity I have with these characters and these universes from my Saturday morning cartoons bolsters my investment in these stories. The sight of these characters on the screen, though they look different from the animated versions I saw as a kid, thrills me as though I'm reencountering childhood best friends.

Saturdays began with Superman, but the series, with all its comparatively positive razzle-dazzle, was never enough to drive me from the comfort of my bed. If I did have an early morning, I watched it dispassionately, taking it in like an appetizer to the main course—because the others were mandatory viewing. I'd skip the tiny, ancient TV in my room, with its constant static and remote control that never seemed to work, and sat at the foot of the bed in my parents' room, in front of their behemoth of a cable TV with all the channels. My mother, who often worked Saturdays, was usually already gone, and my father slept—usually snoring, quite loudly—until it was time for us to watch our favorites together.

I had known other Batmen—Michael Keaton and Val Kilmer on the big screen (I didn't discover Adam West's campy capester until later)—but it was Kevin Conroy's Batman, the Bruce Wayne of *Batman: The Animated Series* (*BTAS*), who indelibly defined the hero in my mind. *BTAS* was never *just* a kids' show; in fact, one could argue that it wasn't a kids' show at all, despite the marketing that indicated otherwise.

When I watched *BTAS* for the first time, when it aired as part of the Saturday morning cartoon block, it distinguished itself by being a darker, more complex show that could be watched by kids but could also appeal to adults. Taking cues from Tim Burton's Batman movies, *BTAS* took a film noir approach to the material, which was brilliantly matched with Danny Elfman's main theme—perfectly arch and suspenseful and reminiscent of the work he did for many of Burton's films, *Batman* included. But the show also boasted its own distinctive style that was graduated from what Burton's Batman films accomplished; not simply noir, this vision of Batman's world sported the sleek and geometric art deco design. The combination was what the show's creators called "dark deco."

The show's complexity lay not only in its unique visual concept but also its composite tone, which combined serious moments of drama with genuinely witty comedy. I'm not talking about slips on banana peels or knock-knock jokes; *BTAS* featured good-spirited sarcasm and ironic dialogue, especially in exchanges between Batman and Alfred, and, later, between Batman and Robin. The show was also full of jokes and innuendos for older kids and adults; Bruce flirts without restraint, and occasionally a comment or two came accompanied with a wink-and-nudge sexual undertone. And *BTAS* wasn't above being cute, though it never became too precious. In the episode "Almost Got 'Im," a group of Batman's villains meet up for a game night and, as they play cards, tell their stories of when they each almost got Batman, comparing their failed attempts. The frame story is self-consciously playful and handled like a treat for the viewer, something more in the scheme of the 1960s *Batman* series, less concerned with gritty realism. But *BTAS* was pleasantly surprising in that way.

The narrative delivered mostly succinct one-offs with some notable exceptions—dramatic two-parters like the Emmy-winning "Robin's Reckoning," addressing the Boy Wonder's backstory and his confrontation with his parents' murderer. Robin's fraught quest for vengeance in that story line was indicative of the show's trenchant approach to character overall. In the enticing episode "Perchance to Dream," we take a dive into the Dark Knight's psychology, watching him question his sanity as he inhabits an alternative dreamworld in which his parents are still alive and he isn't Batman. Though the "it was all a dream" TV episode isn't by any stretch a novel conceit, "Perchance to Dream" doesn't read as a gimmick. It pits Bruce Wayne against his alter ego in order to make the character consider how he defines himself, how much of his identity is molded by his tragedy and his masked self. Batman must also face the price he has paid to be a vigilante hero—a normal life—and make that choice again. At the end of the episode, realizing that he is trapped in this dream reality, Batman guesses that the only way to wake up is to die. He launches himself off a tower, and though he does wake up from the fantasy, the symbolism of the suicidal act is tragic. He must literally kill his dream of a perfect, normal life to go back to being Batman, a haunted hero in a corrupt city.

It was these kinds of episodes that made *BTAS* a game-changer and one of the most notable precursors to Christopher Nolan's popular reimagining of the Dark Knight. *BTAS* won several Emmys, including one for Outstanding Animated Program in 1993. And some of the fresh changes the show made to the source material stuck and even made it into the comics. *BTAS* rebooted the character of Mr. Freeze, a corny two-bit villain in the comics, starting from scratch, giving him a new backstory to make him more sympathetic in the Emmy-winning episode "Heart of Ice." Then Harley Quinn, the bonkers villainess who has in recent years come into her own on both the small and big screens, was born on *BTAS* but became so popular that she was included in the comics.

Ironically, though I remember *BTAS* on those mornings, when I look back, the particulars often elude me. Specific episodes, specific plots are mostly a haze. After all, when the show first premiered, I was barely potty-trained. I came to *BTAS* young, and yet I think about it more than so many others from my youth. Above all I remembered the texture of the show long after: the tone, the color, the shape, and all the other details that came together to form not just a TV show but a moving work of art.

The specifics of *Spider-Man*, on the other hand, I remember, mostly thanks to the show's bold moves into the territory of science fiction. Venom—variable and sludge-like, like a moving oil spill—delighted me the way imaginative villains always have. Venom was creaturely, with its freakishly large mouth, fangs, and long tongue: the very embodiment of wild, insatiable hunger. And Peter's own extended mutation into something more spider than man—the episodes of his transformation made me nervous, perverse as they seemed, using fans' love of the hero against them, as though to say, "You wanted a cute friendly neighborhood Spider-Man? Well, here's an alternate version of that hero, and it's not so pretty."

Spider-Man brought a different kind of flair to my Saturday morning cartoon lineup. It didn't have as sleek of a style as *BTAS*, but rather steered in the aesthetic direction of its comics. Spidey's color palette was brighter, and the animators focused their talents on *Spider-Man*'s star shots of New York City, 3D graphics featuring Spider-Man swinging through the streets of Manhattan. Though the combination of animation styles looks jarring and disjointed to my eyes now, at the time it seemed to me like a futuristic marvel.

While *BTAS* gave off the cool-kid vibe, *Spider-Man* showed up as the nerdy kid who could also hold his own. No Danny Elfman here, but *Spider-Man* did get a theme song performed by Joe Perry, the lead guitarist from Aerosmith, with unforgettable, screeching guitar riffs (what, we may now wonder, could have been more '90s?). *Spider-Man* also kept its hero's personality quirks. This Peter Parker, both a wiseass and a cornball, monologued as he fought and scouted the city. In the first episode of the series, while tracking a villain in the sewers, Spider-Man gripes, "Why can't I be one of those galaxy-hopping superheroes?" He complains about the dirty work he has to do, comparing it to the more glamorous (and cleaner) heroics of his peers: "You don't find the Fantastic Four in a sewer. Or the Avengers! Never have I seen the Avengers in a sewer. Or the Defenders."*

Having its hero make this statement in the first episode doesn't just function on a comic level but also sets up his world and the expectation that we will see Spider-Man encounter other heroes— which he does. *Spider-Man* was full of crossovers with other Marvel characters: Blade, the Fantastic Four, the X-Men, the Punisher, and more. And before Miles Morales could even dream of the Spider-Verse, *Spider-Man*, taking cues from the comics, introduced multiple universes and timelines, opening up the world of the series even more.

In a crossover episode with the X-Men in season two, Spider-Man, fighting his mutation, seeks out Charles Xavier to find out if he can help. In the typical style of a comic book crossover, there's the usual fan service—a fight among the good guys, caused by a simple misunderstanding. When Spider-Man drops in on the X-Men and mistakenly finds himself in the Danger Room, where Xavier's team has to help him defeat Sentinels, the tonal discrepancy between the

---

* *Spider-Man*, "Night of the Lizard" (1994).

shows is made quickly apparent in a short dialogue exchange, as Storm powers up, declaring, "Power of lightning, strike again!" After which Spider-Man follows with, "Um . . . power of web-shooters, get real sticky!"* This is, of course, before the tonal mash-ups that would happen in films like *The Avengers* and *Justice League*. When Tom Holland joined the MCU, he similarly leapt from the playful, light-hearted world of the *Spider-Man* movies to infuse the team dynamic with levity, innocence, and youth. Peter Parker's naivete is a delightful contrast to, say, Tony Stark's sharp cynicism.

But I don't only see my favorite Saturday morning heroes in the MCU; the X-Men film franchise similarly brought me back to those mornings. While *BTAS* had the most style and *Spider-Man* the most character, *X-Men* always had a more substantial heft to its plots, the comics being, as they were, not about a single hero pitted against crime but about a marginalized population pitted against society. Though of course still part of the Saturday morning cartoon block for kids, *X-Men* the animated series kept politics at its heart, asking what is the most effective and moral route to securing civil rights for a group of people who are prejudiced against.

Of all our Saturday morning shows, too, my father took *X-Men* the most seriously, quizzing me on details from the show and from the well of knowledge he had from his childhood reading the comics.

> *Who were the original X-Men?*
> Cyclops, Beast, Jean Grey, Angel, and Iceman.

> *Where did Rogue get her power to fly?*
> Ms. Marvel.

> *What are Wolverine's claws made out of?*
> Adamantium.

---

* *Spider-Man*, "The Mutant Agenda" (1995).

And his powers?

A trick question—the adamantium claws were the result of
an experiment, not his mutation; he had strength, enhanced
senses, and superhuman healing abilities.

Unlike *BTAS* and *Spider-Man*, whose pilot episodes were both tidy
one-offs about well-meaning but dangerously ambitious scientists
who transform themselves into fierce creatures, *X-Men: The Animated Series* kicked off with a two-parter about the teenage X-Man-
to-be Jubilee running away from her foster family because they've
discovered her mutant powers. Jubilee is tracked down and rounded
up by an agency supposedly meant to help mutants, and in just the
second episode of the series, a character on our team of good guys
dies, which leads to conflict among the others. Later in the same arc,
the Beast, standing trial for a break-in, says that he believes in the
justice system and trusts that anti-mutant prejudice won't figure into
the ruling. He declares that he has the same rights as any other citizen, paraphrasing *The Merchant of Venice*, replacing the word "Jew"
with "mutant": "I am a mutant. Hath not a mutant senses, affections,
fed with the same food, warmed and cooled by the same winter and
summer as a human is? If you prick us, do we not bleed? "* The use
of this *Merchant of Venice* quote is striking not simply because of the
fact that one of Shakespeare's more complex and contentious works is
being quoted in a comic book show for kids but because this allusion's
framing of the mutants in the place of Jews further complicates, even
muddles, the show's already substantial racial allegory. In the comics
world, Magneto and Professor X are frequently compared to Malcolm X and Martin Luther King Jr., respectively, in their responses to
their marginalization; the status of mutants is rendered synonymous
with that of Black Americans throughout history. However, this moment in particular conflates the struggles of mutants with those of

---

* *X-Men*, "Enter Magneto" (1992).

Jews. This isn't the first time that happens; Magneto's background as a Holocaust survivor also blatantly links the mutant allegory back to real historical tragedy. This was why the show appealed to my father, who praised comics that used the guise of fiction to talk about subjects that were very real: prejudice, tragedy, death, society, systems of belief. I adopted it too without fully realizing the metaphors at the time; now, as an adult, I return to the X-Men with a renewed sense of admiration for the way the comics broached marginalization and oppression, but also with a newfound critique of the times when those metaphors fail.

And yet the series, and its peers, were not always given the respect they deserved, marketed, as they were, as just kids' cartoons. But the fact of the matter is that these shows, which received strong ratings and were engaging, expert works of television, were popular, and not just among those of us who grew up with these characters. None of the shows began with their heroes' origin stories but all began in medias res, giving us the details as we went along. Each one was an invitation into a world that had already existed, in some form, in comics, with characters and story lines familiar to those fans who knew them, but also with new surprises so well-executed that they became part of the canon. And, between the crossovers in the Marvel shows and their combination into one programming block, this media was positioned in a way that would make it the precursor to the MCU and DCEU superhero boom.

When my father and I got up to watch these shows—him still exhausted from his night shift and me fighting the laziness that came with the arrival of the weekend—we were ready to step into a universe made especially for us. That meant a universe where the spectacular was the norm, where every time the characters we loved met from their different spheres, the landscape expanded until the possibilities seemed endless: these Saturday morning cartoons gave us a universe that was infinite. Before back-to-back episodes and crossovers from the Arrowverse and the Marvel movie marathons, there were Saturday mornings, and shows about heroes that weren't simply child's play.

The Age of Crude Irony

One of my favorite cartoons of my preteen years was Nickelodeon's *SpongeBob SquarePants*. The premise was odd: a square sponge lives in a pineapple under the sea with his pet snail, alongside his cranky squid neighbor and idiotic starfish best friend, and works as a fry cook for a miserly old crab. The adults around me made fun of it— my mother scoffed at SpongeBob's stupidity, and my aunt would call it the show about the "moldy cheese," because whatever SpongeBob was, he definitely did *not* look like a sea sponge. Still, my peers and I watched it. In middle school, my best friend and I would break out into renditions of "Striped Sweater" and the "F.U.N. Song," and I would annoy my mother by prancing around the house singing "Steppin' on the Beach," as SpongeBob did in the season one episode "Walking Small." According to the reliably unreliable rumor mill at my middle school, the oddball show was created when its creators were high.

But when I look back at the early days of *SpongeBob*, when it premiered in 1999, the show wasn't nearly as perplexing as some of the kids' cartoons that came before or after it. In recent years, kids' animated series have seemed to dive even deeper into a well of conceptual curiosities: the trippy, candy-filled postapocalyptic world of *Adventure Time*, the droll *Regular Show*, the cutesy magical *Steven Universe*. But before these series, the animated shows of the '90s ushered in a trend of children's animation that was bold in its weirdness; its myriad absurdities; its grotesque, raunchy humor; and its overall postmodern sensibilities, which mocked genre tropes and forms that came before, defying any one definition of what it was trying to achieve.

At the time, I didn't realize all the particular ways that the shows I watched as a kid drew from and parodied the eras of television that preceded them. Though I sometimes indulged in old cartoons, I didn't often watch the live-action sitcoms from my parents' youth, like *Leave It to Beaver* and *The Brady Bunch*; occasionally I'd leave them on in the background while I did something else—but only if there was nothing else on. My mom, on the other hand, would coo with pleasure when one of the shows came on; her face would light up with a loving nostalgia as she caught it. The show was, as she'd say, "old-school," from when she was a kid. The shows mostly bored me, detached as they seemed from my own life and far-flung from my expectations of riveting entertainment. But they were also curious to me in their wholesomeness: innocent adventures and earnest portrayals of suburban life, portraits of comfortable middle-class American domesticity.

There was an easy formula to many of these *Leave It to Beaver*-style sitcoms: a vaguely saintly, perhaps naive, main character or characters; an emphasis on the nuclear family as a unit and foundation of society; occasional conflicts between old traditions and the newfangled modernizations of contemporary life; minor daily trifles that are solvable in the show's half-hour time slot; and a general innocence and purity of tone, which avoids untidy issues like race, class, politics, etc. Though the family sitcoms of the late '70s and '80s, including *Growing Pains*, *The Cosby Show*, *Who's the Boss?*, *Family Ties*, *Full House*, *Diff'rent Strokes*, and *Family Matters*, among countless others, were all invested in maintaining the same wholesome tone of their predecessors, they also began daring to explore more controversial subject matter in what were called "very special episodes," which became more and more prominent in television shows in the '80s.

Many kids' cartoon shows in the '90s were obsessed with the absurdities of modern life and poked fun at the purity and near-sanctimoniousness of early sitcoms. One of these series, *The Ren*

& Stimpy Show, became a mainstay in the childhood of many '90s kids—and drew the attention of adults as well.

In the series, which premiered on Nickelodeon in 1991, an erratically tempered chihuahua and a moronic cat live together and have adventures—some mundane, some extraordinary and strange. The show's core comedic element was an old reliable one: the odd couple. Almost all of Ren and Stimpy's adventures are incited by complications related to their opposite temperaments and differing levels of intelligence. Most of all, the show stood out for its controversial humor. *Ren & Stimpy* combined sophomoric laugh bait (absurd logic, gross body humor) with jokes that were more risqué (sexual innuendos). In one episode, Stimpy goes on a seemingly endless quest for his "son," a fart, who ends up marrying a rotting fish head. *Ren & Stimpy* could be downright unpleasant to watch, with its close-ups of its characters, their dripping noses, their wrinkles and pimples and hairy moles and veins, the crust around their eyes. The show was willfully contrary in this emphasis on the grotesque yet mundane parts of the body. It's not as though we aren't familiar with all this—mucus and blemishes and farts—but so often TV, acting as a false mirror, presents a glossier version of our lives, an image we can relax into. Cartoons, by their very nature unbound from the limits of reality, exaggerate and emphasize what they see fit, to different ends. (Just consider the disproportionately big-eyed Disney characters, meant to achieve a marketable amount of cuteness.) *Ren & Stimpy* made ugliness and stupidity the joke, even though that kind of joke's a risk; not everyone will find such indelicacies entertaining.

Ren & Stimpy wasn't just about butt jokes. Its characters broke the fourth wall, addressing its viewers like a host would in an educational program: "Hello, boys and girls!" In one short, meant to parody nature shows, Ren serves as the wildlife expert, guiding the viewer through a landscape full of fictional creatures that all somehow look like Ren and Stimpy. But perhaps the most memorable element of the show—at least for me, and surely for others—was the fake commercials and musical interludes. In skits like "Log," a commercial for a children's toy that is, quite simply, a log, *Ren & Stimpy* once again parodied television of yesteryear; the style and music of the commercial are clear rip-offs from the Slinky commercials of the 1960s and '70s. (One may consider that a Slinky, though a childhood amusement of my own, is not much more useful than a log. However, the absurdity of childhood toys, which include slime and defecating puppy dolls and such nightmare fodder as Troll Dolls and Furbys, is its own separate book.)

Perhaps most memorable, and *Ren & Stimpy*'s greatest gift to all of us from the '90s, was the song "Happy Happy Joy Joy," from our "old pal Stinky Wizzleteats." Even now, I recall the thumping butt-bumping of Ren and Stimpy, the former in a mind-control helmet; their unnaturally wide smiles; and the forced frivolity of it. Though the song declares happiness and joy, the singer grows ever more incoherent and even threatening ("I'll teach you to be happy! / I'll teach your grandmother to suck eggs!" was always my favorite part) until the short climaxes to something totally deranged. The singer exclaims, "I told you I'd shoot, but you didn't believe me! / Why didn't you believe me?!" as Ren finds a hammer and brutally bashes it against the helmet on his head, all to the beat of the song. Perhaps part of being a kid in the '90s and loving these shows was also learning to love an antic sense of irony; it's a perverse notion, to be sure, but perhaps there's some "happy happy joy joy" in the aberrant, the outlandish, and the detestable.

At the end of the day, though, the gross, abject humor of *Ren & Stimpy* was a bit too much for me to take. I loved the commercials and Powdered Toast Man and "Happy Happy Joy Joy," but its jokes were jarring for me at five, six years old. The series was too harsh of a contrast to my more openly kid-friendly favorites at the time, like *Rugrats* and *Doug*. However, at the same time *Ren & Stimpy* was on the air, a similar cartoon caught my interest and stayed with me for years: *Rocko's Modern Life*.

Rocko had a similar approach to comedy as *Ren & Stimpy*, with an emphasis on body humor, though *Rocko* was slightly more demure in its absurdist turns. The show was about Rocko, a meek wallaby dealing with the usual trials and tribulations of everyday life: managing a career, maintaining relationships with friends, dating; even things as simple as going to the grocery store or the dentist are the premises of episodes. But *Rocko* was all about finding the eccentricities in even the mundane parts of life. Though the show's visual style was cleaner than that of *Ren & Stimpy*—which went for a crude appearance and a palette of colors reminiscent of the body (various nudes and shades of red)—*Rocko* had a brighter and wilder aesthetic, from Rocko's signature blue-and-purple shirt to his red, yellow, and purple house.

In an update of a classic fish-out-of-water premise, *Rocko* focused on its protagonist's reactions to new technologies and practices, and the struggles of adjusting to the modern world. (In 2019, more than two decades after the show concluded, *Rocko's Modern Life* returned with the Netflix special *Rocko's Modern Life: Static Cling*, which saw Rocko and his friends encountering the twenty-first century after being trapped for twenty years in space. Yet again, adjustment to changing times became the premise behind many of the jokes, which poked fun at Starbucks, iPhones, energy drinks, and more.)

Rocko's world is owned by Conglom-O, an aptly named avatar of capitalism that owns practically everything in Rocko's town and, by extension, its people. (Its slogan: "We own you.") In the season three episode "Zanzibar!," which aired in the mid-'90s, before the threat of environmental catastrophe seemed as imminent as it does now, Rocko and the other citizens of the town try to take on Conglom-O—in musical form—to get the corporation to safely dispose of its waste and recycle. When Rocko's clinically cantankerous neighbor, Ed Bighead, a Conglom-O employee, scoffs at the green talk and contrarily sprays an aerosol can up at the sky, the ozone layer immediately degrades, letting enough sunlight pass through to burn him to a crisp.

Though the show loved to revel in its silly situational comedy and jeer at the evil work of corporations and their henchmen, its satire also ran deeper, to a biting, often cynical, critique of a general erosion of American values—or perhaps a distrust of them to begin with. The show's main criticism was of the American tendency to excess and our obsession with consumption culture. The population of O-Town is greedy, jealous, gluttonous, and lustful, and even our precious everyman Rocko becomes corrupted at times, falling into traps of consumerism while shopping, or, succumbing to the allure of managerial power, transforming into a merciless, cigar-smoking boss. In *Rocko's Modern Life*, every character is afflicted with some vice or another, and no one goes unharmed for it.

A central element of the show's comedic premise, however, is a go-to, low-hanging fruit for children's television, going back to the early days of Bugs Bunny and Mickey Mouse: the adventures of anthropomorphized animals. The humor's ironic: animals behaving in ways that aren't normal. But in shows like *Rocko's Modern Life*, the point isn't just to make a joke of the humanization of animals but also the inverse: to make the point that we humans, with all our technology and laws and so-called civilization, are still no better than animals. An Orwellian approach to kids' comedy, if ever there was one.

That in itself was a trend in the '90s. Shows like *Cow and Chicken*, *The Angry Beavers*, and *CatDog*, among others, featured anthropomorphized animals going about their daily lives, with some surreal twists. Like *Ren & Stimpy*, each one had its own animal odd couple. In *Cow and Chicken*, the eponymous siblings (who are somehow, inexplicably, biologically related) are, respectively, a naive dreamer and a short-tempered grouch, and work their way through middle-school life. In a poke at those classic family sitcoms, at home Cow and Chicken's mother and father, attired in threads of decades past, are only ever depicted from the waist down. Meanwhile, among adult innuendos and bizarre turns of logic, a devil known only as "Red Guy" regularly appears to draw Cow and Chicken into his schemes.

Similarly, *The Angry Beavers* was about two brother beavers—a neurotic one and a lackadaisical one—who are kicked out of the nest and forced to get along in a home of their own, but get into daily hijinks. The show's aesthetic lovingly mimicked or parodied elements from earlier decades: B horror movies from the '50s, comic books from the '60s, the retro style of the '70s.

This approach to humor and style is what really characterized animated kids' shows in the '90s: pastiche. At some point a flurry of animated anthology series started to crop up, all of which welcomed eager young cartoonists to the scene and radically disturbed the old formula of cartoon series that had come before. Cartoon Network and Nickelodeon were pushing forward with new content, taking risks that would come to define a new era of animated shows. On Nickelodeon in the late '90s, there was *KaBlam!* and *Oh Yeah! Cartoons*. At the same time, Cartoon Network had *What a Cartoon!*, then later *The Cartoon Cartoon Show* and other shorts, like the playful cartoon music videos "Cartoon Network Groovies."

These programs adapted the premise of the live-action variety show to animation and took it further, eschewing cohesion to instead pursue shorts that could be more experimental and work totally independently from one another. *KaBlam!*, which dubbed itself "a new kind of cartoon show" and a place "where cartoons and comics collide" in its opening, was such a potpourri of content, with some of the skits using action figures, some 2D animation. The show had a meta frame narrative in the form of a pair of animated hosts, Henry and June, talking and having short adventures, at the end of which they'd turn a comic book page at the bottom of the TV screen to introduce the next cartoon. As a kid, I watched *KaBlam!* with curiosity; it didn't escape me that it was markedly different from the other shows I was used to seeing: *Rugrats, Hey Arnold!, Doug*—shows that were straightforward and coherent. Even *Ren & Stimpy*, which broke the fourth wall and used various narrative styles, was consistent in its animation and characters. But the *Toy Story*-meets-*Justice League* style of the live-action segment *Action*

League Now!, with its beat-up action figures, didn't match the clay figures and mostly dialogue-less *Three Stooges*–style humor of the anthology show's *Prometheus and Bob*.

While *KaBlam!* remained its own separate entity throughout its run, other cartoon samplers served as test runs for possible new series. From *Oh Yeah! Cartoons* came *ChalkZone, My Life as a Teenage Robot*, and my favorite of the bunch, *The Fairly OddParents*, which went on to have a long ten-season run on Nickelodeon. Cartoon Network's *What a Cartoon!*, however, was the variety program that ended up most defining my cartoon tastes during that time. Over two decades later, I still remember watching the Oscar-nominated short *The Chicken from Outer Space*, which became the pilot episode of *Courage the Cowardly Dog*. Though the show later became one of my favorites, as I watched the short at five years old, I was terrified by the suspense and horror-movie aesthetic. The sight of the farmhouse in the middle of nowhere and the bright red eyes of the alien chicken unnerved me and gave me nightmares—but still, perhaps because of my own cowardice, I adored Courage and his emphatic expressions of shock and terror.

What a Cartoon! also offered a misogynistic Elvis-wannabe, a boy genius and his meddling sister, and a kickass trio of magical girls like the ones I loved watching in anime: I ran through every episode of *Johnny Bravo* and *Dexter's Laboratory*, had a much-loved *Powerpuff Girls* sheet and comforter set, and reflexively watched *Courage the Cowardly Dog* whenever it was on. There was a vibrancy to these series: the colors and the tones, and the awareness of the real world, whether in the form of pop culture references or popular tropes. Teetering between juvenile physical humor not unlike the falling anvils from the Acme Corporation and subtler gags that older kids and adults could enjoy, the series also drew from common themes and conceits from various genres, like farcical rom-coms, horror, science fiction, and more. But above all, these '90s series, from the golden age of animation, felt remarkably fresh—weird and experimental, often ironic, occasionally nonsensical, and sometimes even grotesque. Yet that was the thrill: turning the channel to your new favorite show and not knowing what it was going to bring you next.

The Gundanium Age

Though I watched many shows indiscriminately as a kid, switching back and forth between Cartoon Network and Nickelodeon (Disney occasionally, but the channel didn't compare to its competitors), these wildly variable shows, in all their hybrid forms, broadened my understanding of what cartoons could be. In their combinations, there was an enjoyable tension. One after another, you could find something you loved and something you hated; and you couldn't get bored quickly or easily dismiss a show, because even within one program there were so many turns, so many routes it could take, that they were completely unpredictable—at least the most interesting ones.

The multitude of options at the time suggests that this wasn't just a case of a handful of producers and creators aiming to get weird with cartoons; some of this went hand-in-hand with how the networks themselves evolved in the '90s. Cartoon Network in particular began steering its target demographic age a bit older and embraced shows with stranger themes or produced branded commercials and shorts that established the channel as its own slightly more mature brand. It introduced totally different blocks of content, each sporting its own distinctive music and presentation style: Toonami, Adult Swim. On Nickelodeon, the face of the channel's programming block for young kids, Nick Jr., was, appropriately, named Face, and served as the friendly announcer for the upcoming shows.

This change in the approach to branding and marketing cartoons—alongside the often experimental new kinds of content itself—also affected the weekend staple of Saturday morning cartoons. In the early

'90s, the government's restrictions on the kinds of TV content that could be shown to kids (more of an emphasis on educational content and limits on advertising) were already putting a stress on Saturday morning cartoons, which networks were finding less profitable than other forms of programming they could slot in instead. But there were also the threats of changing technologies: cable TV, with ever more channels to choose from, some of which had cartoons on 24/7; and, later, the internet, which would eventually allow kids to find and stream TV whenever they wanted.

As a kid, I hardly noticed when Saturday mornings changed from being an unmissable event to just another day in the week—in fact, chore day, which I dreaded. It seemed to just happen. But I didn't feel the loss so deeply because there was, it seemed, a palpable switch, when the peak time for great cartoons was no longer Saturdays before noon but weekdays after school. Those elementary school-day afternoons became tinged with a sense of urgency (my father, perpetually late to pick me up after the final bell, exacerbated my anxiety). I feared missing even a minute of Toonami, the Cartoon Network programming block that defined so many years of weekday afternoons and had me running to the TV. Toonami gave me my first education in anime.

Anime had already been around in the US long before Toonami, though in a scattershot way. My father spoke of watching *Speed Racer* and *Gigantor* as a kid. (Every time he'd talk about the latter, he'd sing the theme song, "Gigantor, Gigantor, *Gig-aaaaaan-tor*," grinning to himself, though I had no clue what a Gigantor was.) As a toddler, I had watched *The Littl' Bits* and *Maya the Bee*, apparently thrilled at the little animated insect who shared my name. And one day when I was young, I caught my father watching the 1985 movie *Vampire Hunter D*, which I found frightening and scandalous (there was death, blood, and some nudity), but I also found in it a peek into a different world of animation: cartoons that were styled differently, that could be entertainment an adult would watch.

Still, there was never any one destination for that animation—a network or programming block that could properly celebrate anime and package it as media with its own separate identity, unique from the American fare. That is, until Toonami came along.

When the head of programming at Cartoon Network expressed a desire for a block showcasing action cartoons, the Cartoon Network creative director Sean Akins and producer Jason DeMarco were brought on to tackle the task. Akins and DeMarco had grown up on shows like *Voltron* and *Star Blazers* and were looking to bring something different to American TV. Toonami was born on March 17, 1997.

The team faced an uphill battle at first, though; they struggled to get up and running with a small budget but eventually began with the shows *ThunderCats*, *Robotech*, and *Voltron*. Though they didn't have much money, they still had a significant amount of freedom to do what they wanted to and experiment with the block because Cartoon Network, then still a young network, was trying to establish itself and cement its brand.

The aim of Toonami, DeMarco has said, was to introduce young American viewers to animation that was taken seriously, with engrossing storytelling, and illustrated by great artists from the other side of the globe. But Toonami did more than that; it created a comprehensive viewing experience that went beyond just the shows and commercials. When Toonami came on in the afternoons, it was as though the TV had been taken over. The block had hosts: Moltar, then the robot TOM, who piloted the Ghost Planet Spaceship Absolution, and who was killed and brought back in a new form, voiced by Steve Blum, the actor who voiced Spike in the English dub of *Cowboy Bebop*. The graphics were futuristic, and there was a narrative at play, with TOM and his spaceship; even when it aired more dated cartoons, the block gave the impression of a TV experience poached from the future. It wasn't just about the animation but the attitude; here was a block of programming that identified that there was more to the world of animation than what we knew in America. The future of animation, as captured by Toonami, recognizes impactful traditions and classics from overseas, and the brilliant artists who pioneered them; it's more globalized, and it represents the fact that animation isn't a completely insular cultural realm but one that may intersect with others: the music world, the comic book world, etc.

"I will say, I don't think anyone in the network really understood what we were doing, because when we came we said we wanted to use hip-hop; we wanted to use drums and bass; we wanted to interview skaters and comic-book artists. We wanted it to represent all of what we thought was exciting about youth culture at the time. And in a way that didn't talk down to kids and wasn't like, 'Eat your vegetables,'" DeMarco told *Vulture*.*

I was never a big consumer of music; I always put on the radio absentmindedly, just for a bit of noise, and I never sought out new artists or songs, rather just absorbed whatever was popular. But Toonami also brought me some of my first encounters with music that wasn't just the same recycled hits on the radio. The block aired animated music videos from Daft Punk and the Gorillaz, and my earliest memories of those artists are, ironically, not of the songs but the videos. I had never seen animation paired with music in such a way; I was lured in by the visual narrative. In 2001 I became obsessed with two albums. One was *Gorillaz*, which I asked for and got, to my surprise, despite the "Parental Advisory" label; it was my first explicit album, and I was unsure of what I'd be doing to my virgin ears. I had, after all, asked for the album purely based on my fascination with the video for "Clint Eastwood," with its zombie, "Thriller"-dancing apes. But when I listened to the album, I loved it, and I played "Clint Eastwood" on repeat until I couldn't get it out of my head. It took a bit more research for me to figure out the band behind the blue

---

* Emily Yoshida, "How Toonami Became an Anime Gateway for Millennials," *Vulture*, March 17, 2017, vulture.com/2017/03/toonami-was-an-anime-gate-way-for-millennials.html.

aliens in the anime video for Daft Punk's "One More Time," but I was eventually gifted *Discovery*, and it lived in my Discman for the better part of that year.

Thus was the power of Toonami, with its novel catalog and extensive world-building. Toonami started blowing up with *Sailor Moon*, *Dragon Ball Z*, and then *Mobile Suit Gundam Wing* in the late '90s and early 2000s. For the years that these shows were on, they became my nerdy lifeblood, my meat and potatoes (or the vegetarian equivalent) in television entertainment. A large part of what now defines me as a nerd came from me watching Usagi, Goku, and Heero Yuy on those afternoons after school. They invited me in, so I wanted more: I quoted Heero in the schoolyard during recess, went to the FYE store in the mall to buy VHS tapes of *Sailor Moon SuperS: The Movie* and *Dragon Ball Z: The History of Trunks*. I built mobile suit models. One of my first DVD purchases was *Mobile Suit Gundam Wing: Endless Waltz*, which I still have sitting on my bookshelf today.

Though *Sailor Moon* remains in the pantheon of great, influential shojo (anime aimed at young girls) and *Dragon Ball Z* remains a mainstream anime standby today, Toonami also notably brought mecha to the US in shows that redefined our relationship to machines.

When Bandai, the colossal Japanese toy company, came to Cartoon Network with the first few episodes of *Gundam Wing*, DeMarco, who had been searching for Gundam content, was thrilled. Gundam, after all, was and still is one of the largest media franchises in Japan. "It was a more realistic approach to using giant robots as weapons of war when compared to the things that we as Americans have been exposed to, which are your Voltrons and all the '70s fun giant robot stuff," DeMarco told IGN.[*] In 2003 the network even ran a "Giant Robot Week," celebrating the genre.

DeMarco wrote a trailer to the series to run on Cartoon Network,

---

[*] Christopher L. Inoa, "How Gundam Wing Found Its Home on Toonami 20 Years Ago Today," *IGN*, March 9, 2020, ign.com/articles/how-gundam-wing-found-its-home-on-toonami-20-years-ago-today.

one that reflected the show's expansive world of war and action: "We just wanted to make sure people understood that this wasn't the sort of same cartoon that they had been used to seeing; this was a different beast, this is Gundam, it's almost a genre unto itself, and luckily there were no grown-ups around to tell us, 'You can't do that for a kid show.'"* In its first week, it was the highest-rated program on Toonami. But of course, it wasn't the only mecha Toonami brought to the US. After the success of *Gundam Wing*, there were other *Gundam* shows, along with the old classic *Voltron*, the seamlessly stylish *The Big O*, and one of the seminal mecha in the genre: *Neon Genesis Evangelion*.

I personally never much cared for big robots; *Transformers* and *Voltron* always looked too campy and dull. But in Gundam shows and Evangelion I found a new appreciation for the genre. The shows created a metaphor of the human-machine relationship: humans create weapons in their own image, as vehicles for a violence inherent to our species. But in a terrible uncanny valley, the machines resemble humans but surpass them in their capacity for destruction. The shows suggested that the further humans walk on the path of advancement, the more dangerous their primitive urges become. *Evangelion* then also incorporated religious imagery and existential, psychological themes. The show asked whether humans define machines or the machines define us and, in its hormonal young protagonists, conflated the process of human maturation with militaristic advancement. These shows were not just simple fighting cartoons.

One afternoon, as I watched a tense *Gundam Wing* episode where one of the pilots seemed to have died, I ran to my mother crying during a commercial break, babbling about a fictional war and its casualties. Later, I ran back to her with an update: the pilot wasn't dead, so everything was okay after all. She looked at me quizzically as she continued folding the laundry. What cartoon could elicit such emo-

---

* Inoa, "Gundam Wing."

tional whiplash? But these anime shows spoke differently to me than even my favorite American cartoons; these characters were real to me in an undefinable sense, and I held them and their fates precious.

The most valuable part of these shows wasn't just the emotional resonance they had with me but how, even early on, they linked me to a community of fans, before I could even define fandom or identify myself as part of one. I unconsciously seemed to seek out the kids in school who watched anime too. When I discovered someone else who also raced home and turned on the TV to watch Toonami, they became different in my eyes; even the kids I found obnoxious or annoying, once they said they watched *Yu Yu Hakusho* or *Outlaw Star* or *Tenchi Muyo!*, they were kin. One elementary school friend would meet with me at recess so we could discuss the episodes of *Sailor Moon* and *Gundam Wing* from the previous day. We disagreed on our favorite pilots: hers was Trowa Barton, while I was downright obsessed with the stone-cold Heero Yuy. In middle school another friend, a fan of horror and battle anime, would animatedly recount all the best fight scenes in whatever shows we were watching at the time; we later studied martial arts together.

Toonami, of course, was just the beginning. It began a programming segment called "Midnight Run," of uncensored anime that was targeted to an audience of older kids and adults. So in 2001, Cartoon Network was inspired to introduce Adult Swim, a nighttime block dedicated to the older demographic.

I discovered Adult Swim while flipping channels late one night during that first year of its premiere. I caught a cartoon, one I'd never seen before, and was thrilled because I didn't know there were kids' shows still on at that time of night. I quickly found out—when a football-headed baby with a British accent piloted a ship shaped like a sperm—that this was no kids' show, and that Cartoon Network had introduced something new to late night.

Despite my shock at that first encounter with Adult Swim programming, I ended up watching the show—which I later discovered was *Family Guy*—and found a wealth of new anime to consume. Though Adult Swim would grow to develop its own distinct identity, in the early days it still had some of the feel of Toonami, with a new tone—a simple black screen that, when I watched in the tiny television in my room with my lamp off, would momentarily cloak my whole room in darkness. And one of the block's earliest offerings, *Cowboy Bebop*, with its inventive incorporation of music into its themes, drawing from jazz and film noir to deliver a futuristic Western-style story about bounty hunters in space, felt like an appropriate hodgepodge of mediums and influences—just the approach that it seemed the network was aiming to embody.

By my teen years, Saturday morning cartoons seemed like long a thing of the past, but by then I already had a new Saturday tradition: after the rest of the house was quiet and dark, everyone having said their good nights after a long week, I stayed up, the volume on my old television set on low, just high enough that I could hear, but not so loud that my mother, who would question my late-night viewing, would catch me. Once I heard the snoring through the wall, though, I'd chance turning up the volume a bit higher, and lean in, sitting cross-legged on the carpet and staring up at the screen. I watched the Elric brothers learn alchemy and cried over the tragedies of Nina Tucker and Maes Hughes (RIP); tagged along for hundreds of episodes of a series about an irascible redheaded schoolboy fighting ghouls in the spirit world; cowered during the frightful matches between a girl named Saya Otonashi and vampiric beasts; and gleefully dived into the intricate cat-and-mouse detective story between two geniuses named Light and L. As the popularity of anime grew, I visited the mall in search of more tokens, usually in the form of accessories, buttons, or key rings: a transmutation circle, a tiny version of Hagi's coffin-like cello case, a chibi L, predictably barefoot and in a crouch, holding the stem of a ruby-red apple between his index finger and thumb. In his *Vulture* interview, DeMarco said that Toonami led fans to their new fandoms: "You're watching *Yuri on Ice* because you saw *Dragon Ball* when you were ten."[*] For me, this has always been true, from Saturday mornings to Saturday nights.

The Age of Silver Bullets

At some point near the end of middle school, anxious about the torrent of hormonal changes I was facing and all the related hype around adolescence, I decided that, being at the threshold of adulthood, I could no longer watch cartoons. The Adamantium Age, my playground years of pre-noon Saturdays with capes, was far behind me. The Crude Iron Age, with all its screwball antics, had already had its time in my elementary years. And from my elementary to middle school years, Toonami ushered me into the Age of Gundanium, of mobile suits, Sailor Senshi and Saiyans. Now, I determined, was time to cut the toons and grow up.

This didn't last very long at all. A life without cartoons was unbearably bland, like the black-and-white portion before the colorful awakening in *The Wizard of Oz*.

However, I found that there were other kinds of entertainment to explore. Easily spooked, I was late to horror. I watched the fantastic Disney Channel series *So Weird*, able to handle the show only because most of its episodes skewed more toward science fiction than horror. I missed out on *Goosebumps* and *Are You Afraid of the Dark?* while they were enjoying peak popularity among my classmates. But one hot summer, while my mother worked and my dad slept off his night shifts, I ripped every *Goosebumps* title I could find off the shelves at the library, and I braved reruns of *Are You Afraid of the Dark?* I read *Dracula* and *Frankenstein* and, one fateful day, having exhausted all the interesting options in the children's room in the library, hesitantly crossed the threshold to the main room, larger and quieter and substantially more solemn. There I discovered, to my ecstatic pleasure, multitudes of new options. The aisle closest to the doorway separating the children's room and the adult section was labeled "YA," though it didn't even comprise the whole aisle, just a few shelves, and some of the first books I picked were Annette Curtis Klause's teen horror romances *Blood and Chocolate* and *The Silver Kiss*. (This was, of course, years before *Twilight*.)

I was at the cusp of adolescence and curious about horrors, real and imagined: high school, vampires, witchcraft, boyfriends, demons, dances, PE. When I discovered *Buffy the Vampire Slayer*, it was just what I needed.

Buffy found me on a Halloween night near the end of middle school in the early aughts, around the time it was finishing its first run. Halloween has always been a tricky holiday for me: it's my favorite (how could a holiday that involves candy and costumes not be?), but when I aged out of my tradition of trick-or-treating with my friend in her beautiful suburban cul-de-sac, and the bartering of M&Ms and 3 Musketeers that followed at her kitchen table, I struggled to find a way to celebrate. Scary movies were out of the question, even on my bravest days. (The fear I met during a viewing of *The Grudge* on a sunny, picturesque weekend afternoon when I was a teen was an unfortunate companion for years after.) Sure, there were the old favorites that offered more G-rated takes on horror—*Scooby-Doo*, *Alvin and the Chipmunks Meet the Wolfman*, *Alvin and the Chipmunks Meet Frankenstein*, *The Nightmare Before Christmas*, *Halloweentown*—but one year, desperate for something new, I flipped to a marathon of *Buffy*.

Buffy, a reboot of the 1992 movie of the same name starring Kristy Swanson, dropped the unbridled camp of the film, making a teen horror show that still had a sense of humor. In it, Buffy Summers, a teenager who has been chosen to be the legendary slayer, fighter of vampires, demons, and various other agents of evil, and her friends juggle researching spells and patrolling graveyards with getting through high school—a high school inconveniently situated over a hellmouth.

On paper, *Buffy* may not have seemed like much. After all, it did follow a popular tradition of horror movies featuring teens fighting, being terrorized by, or themselves becoming, monsters. The '70s and '80s had brought us classic teen terrors in the form of *Carrie, Halloween, Prom Night, The House on Sorority Row, The Texas Chainsaw Massacre,* and *A Nightmare on Elm Street,* among others, and the '90s fixed its attention on teens for a spate of horror movies like *Scream, I Know What You Did Last Summer, Idle Hands,* and *The Craft.* Movies served up menus of teen deaths in all shapes and sizes: slit throats, stabbings, and impalements. Often the quotidian conflicts and concerns of adolescent life were paired with this terror to minimize and undercut such trifles, emphasizing the petty self-absorption of youth, or to accentuate and dramatize the viciousness that can be found within the halls of a high school.

These movies positioned teens' transformations—their own change to something monstrous or their brutal dismembering, torture, and murder at the hand of some external evil—as morbid metaphors for the transformation they were already facing, from youth to adulthood. In *Carrie,* the teen protagonist struggles with her shame at menstruating and her hormonal urges and changes, alongside her psychic awakening. Afraid of her womanhood, which her religious fanatic mother equates with sinfulness and monstrosity, Carrie then embodies a true monster, callously killing her peers, her mother, and ultimately herself. In *Halloween,* too, teen sexuality becomes linked with a dire fate; teens have sex, and Jason comes for them. More recently, in the 2020 Netflix series *I Am Not Okay with This,* adapted from Charles Forsman's comic, the main character, Sydney Novak, becomes awakened to her telekinetic powers at the same time that she becomes awakened to her sexuality.

In 2006, when I myself was in high school, one of my favorite bands at the time, My Chemical Romance, sang "Teenagers scare the living shit out of me," and there *is* something particularly frightful about that time.* There is a persisting idea that high school is a horror show.

In middle school, faced with the looming prospect of high school, I became obsessed with teen shows like *My So-Called Life* and *Degrassi: The Next Generation*. I looked to them as a guide to what I should prepare myself for. I needed tips for how one could survive. In these shows, high school was its own self-contained universe, where the stakes were always high. Teens were trapped within their bubbles, and you had no choice but to be invested in the petty minutiae of these fictional characters' lives: what classes they were taking together, who was taking whom to the dance, who spread a rumor, who had a pregnancy scare.

These fictional high schools were like giant games of *Minefield*, where one must maneuver around the explosive traps, hoping not to get hit by the shrapnel. One gained allies and plotted against foes, navigated around pressures like drugs, alcohol, and sex. (Somehow grades never really seemed to figure in.) Everyone had an assigned role: nerd, jock, cheerleader, etc. I hoped to arrive on the first day of high school, feet firmly planted in the safe space between popular high school snob, à la Paige Michalchuk, and successful yet insufferable nerd, à la Liberty Van Zandt. In other words, a moody and smart Angela Chase.

Enter Buffy Summers. Our first introduction to Sunnydale High, with its ironically positive name, is at night, in darkness. The first few minutes of the first episode give us a quick tour of the grounds, starting out front and then moving around inside. The music is eerie and discordant—what you'd expect of the score to any horror movie—with intermittent double beats of percussion that resemble the sound of a heartbeat. The camera moves furtively, around and high and low,

---

* My Chemical Romance, "Teenagers," track 11 on *The Black Parade*, Reprise Records, 2006, compact disc.

until it fixes on the sight of a young couple breaking in, with the usual scary movie cliché: the boy urges the girl to join him in some mischief and romantic action, while the girl looks scared and unsure. Of course, in the world of *Buffy*, this setup ends with an ironic twist on the helpless female trope; the girl ends up being the vampire, making a woman the predator and the man the defenseless prey.

In Sunnydale, writer-director Joss Whedon (a nerd champion until his abusive behavior on set came to light in recent years) created a bubble world, intentionally small and, for the first few seasons of the show, completely high-school-centric. The number of locations we encounter in Sunnydale are few. Outside of the school, we find the local hangout spot the Bronze, some suburban streets, the alley behind the Bronze, graveyards, and the occasional shop or so. Sunnydale High, positioned on top of a hellmouth, is the origin site of the show's main conflicts and the source of its narrative drive. Just as it sits at the juncture between youth and early adulthood, so does the hellmouth sit at the juncture between one world and another. Both are unstable, places of chaos. High school is truly, and literally, hell.

Buffy was never just a high school show with monsters; the show created a mythology around the town, the teens, and the high school, emphasizing the sense that there were outside forces always at work. The show's opening contains its dramatic pitch: "In every generation there is a chosen one. She alone will stand against the vampires, the demons, and the forces of darkness. She is the slayer."* Though the Scooby Gang takes its team name from the beloved animated series about those meddling teen monster-hunters and their talking dog, they aren't simply going to classes and fighting evil on the side as a fun extracurricular; tagged to the show's emphasis on fate is a sense of responsibility. *Buffy* always had real stakes.

For all the fun *Buffy* had, in its characters' quick, lively banter and its occasional odd, campy turns (i.e., "Once More, with Feel-

---

* *Buffy the Vampire Slayer*, "The Harvest," March 10, 1997.

ing"), when the show wanted to get serious, it was devastating. The deaths of the technopagan and honorary Scooby Gang member Jenny Calendar; Buffy's mother, Joyce; and Buffy herself, more than once, reinforced how the show's fictional narrative didn't undercut its portrayal of tragedy. *Buffy's* juxtaposition of horror and supernatural elements with everyday fears highlighted the latter and made them appear scarier than vampires or demons. Spike, who, for a substantial portion of the series, was a central antagonist to the Scoobies, becomes reformed (unwillingly, then more willingly), but then attempts to rape Buffy, a moment that is disconcerting because it's an act of violence that's not even unique to a vampire. Even a powerful monster-slaying heroine and a supernatural villain who have fought with kicks, punches, and spells find themselves in an unfortunately more common situation: sexual assault.

The world of *Buffy* exists in a heightened state of irony, where a group of teens regularly faces and defeats the forces of evil but can't stop some of the pedestrian frights that come with growing up. Though Buffy is the slayer and often does the impossible, she is unable to do anything to prevent her mother's death, which is due not to a demon or supernatural entity, but a brain aneurysm. The gang defeats monsters, but when one member of the Trio, a wannabe-supervillain group of regular boys, shoots a gun and kills Scooby member Tara with a stray bullet, it shows that horror need not be all supernatural fiends but also human evil, which isn't overcome as easily. Indeed, Giles's reveal in the episode "Halloween" that the holiday is ironically quiet for demons and vampires implies that even monsters can be scared off by the normal ruckus and goings-on of humans. I can empathize: A scary scene in a movie or TV show will eventually fade from memory, but a Halloween party incident? Or a social snafu? The marks left on us by the people in our lives are much more indelible. When compared to the depths and imagination of human cruelty, monsters can seem totally harmless.

Buffy delivered an alternative to the teen horror movies and slasher flicks from earlier decades, using the extended format to combine comedy and tragedy, terrors fictional and real, and plots and characters that challenged the tropes that so dominated the form, from the damsel in distress to the meek, helpless nerd. But *Buffy* would become the progenitor for a whole new genre of TV show, the high school horror-thriller, providing an example of the form that would not be matched.

The 2000s brought on an endless cascade of teen shows, seemingly out of nowhere. Perhaps we can blame the popularity of *Gossip Girl*, which engrossed viewers in the happenings of rich young socialites. But Serena van der Woodsen wasn't tracking down murderers or fighting demons (at least not real ones). In 2010 *Pretty Little Liars* similarly presented a group of attractive teens keeping secrets and facing rumors, though the narrative amped up the drama with convoluted mysteries, murders, mistaken identities, and blackmail—a glossy teen soap on cable TV. Soon shows began directly transitioning into teen horror in the vein of *Buffy*, like the popular series *The Vampire Diaries*. Others revisited horror movies or TV shows that had already been done, rewriting the stories with a new teen cast, like *Scream*, *Teen Wolf*, *Bates Motel*, and *Charmed*. In 2017 *Riverdale* became an unexpected sensation, reviving Archie and the gang from their modest, wholesome lives within the pages of the 1940s comic books, re-creating the original series as a brooding high-school drama full of sex and murder. That was followed by the *Chilling Adventures of Sabrina*, which went for a red and black gothic-chic palette, and very obviously and indelicately announced its relevance to the contemporary age by plying its plot and dialogue with rudimentary feminist takes. And there have been many others: *Shadowhunters*, *Ravenswood*, *Motherland: Fort Salem*, and more.

But this rollout of teen shows, one after the other, all in the span of about a decade, has felt, for the most part, like a barrage, with the shows fundamentally indistinguishable from each other. The issue is the extent to which these teen horror-thrillers became part of a trend more than anything else—let's say the teenage gothic. Teenage gothic is primarily an aesthetic: dark lighting, attractive young people, convoluted plots full of sex, murder, mysteries, and betrayals. It may be ironic but perhaps not even confident in its irony, because it does still subscribe to the superficial trappings of the genre.

The post-*Buffy* rise of the teenage gothic in the late 2000s to 2010s raises the question of how the trend came to be in the first place. What attracted me to teen shows was the idea that they were peeks—however unlikely and however bizarre—into what my adolescence and high school life could be. In high school, I continued to watch some teen shows but had mostly stopped by the time I got to junior year. I had faithfully watched the first five seasons of *Degrassi: The Next Generation* but started losing interest around the sixth, and I watched a short-lived drama called *Beautiful People*, but shows like *The O.C.*, *One Tree Hill*, and *Gilmore Girls*, which were so popular with my peers, passed me by. By my junior year of high school, the high-school drama had lost its appeal. Perhaps that's because, being in the thick of it, in my conservative Catholic school, worrying only about exams and college applications and our tyrannical dean who seemed to magically apparate in the hallways to issue detentions, I saw through the thin veneer of drama cast over these fictional adolescent lives. High school was neither as dramatic nor horrific as I had been made to think. When I held up my experiences to those I saw depicted on the screen, they looked so different that I winced at the disparities. They looked to me like crudely drawn portraits of what adolescence was supposed to be.

And yet the lasting popularity of teen dramas, and the recent uptick in the teenage gothic, seem to indicate that many people have not had the same experience I had with the genre. There is a cultural fascination with adolescence; entertainment media loves to romanticize high school, as do many people. There's the notion of someone's "glory days," say, back when they were the star jock or the head cheerleader or the top of the class. There's comfort in the reminiscence, though it is an intentionally misleading fantasy. Adolescence includes the freedom and liveliness and daring of childhood without the burdens of responsibility that come with adulthood—at least in the ideal fantasy of adolescence so often depicted in teen shows. Teen dramas capture the bubble that is a privileged adolescent life, full of superficial concerns and conflicts. The teenage gothic is an extension of that, delivering episodes rife with murders and vampires and werewolves and witches all stylized in the same way as the kiss-and-tell story lines. This is no place for realism.

But that's also what distinguished *Buffy* as the first and last of its kind: the series incorporated horror not as an extension of some exaggerated simulation of adolescent life but as a means toward highlighting the real human drama. That's why, even when I lost my interest in my other high-school dramas, or forgot them altogether, *Buffy* remained with me.

On Halloween, when I'm still lost for things to do, even now, more than a decade removed from high school, I watch old episodes of *Buffy*. When I think of *Buffy* I do still think of high school, but more than that, I think of how the Gentlemen, in muting the residents of Sunnydale, serve as a metaphor about the power our voices hold. I think of Buffy dragging herself through a toxic relationship (with a vampire man, but a man nevertheless). I think of Buffy sinking in her grief for her mother. I think of Willow's innocent interest in magic, which soon turns to a harmful addiction. I think of Buffy depressed and angry and withdrawn from the world, even though she's meant to be its hero. My high school experience wasn't Sunnydale, but at times it was fear and depression and grief, just like *Buffy* was. Bearing the series like a stake in a handbag, I went into adolescence armed with *Buffy* and have carried the slayer with me ever since—to hell and back.

III.

Moon Prism Power, Make Up!

Power, gender, sexuality, and identity in anime and manga

In the fall of 2019, while in Boston for a few readings, I paid a visit to a friend and crashed on her living room couch. Once she, her husband, and I were settled in for the evening, we sank into the couch to watch some TV. She was in the mood for anime and flipped through the offerings on Hulu, stopping at the '90s dub of *Sailor Moon*. "You know, I've never actually watched this," she said. I insisted she watch the first episode, in which Usagi Tsukino, a teenage girl with a reputation for laziness, tardiness, klutziness, and bad grades, discovers that she is actually the monster-battling guardian of justice Sailor Moon.

My friend laughed mirthfully throughout the whole episode. Occasionally she'd pause and say, "Wait, what—," never with displeasure, always glee. The show knew it was ridiculous, she pointed out afterward; I agreed. And yet, unlike many other shows of my youth, I can watch *Sailor Moon* again and again unironically, in total earnest, and enjoy it with the same wholehearted pleasure.

In fact, I have done just that. I watched a few episodes with my friend that night, but I had also watched the occasional episode on my own over the years. In my freshman year of college, before everything was easily streamable, my friend and I watched as many episodes as we could find, revisiting the arcs we knew from our youths and going beyond that, to the ones that never aired in the conservatively censored US versions. My enthusiasm hadn't waned.

As soon as *Sailor Moon* premiered on Toonami in 1998, it was my favorite show. I sang along to the English opening theme and mimicked Sailor Moon's signature action poses during fight scenes.

The battle stances and the mid-fight hero speeches were all part of the show's glamour. Clark Kent simply ran into a phone booth and emerged in his Superman costume—what a lack of finesse. In *Sailor Moon*, there were countless transformations: with a declaration and the help of an enchanted compact or pen, the girls were rendered as nude silhouettes, dressed piece by piece, from heeled boots or pumps to earrings and gloves. When I was young, *Sailor Moon* wasn't just a show to me; it represented a whole world in which young girls had power and were the heroes of the story. I craved the magic of it all, wishing to be a pretty sailor guardian too.

I did, however, get the sense early on that my love for the show could be something to be ashamed of. My father would make fun of it relentlessly, calling out in a shrill approximation of Usagi's voice, "*Darius! What are we gonna do, Darius?!*" intentionally getting Mamoru's English name, Darien, incorrect, to my irritation. He'd call me "Sailor Earth" with a broad grin. I was obliquely aware that my dad's teasing likely had something to do with gender; we watched shows about male heroes together on Saturday mornings, but he would jest at the expense of my beloved Sailor Scouts. *Sailor Moon* was unabashedly girly, after all, and I was always notoriously opposed to anything too feminine. For years I fought my mother on dresses and skirts. I still can't walk in heels and have never worn makeup or nail polish a day in my life.

So when I fantasized about my own transformation to a Sailor Scout, I imagined opting out of the steps that included magically applied nail polish and lip gloss. I liked the style of Jupiter's and Uranus's boots but wondered if I could get a version in flats. These were just traditional, stereotypical markers of femininity, of course, and the casual observer of the show might accuse it of pandering to this blush-pink image of girlhood, with girls who fight with the help of accessories like tiaras.

This is only part of the story, in *Sailor Moon* and in shojo in general. Shojo, which roughly translates to "young woman" or "girl," is manga or anime that is targeted toward that very demographic. In these series, female protagonists navigate school and romance, and oftentimes the shows have a bubblegum aesthetic. A popular subgenre, magical girl shojo, like *Sailor Moon*, depicts young school-age girls who are imbued with magical abilities and must save the world.

At first glance, the form appears superficial, as it seems to draw from gender norms: the girls wear cute outfits and wield the power of love. But the genre is often quietly (and sometimes not so quietly) subversive, showing girls who fight courageously while also being vulnerable. Shojo performs a version of femininity that manipulates traditional ideas of womanhood and girlhood to broaden the idea of what is female and what is female power.

The Scouts themselves are more complex than they may at first seem. Makoto, Sailor Jupiter, my favorite Scout of the inner planets, is tough and tomboyish. The tiny conducting rod that would rise from the middle of her tiara before her lightning attacks thrilled me as a kid; it was my favorite feature of the Scouts' gear. And yet Makoto is also sensitive and a hopeless romantic, showing that a woman can embody both sides. Minako, too—though as a kid I dismissed Sailor Venus because of her bubbly popular-girl persona—is a romantic and, of course, the Sailor Scout of love, even though she has a tragic backstory full of heartbreak. And later the young, seemingly weak Hotaru turns out to have the awesome power of Sailor Saturn, the bringer of life and destruction. And at the center of it all is Usagi, who is clumsy and cowardly and quick to cry, especially in the early episodes of the show, but who is ultimately revealed to have unflappable fortitude and an endless capacity for compassion. She fights for love—and not just romantic love, but a love for her friends and for the world at large.

At the end of the show's first season, the Sailor Scouts travel to the North Pole to infiltrate the fortress of the villain, Queen Beryl, who has taken Mamoru, aka Tuxedo Mask, Usagi's boyfriend and future husband, hostage. The Scouts face Beryl's henchmen and, one by one, are picked off and killed, until Usagi is the only one left. Each death nearly breaks her, but she continues. In the end, Usagi, awoken to her true form as Princess Serenity, fights Beryl but finds her power waning. In an iconic scene—perhaps my favorite of the series—the Scouts materialize as apparitions at her side, and each lends a hand to power her through.

So often our stories in books and entertainment media value the idea of singular strength, of an individual making moves and battling to the top. But power—whether in a fictional world or in a real society—is rooted in community. No Sailor Scout is an island—so said John Donne. Well, *sort of*.

Sailor Moon also granted its female heroes the power of gods, quite literally, as the show drew freely from Greco-Roman mythology. The story of Usagi and Mamoru's love in their past lives as Princess Serenity and Prince Endymion is an explicit reference to the Greek love story of Selene, the goddess of the moon, and the shepherd-prince Endymion. Each of the Scouts' abilities, and occasionally their temperaments, match those of their Greco-Roman counterparts: the fierce, petulant Mars recalls the god of war; the powerful Jupiter fights with lightning like the father of the gods; Venus fights with love like her counterpart. Either way, they are soldiers and guardians—not just pretty princesses who stay locked in towers.

The whole premise of the show's first season is the Scouts' mission to find the legendary Silver Crystal and figure out who their princess is, since they don't realize that the princess is in fact Sailor Moon (a fact I found impossible to believe as a child, obvious as it seemed to me, even at seven years old). The princess is one of them: a fighter, the commander of her troops. Compared to these soldiers, who are bestowed with the powers of the universe, the men seem lesser, mundane. Even the main villains are female, as though in the world of *Sailor Moon*, both the sides of good and evil recognize that the most power lies in the hands of women. (Comparatively, Mamoru, a reborn prince who runs around in a tux throwing roses during battles before promptly disappearing, is a letdown. A meme depicting his declaration, "My job is done," and Sailor Moon responding, "But you didn't do anything," is popular for good reason.)

Usagi isn't the natural-born champion that we're granted in so many hero stories featuring men, but that formula wouldn't have been as interesting anyway. Usagi is often scared, lazy, confused—and yet still rises to the occasion because she has to. What makes characters engaging is not when they are the crowning image of themselves, totally unblemished, but when they are forced to confront the limits of how they're defined—when they try, and sometimes fail, to be better and we see their full potential shine through.

In *Sailor Moon SuperS: The Movie*, which I owned as a much-beloved VHS in the '90s, Usagi fights with Chibiusa, aka Sailor Mini Moon, her daughter from the future, and childishly competes with her for Mamoru's attention. And yet, by the end of the movie, Usagi risks everything to save her. Even as she carries Chibiusa, making her defenseless against her enemy's attacks, she continues to fight forward and shield Chibiusa from the blasts. When Chibiusa is first abducted by the villains, in a giant flying gondola, the perspective of the scene switches from below to up above, from Chibiusa's view. Usagi remains down below, scrambling fruitlessly, frantically yelling for Chibiusa as she floats farther away. But we're then brought closer to her face, which looks shattered, like every part of her is at the point of collapse. Her hands shake and her head turns down and to the side as though she has resigned herself to utter defeat. But the moment I love comes next: she shakes her head, ever so slightly, balls a fist, and looks up to the sky with a new resolve, her face firm and defiant.

The whole change happens in the span of just a couple of seconds before the movie continues with the rest of the action, but it shows the very point at which Usagi thinks beyond herself and girds herself for battle. She makes the choice to be brave and fight—to be the hero.

But this isn't the only thing these magical-girl shojo have to offer. One of the most important things the genre has done is take on queer representation, embracing a spectrum of sexualities and gender expressions. *Sailor Moon* depicted several openly gay characters, including villains (two of Queen Beryl's minions, Kunzite and Zoisite) and heroes, like two of the Scouts themselves: Haruka (Uranus) and Michiru (Neptune), who were in a relationship—at least in the original manga.

Though *Sailor Moon*'s creator, Naoko Takeuchi, confirmed that the two Scouts were romantically involved, the dubbed version that came to the US said differently. The American dub made significant changes to the show, some allegedly to make it more accessible to a Western audience but others to make a more heteronormative product. As a result, genders and the nature of some relationships were changed.

When Haruka is introduced, dressed in a boys' school uniform, Usagi and Minako are enamored with her, assuming she's a guy. Haruka flirts back, and it's not until later that the Scouts realize that Haruka is actually female. Whether the depiction of a queer relationship would have shocked and confused my young self as the show's North American distributors surely assumed it would is moot (though unlikely); what the egregious queer erasure did do was unnecessarily complicate the show in the service of creating a less diverse and thus less taboo world.

As a kid, I loved Haruka's androgyny, which the animation style served as it seemed fit. In some scenes, like the early ones, when she's meant to present as a man, her features are drawn sharper, but later her face becomes more rounded, her eyelashes more prominent. Haruka raced cars and motorcycles and could rock a pair of slacks and a button-down shirt. And in her more feminine sailor form too she exuded power; she wielded a sword and had impressive offensive attacks. The physicality of the Scouts' attacks varied, but many of the moves involved soft motions—arms crossed defensively or fanned out more like a deflection. Uranus's attack, World Shaking, involved a clenched fist and a torrent of energy ferociously slammed down to the ground.

The American dub named Haruka and Michiru cousins, not only shoving them back into the closet but also making up an odd, non-sensical alternative relationship to account for the change. Though the show erased the Scouts' queerness, it wasn't able to totally censor out the chemistry between them. The now incestuous flirtation between Neptune and Uranus baffled and disconcerted me. The blushes and small smiles were inexplicable.

This erasure seemed especially flagrant because of what Neptune and Uranus represented. So often depictions of queerness in the media are burdened with problematic tropes: the gay best friend, the promiscuous bisexual, the "buried gay," etc. Lesbians in particular are framed as objects of a straight male gaze, as though female pleasure cannot exist independent of men. In *Sailor Moon*, however, a show that celebrated the power and importance of female relationships, Haruka and Michiru have a mature relationship that is simply stated as fact, without any shock value or fetishization.

Though the revision of Haruka and Michiru from lovers to kin is likely familiar to most American fans of the show, another set of queer-presenting characters—and the entire arc of the show that featured them—was nixed completely. When my friend and I revisited the series in college, watching beyond where the American dub had stopped, we were shocked to see a season begin with the implied death of Mamoru. But even more surprising was how the show provided Usagi with another love interest, a boy named Seiya, the lead singer of a boy band trio that actually turned out to be a special group of Sailor Scouts called the Sailor Starlights.

While Takeuchi insisted that Sailor Scouts could only be women (and so, in the manga, the Starlights were simply women who cross-dressed as men), the anime introduced a more dramatic transformation, allowing that the Starlights actually changed their sex as well. They appear in pronounced masculine attire: suits that showcase their streamlined physiques and broad shoulders. In their transformation sequences their silhouettes change to include breasts and waists and curves. The costumes, too, are unforgettably risqué: short shorts, thigh-high boots, bikini tops, and what appears to be a whole lot of latex. They're imposing figures—tall and slender, with long, dramatic wisps of hair—and their costumes emphasize their transsexuality. (Not to mention their attacks, including Starlight Honeymoon Therapy Kiss, and my personal favorite, Star Gentle Uterus. Coming from characters who swap sexes, the attacks seem like a bold-faced joke about how female power is defined. The Starlights may appear as men in their daily lives, but in order to have real power in the world of the show, they need to have the most arrant display of femininity.) Though the show's inclusion of what were essentially trans characters proved how uniquely representative Sailor Moon was, it still struggled to allow the Starlights to fully occupy a trans or nonbinary space. Their attacks fall in line with the show's interest in elevating female power, but the sailor uniform is also a trap: for a tomboy like me, who wanted to be a Sailor Scout, it was surprising that despite the show's embrace of Haruka's everyday butch look and, later, the male-presenting Starlights, whenever a character transformed into their star-warrior form, they reverted to a heterogenous vision of femininity. In one sense, it's still a wonderful alternative to the many stories that fail to portray female power at all. But in another sense the series fully commits to one kind of female gender presentation as the ideal, leaving not much wiggle room for, say, the queer characters to be powerful without makeup and heels. In so many ways, *Sailor Moon* broke the mold, but its embrace of girl power also wouldn't fully hold up to the more nuanced, contemporary politics we have about gender performance and stereotypes today, especially when it comes to queer individuals.

Another of my go-to magical girl shojo as a kid, *Cardcaptor Sakura*, also erased its queer characters. In the show, a young girl named Sakura discovers a magic book—the Clow—full of sentient cards that grant its wielder their abilities. The cards, however, escape, and she must collect them all to prevent them from wreaking havoc on the world. I loved the show and had my own Clow book that sat on my bookshelf—a fake plastic book with a clasp that was full of cards. When the show came on, I'd take out my favorite cards (the Windy, the Fly, the Time, the Shadow), flinging them down onto my carpet, pretending to activate them in just the way Sakura did. I didn't have her magical wand, so I used what I had handy—anything vaguely talismanic that I could use to tap the glossy illustrated bits of card stock and pretend that they could be my source of power, like they were for Sakura.

Cardcaptor Sakura embraced many shojo tropes, keeping its female protagonist in the spotlight, with her infinite costume changes (Lolita-style frills and bows that even I, with my contempt for anything too feminine, found irresistibly cute) and fantastical adventures, but also incidents from her regular life. Tender relationships and romances abounded: Sakura has a contentious relationship with Syaoran Li, another cardcaptor with a better handle on his magical abilities, until it turns to romance. Sakura's best friend, Tomoyo, who supplies Sakura's cardcaptor outfits and enthusiastically films her missions, has a crush on her. Sakura and Syaoran both have crushes on Yukito, the best friend of Sakura's older brother, Toya. But Toya and Yukito—who is actually the human alter ego of an androgynous angel-guardian of the Clow—are in love. And there are many more to speak of.

But as with *Sailor Moon*, *Cardcaptor Sakura* was totally transformed when it was brought to the States. The version that aired when I was a kid was dramatically edited down, and personalities were altered to be more in line with what was thought to be an American sensibility. Even the show's name was changed, to *Cardcaptors*. Not only did the series censor the original's queer relationships, it also reframed the show's perspective entirely. The new dub was meant to appeal to both boys and girls, and so it was edited in a way that more strongly aligned it with shonen, or series for young boys, than shojo. Romances and sequences depicting Sakura's daily life were downplayed, changed, or cut completely, and Syaoran was introduced sooner with the hope that he would draw in young boys in a way a young female protagonist presumably wouldn't. Fight scenes also became more the focus, as in shonen like *Pokémon* and *Dragon Ball Z*.

Though I loved *Cardcaptors*, it felt incomplete, seeing as it was just that—pulled apart, revised, and cobbled back together into something so much lesser than what it originally had been. These edits were indicative not only of the narrow-sighted gender politics of the media, but also of how young fans were yet again underestimated. The pandering edits and cuts of episodes to fit gender stereotypes and conservative views of sexuality were done with the assumption that kids wouldn't notice the difference. Or that even if they did notice the signs of things conspicuously absent or unspoken, they were better off with holey narratives and simplified characters, because anything other than that would be to risk enabling a hasty maturation and perhaps even perversion. Fans did notice, though. The DVD and VHS releases of the dubbed American version of the show were canceled because of poor sales. Ultimately the original subtitled show outsold the dub.

Coinciding with the run of *Cardcaptor Sakura* was another magical girl shojo, *Revolutionary Girl Utena*, which also revolutionized the genre with its take on sexuality and gender expression. I was late to *RGU*, having only heard of it for the first time at my first New York Comic Con. I went with two friends, my college roommates at the time, one of whom then became my annual Comic Con companion. At the end of one long day, as we looked through the Con schedule, trying to figure out if there was anything left that we wanted to see, our roommate pointed out a screening of *Revolutionary Girl Utena*. We didn't know what it was, so she pitched it as a ridiculous, super-queer *Sailor Moon*. So we went to the screening room in the Javits Center, where there was no panel, no celebrities, just a big screen playing episodes of *RGU* as a bunch of nerds sat intently watching in the dark. Even though I'd watched plenty of campy magical girl shojo growing up, *RGU* seemed unreal: the concept, of a girl who dresses up like a prince and goes to a school where she must duel other princes to win a girl known as the "Rose Bride," was absolutely nonsensical. And the queerness of it was remarkably explicit. As we watched in the dark room of whooping longtime fans of the series, we wondered how such a '90s show was even real.

From the very start of the first episode, as the show introduces its heroine's backstory, *RGU* subverts the typical fairy-tale setup. The young Utena encounters a valiant prince whom she becomes enamored with and goes on a mission to find. But, ironically, she expresses her love for this mysterious prince by deciding to become a prince herself. Years later, as she attends Ohtori Academy, she wears a boys' uniform, though with playful modifications. Her military-style jacket is broad in the shoulders but narrows down to an impossibly slim waist before fanning out slightly at her hips, and beneath the jacket peeks not slacks but what looks like a pair of red biking shorts.

Utena's search for her prince brings her to Ohtori Academy, where students inexplicably duel to win an engagement with, and ownership of, the obedient Rose Bride, Anthy. While defending Anthy from her abusive current fiancé, Utena gets drawn into the duels and wins her first match and thus Anthy's hand in marriage. Though Utena is searching for her own prince, along the way she becomes the prince who saves Anthy. This is just one of many ways the show subverts fairy-tale tropes. When Utena discovers the dueling arena, in a forest by the school, an upside-down castle dangles above the ring like a chandelier—a symbol of a fairy tale literally turned on its head.

Utena is popular and alluring to both men and women. Girls around her flirt and swoon as though she's a celebrity, and male characters plot to capture her interest. Though Utena plucks traits from either side of the gender binary, her flexibility along that line erases it. *RGU*'s two central female characters, Utena and Anthy, have parallel journeys. Anthy, who is emotionally, physically, and sexually abused, must discover her agency. Utena must discover what kind of power she wields and how she may use it, as a prince or princess. Here the implied queerness of Utena and Anthy equates to freedom: they are free to define themselves, their relationship to each other, and their power within an institution that would have them just serve as damsels in distress waiting for men to save them.

Despite my love for magical-girl shojo as a kid, by the time I hit my teens I had stopped watching them. Though I retained my love for *Sailor Moon*, I didn't seek out any new shojo, which I dismissed as too girly and too juvenile, with their transformations and focus on love and friendship. Shojo like *Sailor Moon*, *Cardcaptor Sakura*, and *Revolutionary Girl Utena* were progressive in their portrayals of gender and sexuality, but I missed much of that, having watched the censored versions, which reinforced the antiquated (and offensive) narrative that non-heterotypical relationships or behaviors were abnormal. What I was left with was fun and impressive but less explicit in the ways it subverted the conventions of the form. In the past decade, however, I have been surprised by shojo again and again. Recent shojo have taken more blatant jabs at this kind of conventionality.

The plot of *Kill la Kill* is absurd: a girl named Ryuko with a giant scissor blade shows up at a school searching for the person who murdered her father. But that school has a frightening hierarchy. Battles determine not only the superiority of certain students but also how those students and their families can advance economically.

Oh, and there's magical clothing. The top students wear magical sentient clothing that Autobots them into fighters with advanced abilities. Meanwhile, an underground movement of scantily clad rebels called Nudist Beach keeps an eye on the school, its students, and its villainous lady in charge.

In *Kill la Kill*, one can see the points at which the show took magical-girl tropes and ran off with them. Like *Sailor Moon, Kill la Kill* has its female protagonist transform in battle; the costume change empowers her. But Ryuko's costuming is absurdly revealing. Instead of the outfit changing into full-body armor, it shrinks on her body to something that resembles fetish gear more than anything else. Instead of the usual cute outfits that magical girls don, Ryuko is stripped down. The series pokes fun at the notion of the magical makeover by making it something obscene.

And when it comes to our heroine herself, she challenges the trope of the cute, girly shojo protagonist; Ryuko is tough and tomboyish and quick to fight. I immediately related to her, with her combativeness and nerve. And I admired her footwear—sneakers seemed much more practical than kitten heels, and would be my own choice if I lived in a world of magical girls. The series pushes back against the magical-girl shojo tropes by instead resembling shonen, with the emphasis on battles and the starker, bleaker animation style. There are no blush pinks or purples, and no frilly dresses here—that is, with the exception of, ironically, one of the series' antagonists, Nui Harime. With her big curly ponytails (reminiscent of Usagi's), her giant pink bows, heart choker, and pink ruffle dress, Nui more closely resembles the typical magical-girl heroine, though her sugar-sweet appearance and bubbly persona are just covers for her sadism and cruelty.

Magical girls, after all, are full of surprises.

I know this as a fact, as a veteran anime fan, and yet I was still somehow unprepared for the shock of magical-girl irony that was *Puella Magi Madoka Magica* when I watched it a few years ago. I came to the show two or three years late, having dismissed it as a juvenile shojo, a cloyingly cute magical-girl offering that would inevitably fail to measure up to its '90s predecessors. Very early on, however, *Madoka Magica* showed that it had something unique to offer.

In the series, a group of middle-school students decide to become magical girls to fight witches. In exchange, they're granted any wish they desire. All of that seems like typical fare—the girls fight evil while wearing cute outfits, and there's even a cute magical-creature guide, Kyubey, to accompany them. And yet I noticed hints in the visuals that something about this magical-girl show was peculiar. The sleekness of the show's main style of animation stands in such stark contrast to scenes depicting the witches, who are not actual characters—no Sabrina or Sanderson sisters here. Each one is a trippy hodgepodge of colors and shapes, inconsistent with the rest of the show's aesthetic; instead, a cut-and-paste collage of images with different patterns and textures like a patchwork quilt of animation.

I found the contrast off-putting, especially for a show that appeared to me like a very basic magical-girl shojo. A few episodes in, however, *Madoka Magica* abruptly reveals what it is really about. When two schoolgirls, Madoka and Sayaka, are recruited by Kyubey to become magical girls, they shadow Mami, an upperclassman who is already a magical girl and fights witches. The ringlet-ponytailed Mami looks the part of the cheerful, self-assured magical girl, though her cute costume is also a bit out of the ordinary for the genre. Browns and tans, a corset, and footwear recalling cowboy boots: it's Lolita meets the American frontier. Instead of wands or tiaras, or even stately swords, she bears guns, which creates another striking contrast, between the cute teenage magical girl and the violent real-world weapon she uses.

Not long after she's introduced to us and makes friends with Madoka and Sayaka, she goes off into battle. Mami blasts the witch, but not before it transforms into a grinning clown-faced creature with a caterpillar body. It faces Mami, opens its mouth of sharp teeth, and decapitates her. We don't see the gory details up close, but we see her limp, lifeless body suspended from the top of the screen, first in her magical-girl outfit, then in her regular school uniform, before the witch drops her body in the distance. The shock is twofold: the gruesome death itself, so out of character for a shojo, and the touching scene among the girls that precedes it, setting us up for the tragedy. Mami's death joins the ranks of the most disturbing anime demises, and not because anime doesn't have more unsettling death scenes to offer (it certainly has plenty), but because *Madoka Magica* builds its story and characters from the traditions of the genre just to surprise viewers in its subversion of those same tropes. (And to the cosplayer I saw at 2019 New York Comic Con dressed as the witch holding Mami's dead body dangling from its mouth, I would like to say, "Well done, but too soon.")

Just as *Revolutionary Girl Utena* provided a dark alternative to the fairy-tale narrative, *Madoka Magica* showed the cost that comes with being a magical girl. Kyubey is not the cute, benevolent creature he seems to be. The wishes the magical girls get are monkey's paws, granted with unknown consequences. The girls themselves won't always necessarily save the day or even get out alive. And the truth about the witches—that they are former magical girls who've been tainted with despair—rejects the idea that these magical girls are always unimpeachably pure and good. Each is burdened with something, and the specter of the show isn't the witches but the feelings of isolation and hopelessness that they summon from the girls. The girls must fight, and yet they are also the most vulnerable to transforming into the very thing they fight.

Every year for the past several years, me and my Comic Con partner discuss our cosplay plans. Since day one our list has included magical girls. Sailor Scouts. Cardcaptors. Even now, I hesitate, considering the skirts and the boots and the frills. More often I cosplay as male characters, either as is or gender-bent, but I'm ashamed to admit there are times when I question how well or comfortably I will fit the mold of these magical girls, even for a casual game of dress-up among a convention center full of nerds.

But part of that is just me internalizing a false narrative about female power—that it's less strong, less valuable, and less interesting in our society. The magical-girl shojo don't just say that women can be strong; they say that we, too, have battles to fight, and can fight harder and longer than the boys because for us there's always been more at stake.

I am Generation Pikachu. Which is to say that I grew up with the cultural phenomenon that is *Pokémon* as its popularity began to expand from its native Japan over to the States. When the *Pokémon* TV series aired in America, when I was in elementary school, it became an immediate hit with the boys in my class.

Ever the critic, even then, I was nonplussed by the hype and decided the show wasn't worth my eight-year-old attention. My mind remained unchanged until, one day at school, I walked up to a group of boys who were having a lively *Pokémon* debate. I stopped, curious, but suddenly one turned to me and declared, with a tone of glib self-satisfaction, "*You* don't know about *Pokémon*. *Girls* don't know about *Pokémon*." He was right, at least in the sense that the girls in our class hadn't seemed to have caught on to *Pokémon* yet, though I doubt that he'd surveyed them to confirm it as fact. And he was certainly right that I didn't know anything about *Pokémon*. Still, I found the very implication that something was unavailable to me because of my gender infuriating. That afternoon after school, I dutifully watched the new episode of *Pokémon*. I took mental note of five Pokémon as though I were preparing for a quiz. The next day, I proudly marched up to the boys and recited the list of the five Pokémon I knew. They were shocked (eight-year-old boys are easy to impress) and I felt vindicated; their confusion and awe seemed like points in my book, a mark of respect. I had always chafed at stereotypes of femininity and so relished the fact that I had apparently transcended the limits of my gender—at least as defined by these boys—and granted myself, in this small way, a token of androgyny, which I loved. Here I was "one of the boys."

Having proved my point, I could have returned to a *Pokémon*-less existence, but I kept watching, and it became a genuine fandom of my own. I got *Pokémon* games for my Game Boy, had a collection of tiny Poké Ball toys, and had a Pikachu plushie. My mom planned out a whole *Pokémon*-themed basket for me for Easter. Even though I didn't actually understand the card game, I nevertheless collected the cards in a frenzy and organized them in a card-collector book: blue with Charmander on the cover. The book was so packed that its little buckle barely held. When I went to summer camp and brought my cards to show off to a group of boys, laying them out across the table, I was devastated when my holographic Blastoise and Charizard inexplicably went missing. And in 1999, I had my very first devastating theatrical experience, when I saw *Pokémon: The First Movie.* Watching Ash get caught in the crossfire of the battle between Mew and Mewtwo while Pikachu desperately tried to revive him broke me in a way my parents were wholly unprepared to deal with. "You must really like Ash??" my father said, quizzically. No, I corrected him in a garbled voice, trying to speak through my downright funereal weeping, I couldn't bear the sight of Pikachu's grief.

My love affair with *Pokémon* was passionate, all-encompassing, and yet brief. After about two years of everything Pikachu, my peers and I began to lose interest. The arcs of the show quickly became familiar, and the Pokémon themselves kept multiplying. I soon found my trusty edition of *The Official Pokémon Handbook* outdated and began resenting how the growth of the fandom outpaced my interest. I turned to the "I liked it before it was cool" defense, and when my parents pointed out a new Pokémon, appearing on a poster or commercial or as a toy in my cereal box, I'd scoff, saying I didn't know it because it wasn't one of the "originals."

Still, *Pokémon* was an essential part of my nerd evolution. It was my first introduction to shonen. The genre has become increasingly popular since *Pokémon* arrived on the scene in America. Shonen follow a formula not too far removed from that of superhero stories. The heroes are always boys, usually outsiders, underdogs endowed with some secret ability, falling into the trope of the "chosen one." They venture forth on Odyssean quests, usually in the pursuit of a vague notion of "greatness." (In *Pokémon*, this was plainly announced in the unforgettable theme song: "I wanna be the very best, / like no one ever was . . ."*) There is an endless refrain of adventures and battles, adventures and battles, so most shonen are known for their sizable arcs, some going for decades. Though the ever-recurring "Nurse Joys" and "Officer Jennys" in *Pokémon* are more a holdover from the video-game tradition of reusing character designs, they could also work as a self-aware joke about the shonen show's relentless repetitions.

Another shonen, *Digimon: Digital Monsters*, which premiered in the US in 1999, had infinitely more defined characters and more complex story lines, along with a futuristic-fantasy twist, but at its roots it still recalled *Pokémon and* fell into the more popular show's shadow. Kids are teamed up with a "digital monster" and have battles, and their Digimon evolve into larger, more powerful forms. Unlike *Pokémon*, which existed in its own simple world, *Digimon* had a narrative that crossed between the "real world" and the Digital World of the Digimon. While *Pokémon* seemed to be a world built on a principle of magic, *Digimon* proposed a world built by technology. Neither

---

* *Pokémon*, "Pokémon, I Choose You!" 1997.

was perfect in either respect, but both shared fundamental traits that distinguish shonen and supposedly make them most appealing to young boys.

I hate to admit how much my male peers influenced my anime preferences as a kid, but the fact remains that they drew me into not only *Pokémon* but also, a few years later, the shonen *Dragon Ball Z*. I was aware of the show, which aired as part of the Toonami block I was so attached to, but again, I hesitated to start it.

In fifth grade, for some reason or another, our teacher made us move our desks. In the new arrangement, I was the second seat in a row of desks perpendicular to the board and across from the windows. In the first seat, by the door, sitting to my right, was a boy I wasn't thrilled to be near. He wasn't the worst option to have, but also certainly not the best. He was small, short and skinny, with a round head and knobby knees, jet-black hair and thick, dark eyebrows. He spoke quickly and incessantly once he got going. And he loved two things with all his being: the *Redwall* series and *Dragon Ball Z*.

Thanks to my deskmate, I was familiar with the Z Fighters even before I watched the show. Known as the class artist, he drew constantly, and I watched: he'd sit in the chair with one leg folded beneath him, and his body would arch over the desk, his shoulders rounded in and elbows out as though he were huddling over some secret treasure. He drew the way he spoke—rapidly, sharply, with quick strokes dashed out like attacks. And though we were years past the days of handwriting exercises, he held the pencil wrong—between his ring finger and his pinky, his whole fist clasped around it as though he were bearing a weapon. He drew Goku making attacks, Goku powering up, Goku in his Super Saiyan forms. And he made his love for the show a whole theatrical performance: he'd draw the characters and then recount everything that had happened the afternoon before. He gestured, made sound effects (though I never actually asked for these play-by-plays), and I found his excitement unnerving. It was loud and violent in its display, so unlike the way me and my girl friends fawned over the details of the romantic subplots in *Sailor Moon*. He loved miming Goku's signature attack: the "kamehameha," with its enunciated, drawn-out roar and inciting motion, hands drawn back to grasp an invisible ball of energy, then arms thrust forward with the palms meeting, fingers curled in.

He wore me down with his constant talk about the Z Fighters; I watched the show to try to understand it all. Soon I was wrapped up in it too. Even though we joked about how the battles were so shamelessly drawn out, with Goku powering up for what seemed like episodes on end, we also readily yielded to the suspense, tuning in religiously every day to watch and wait for the final blow to land. We ate up the big bads: we treasured evil Vegeta, lost our minds with Frieza, and relished the Androids and Cell.

With the introduction of each new villain, however, there was a case of diminishing returns. By adhering so closely to the simplest, bare-bones shonen formula, the show constantly undermined the stakes it kept trying to raise. In order to keep the fights interesting and ensure that the heroes kept reaching new levels of power, the conflicts had to be built on a steadily increasing incline. But to say each new villain was the most powerful our heroes had faced and posed an immediate danger to the world, the series had to build up the audience's trust that this would be an entirely fresh, dangerous challenge while also downplaying the earlier villains, who themselves were so recently the cream of the crop.

There is a larger problem here, of the limitations the genre puts on itself in its relationship to gender and power. Despite their main conceit often being a boy fighting his way to greatness, the nature of how power is often portrayed in shonen provides only one rote avenue to travel from beginning to end. The male heroes must journey and get stronger and fight and win, because brute force is valuable. Even the conditions of the world so rarely change. We learn more of the world and its characters, but there is no alternative way for the hero to navigate it. Things remain stubbornly static.

Throughout the years, I watched as many episodes as I could stand of the shonen I encountered: *Inuyasha, Yu Yu Hakusho, Rurouni Kenshin, Bleach, Naruto*. The formula was a comfort, especially when I watched in my preteen and teen years, struggling with my adolescent feelings of displacement. The heroes were black sheep in one sense or another, and yet they had infinite potential; they could change the world. Inuyasha, half human and half demon, grew up shunned by both worlds. Ichigo Kurosaki, gruff and ornery and isolated from his classmates, stands out for his bad attitude and red hair. Naruto is rejected by his peers because he houses within his body a dangerous nine-tailed fox demon. While magical-girl shojo so often feature girls who are in more uplifting circumstances, and who gradually stumble into power, shonen often create a mythology around their male protagonists from the start.

The difference in the very shape of the narratives, too, creates a notable discrepancy in the size of the worlds depicted in shonen versus shojo. Shojo don't as often adopt the mode of journeying; we see just a sliver of the world, with our female heroine at the center. In shonen, the heroes almost always venture forth from their homes—Monkey D. Luffy pirating the oceans, Yusuke Urameshi and Ichigo Kurosaki both venturing through the worlds of the living and the dead, garnering friends and foes along the way—making their worlds larger. In shonen, the world is there to be conquered and owned by our hero, while in shojo, the world is simply there to be defended, saved. The two genres, then, approach their stories from fundamentally different positions: offensive versus defensive, warriors versus caretakers.

And yet, for all of shonen's emphasis on the boy-hero-on-the-path-to-glory narrative, these shows also resist the wholly singular approach. Even if the hero starts off totally alone, he gains a posse along the way, forming a whole central cast of hero characters who may squabble and support one another in the battles to come. That's especially true in sports shonen. One of my favorite anime of the past couple years is *Haikyu!!*, about a short young man named Shoyo Hinata who wants to be a great volleyball player. He joins a high school team that has fallen far from the heights it reached in its heyday. The eager underdog, the fierce battle-like competitions, the ever-broadening cast of characters: *Haikyu!!* has all the usual traits of shonen but improves the formula. The team doesn't always win against its competitors; sometimes they lose, making the stakes in each game higher. The show doesn't just get lost in its love for its protagonist but constantly shifts its perspective to show us the backstories and growth of the other members of the team. And each opposing team is distinguished with a particular style and character, with even seemingly unimportant tertiary players given enough development and background to provide every matchup new heft.

Part of the popularity boom of shonen in America in the past three decades is perhaps correlated to the growing focus on super-hero stories in pop culture. The earnest adventures of these boy-heroes simply represent a longer-form iteration of the narratives of the grown, masked heroes who have become inescapable in TV and movies. One can see the likeness of Superman in Goku, another alien who arrives on Earth, becomes adopted by humans, and comes to believe himself to be the defender of humankind.

But the recent superhero boom has also produced a contrary effect: shonen that increasingly satirize comic-book-hero stories. One ironic conceit that has been popular in recent years has been the impotent superhero, as in 2013's *Samurai Flamenco*, in which a male model decides to become a hero despite his total lack of abilities. On the other end of the spectrum, 2015 brought the hit series *One-Punch Man*, in which an underwhelming-looking hero named Saitama, who does hero work just for fun, is so powerful that he spends most of his time bored. Taking the "chosen one" trope to the extreme, *One-Punch Man* provides a main character who is so inexplicably power-ful from the start (when asked how he got so strong, his response is a confoundingly simple daily routine of basic workouts like running, push-ups, squats and sit-ups) that he has nowhere else to go. Unlike the heroes who train and level up, facing harrowing obstacles on the route to saving the world, Saitama indifferently pummels villains on his way to the grocery store, more concerned about coupons and discounts than his opponents.

The trope of the theatrical leveling up also becomes a source of parody in the animation itself. Saitama, who is usually drawn with a dolt-like expression, and whose head is styled as perfectly round, with simple, undefined features, transforms in the rare times when he is being serious. His facial features become more detailed, with shading and sharper line work revealing fresh contours in his forehead, chin, and cheeks. His eyes are narrowed and focused, and his eyebrows angle downward, creasing his brow. Though by its very conceit the show seems to write itself into a corner (what can possibly happen when a hero can't be beaten?), *One-Punch Man* releases itself from its genre's prerequisite of long, drawn-out battle sequences, instead spotlighting the colorful characters and their machinations as a source of humor. Instead of being a celebrated public figure for repeatedly saving the day, Saitama is a low-ranked hero in this society of fighters; his abilities and victories go unnoticed, and he gets tangled up in the bureaucracy of the show's governing body of crime-fighting superstars, the Hero Association.

The year after *One-Punch Man* premiered, *My Hero Academia* landed on the scene and quickly became a mass sensation, hitting the list of top-selling franchises in Japan. In *MHA*, like *One-Punch Man*, heroism is so common that it's a profession, and individuals with silly, useless powers are juxtaposed with the extraordinary sort. In the world of *MHA*, almost everyone has a "quirk," or power, except for our protagonist, the shy and studious Izuku Midoriya, who idolizes the number-one-ranked hero, All Might. Midoriya desperately wants to become the top hero, and when he finally gets a quirk of his own, he enrolls in the top-ranked hero academy and trains to become a professional hero, fighting villains and making friends along the way.

Even though he falls into the trope of the underdog outsider, Midoriya subverts the trope of the "chosen one," because he is not powerful, and when he does inherit his quirk—the powers of All Might, willingly passed on to him—he has to train extensively to even bear it. He can't just level up; his body is too weak to sustain the power, so his muscles tear and his bones break. And later, he discovers that he was not the top candidate to inherit All Might's powers. There was another, who already had an impressive quirk and was strong and the perfect hero. Midoriya does, of course, prove he's worthy again and again throughout the series.

The show presents the richest parody of American comics through All Might, who turns out to be a clear analog for such American comic-book heroes as Captain America and Superman. (His attacks, in a hilarious callout to American nationalism, are named after US states and cities, as in "Texas Smash.") Donning a red, white, and blue costume and sporting a dramatic blond mane, All Might looks like the quintessential American superhero. Yet there's something about him that looks slightly deranged. Beneath that mane is a disconcertingly wide grin, and there are his black eyes, which make him appear devious. He is a caricature of America's obsession with its own power. And yet he, like Midoriya, is nothing without the quirk that was passed down to him.

My Hero Academia is surprising too for the way it quietly dissects the American superhero narrative's tendency to herald the individuality of its hero over the team. Despite our culture's recent obsession with team-ups and crossovers—the Avengers, the Defenders, the Justice League, the Arrowverse—they are forced, written not with narrative continuity or development in mind but with a glut of fireworks and effects that will pull in audiences' attention. Ultimately, with our American sensibility so ingrained in the stories we tell, the strength of a community is subordinated to the strength of the individual. *MHA* isn't all that interested in single heroes but rather in how heroism is fostered through community.

Midoriya strives to become the number one hero but still celebrates his classmates' successes and eagerly learns from the older heroes around him. The young heroes-in-training have much to learn and yet still make themselves indispensable to the more established folks, using their quirks to help investigate crimes and bag villains. There's an openhearted earnestness to the show for this reason; *MHA* has brought the superhero story back to its roots, focusing on themes of resilience and hope.

The show's earnest enthusiasm is also embodied in its star himself. In a genre where masculinity is limited to one look or attitude—brute strength and aggression—*MHA* dares to present a male protagonist who is precious and vulnerable. Midoriya loves heroes so much that he is an unapologetic fanboy, studious to the point of obsessive. He has a bottomless reserve of faith in his mentor, All Might, and the role of the hero as a symbol of hope in the darkness.

My friend and I watched the first episode of the series together one late night after a day of Comic Con adventuring. We had heard of this new series that was quickly becoming popular, about a boy who goes to a school full of heroes. We tried it not expecting much—just the usual shonen fare. Midoriya is introduced as a quirkless young child who is bullied by his peers but who, through a face full of tears, asks his mother if he can still be a hero like All Might. When we watched the little Midoriya crying because he realized he might not become the exceptional hero he hoped he would be, we let out a simultaneous sympathetic wail. Here was a sensitive, emotive shonen hero, and we related to him more than we did our favorite heroes of shonen past. If only I had seen something like *MHA* as a kid, knowing that the boy could be strong because of and not despite his emotionality, and that the girl could wield power that was more than just fluff. At their best, these genres transcend gender stereotypes and heteronormative frameworks to reveal worlds more flexible and thus inclusive. We dream of heroes so much greater than ourselves, so why would gender restrictions apply?

When I was young, I would go with my mother to the salon to get my hair braided. It was always an hours-long ordeal, so dull that I would bring any kind of distraction I could: schoolbooks, side reading, my Game Boy. Once I got in the salon chair, however, I could at least direct my attention to the grown folks' talk, their gossip about people in the salon I had seen or people I knew nothing about.

One afternoon, my stylist told my mother and my mom's hairdresser about a problem she'd had with her son, who was around my age. Their family desktop wasn't working as it should, and when she and her husband inspected it, they found files and files of sexually explicit anime. I don't remember the exact reactions of the other women but rather how the air changed in the room. A preteen boy discovering porn would have been one kind of embarrassment—shameful, sure, but mundane, expected. But anime—there was something perverse in that. The particular shade of my mother's judgment as she considered it struck me personally, as though I, too, another preteen anime fan, had committed some crime. But our own family computer had parental locks that made even innocuous school research a hassle, and the prospect of searching for anime porn—or porn in general—had not even occurred to me. And yet it was the fact that it was anime—something I loved and watched religiously—that made it most taboo. This boy was surely an aberration, already steeped in who knew what fetishes, though he was barely adolescent. So if I enjoyed these anime, what the salon women and my mother called "cartoons," then was I an aberration as well?

Having grown up before our recent nerd renaissance, I was used to the cliché assumptions that usually came with fandoms: nerds were lame, uncool, socially awkward, didn't have any friends, etc. But with anime there was the bonus assumption that if you were a fan, you had some odd sexual fetishes.

This was one of the reasons why I was wary of otaku, or super-passionate anime fans, even as I identified as one myself. Early in my freshman year of high school, I went to a meeting of the anime club, which I had been thrilled to find listed among the extracurriculars in the school handbook before the start of classes. I found the anime club tucked away in the art classroom in the far hallway, the territory of the middle schoolers. I was sorely disappointed. Some TV show or movie was playing, but no one was really paying attention; students were drawing and chatting among themselves in small groups. A teacher was there, who I recognized as the middle school art teacher, but she seemed to just be hanging out like everyone else. I heard some girls arguing over who had the more legitimate claim to the white-haired fox demon Sesshōmaru. At one of the desks, I saw a classmate who took the same bus as me—a short, quiet bespectacled boy who bore a strong resemblance to Filburt from *Rocko's Modern Life*. He was also surprisingly crude. Whenever he made a perverted joke, a broad grin would spread across his face and his ever-slouched shoulders would hop up and down in quick succession as he chuckled like Muttley from *Wacky Races*. He loved drawing and was a pretty good artist—but he almost exclusively drew buxom anime women. He and his friend were hunched over a drawing at one desk, snickering. I settled down at a desk by myself, working on a Wing Gundam Zero sketch I had started but never finished. I didn't return to the anime club.

This, I decided, was why I had to be careful with revealing my fandoms. Anime still seemed too niche, so I brought it up to people with hesitation, if at all. Almost exactly four years after my anime club adventure, a few days into my freshman year of college, I was hanging out with a transfer student I had met during one of the orientation events. He had hair that inexplicably seemed to both swoop upward and hang limply at the same time, and an eyebrow piercing.

He caught a glance at my lanyard, which was heavy with my collection of key chains.

He held one up, Maya Natsume from *Tenjho Tenge*, which sat alongside my L key chain and alchemy circle. "Are you into those *cartoons*?" he asked mockingly, and the shame shot through me as I snatched my lanyard away.

In truth, I have always been unabashed in my love for *Death Note* and *Fullmetal Alchemist*, despite my momentary embarrassment, but part of what made me second-guess myself then, in front of this eyebrow-ring-wearing sound-design major, was that particular key chain. Maya was kneeling, one knee down, in a tiny skirt. Her right arm reached behind her head, bearing a weapon. And her shirt was tied up under her breasts, which poured almost completely out of the top.

Ironically, I wasn't even a fan of the show. I had watched a few episodes of *Tenjho Tenge* but found it gross. It had a typical shonen setup: two friends enroll at a high school where they quickly discover that all the students are there to develop and hone combat skills. They face off against an authoritarian body of fighters that rule the school—the Executive Council—and join the only club that dares oppose them, the Juken Club.

Instead of being a fighting show with the occasional panty shot, which was what I'd come to expect, *Tenjho Tenge* was explicitly sexual all the way through. Maya, the powerful leader of the Juken Club, is introduced in chibi form, as a small child, but we learn she takes on the form just to conserve her chi. When she transforms to her regular full-figured teenage size, her outfit shrinks and she spills out of it.

In one multi-episode-spanning battle, during which the Juken Club is ambushed by members of the Executive Council, Maya, wearing a short black dress with side cutouts and heeled sandals, faces off against the council's vice president, who also wears a short dress with heeled sandals. The fight is full of nearly constant panty shots, and during combat Maya changes to her chibi form and back, making the revealing shots of her jumping and crouching in her dress even more disturbing. The vice president, an expert with knives, seems to draw the weapons out of thin air, but her trick is eventually revealed: she's extremely obese and uses her chi to maintain her usually slim (and yet still large-breasted) figure, and hides the knives in the folds of her fat. Once defeated, she can no longer hold her body shape together, and her fat explodes outward, releasing the rest of her hidden knives, so that both girls are left beaten, with their clothes totally shredded.

Even if we disregard the grossly fatphobic plot development with the vice president, the show's misogyny and male pandering is clear. I stopped watching, aware that the show was less about plot than it was about sex. It permeated nearly every scene—and certainly every scene involving women.

But this is what we anime fans would call fan service with a shrug and a sigh. Anime maintains a short leash between its creators and its fans, with shows constantly catering, in big ways and small, to what they think their viewers most want to see. It's done with a sense of generosity—it is called a "service" after all—to show gratitude to loyal fans. And yet fan service is often based on assumptions grounded in heteronormative gender norms: boys want to see boobs and panty shots, and girls want to see Adonis-like bare-chested men. So fan service only serves a very particular kind of fan, often alienating the rest.

Tenjho Tenge was an extreme example of fan service gone wild, but it is pervasive in anime, especially in shonen. Though *Bleach* was relatively tame, it also dipped into a similar trope in fan service: the hot-girl transformation. Instead of a transformation like Maya's, from an innocent chibi form to a full woman, *Bleach* had the transformation of Yoruichi, Ichigo's ally and mentor, from a cat to a naked woman. In *My Hero Academia*, fan service comes in the form of the "R-rated" superhero Midnight, who wears a dominatrix-style outfit that prominently features her breasts, with garters, handcuffs, and a whip.

And one of the most reliable character types one finds in anime is the "lovable pervert." *Inuyasha* has Miroku, the horny cursed monk. *Bleach* has Kon, the cleavage-loving soul who mostly inhabits a stuffed lion doll. *Dragon Ball Z* has Master Roshi. *Naruto* has Jiraiya. In *My Hero Academia*, it's Midoriya's classmate Minoru Mineta. Even in shojo we find this character: In *Fruits Basket*, Shigure, an older male figure, is known for his love of teen girls (in one episode, thinking about the young female guests he'll be seeing, he sings to himself gleefully, "High school girls! High school girls!"*). And in *Kill la Kill*, Ryuko's teacher, Aikuro Mikisugi, who is also part of the revolutionary group Nudist Beach, aggressively flirts with his underage student and strips.

Fan service is so built into the industry that for years I bore it without questioning it. It wasn't until I watched *Tenjho Tenge* that I realized there would be shows I would find totally unacceptable for the ways they so often made objects of their female characters, hoping to catch the male gaze. In recent years, I've noticed that fan service has become unbearable to me and affects how I view the quality of the show.

Fairy Tail, a fun, whimsical anime about a guild of magicians who train together, take jobs that make use of their magical abilities, and often save the world (which is full of various other guilds, magical creatures, and fantastical locations), is another one of my favorite shonen. It suffers from some of the usual pitfalls of shonen: it goes on for way too many episodes, the battles sometimes seem endless, some story details are awkwardly incorporated. And yet the characters are vibrant and ceaselessly supportive of each other. Though plenty of male characters take the spotlight, the women, too, prove themselves to be fearless and indomitable. The whole world, with its magic and mythology and familiar faces—characters we meet and who return again and again, like family—is like comfort food.

My friend and I started it together years ago, one night during

---

* *Fruits Basket*, "Make It Clear If It's Black or White," September 6, 2001.

our second Comic Con. We found it heartwarming and funny: the (literally) hotheaded dragon slayer mage Natsu Dragneel; his adorable sidekick, Happy; the earnest Lucy, with her cohort of magical zodiac figures; the ferocious Erza Scarlet, whose power is the magical-girl-style costume change, but with armor and weaponry; and the curmudgeonly Gray Fullbuster, an ice mage who provides some comical—and well-deserved—fan service. Gray unconsciously strips to cool off and is forever surprised by his sudden nudity.

Fairy Tail was our first cosplay: I donned a wild pink wig and Natsu's signature scarf, vest, and trousers to be the dragon slayer. My friend chose the mighty Erza, who had several costume options available. She chose the Robe of Yuen, a cute purple-and-pink outfit resembling a kimono. As we prepared for our first convention outing in cosplay, I watched my friend fuss with her outfit, making seemingly endless modifications. The neckline was impossibly low and the leg slits were brazenly high. She walked to and from the mirror with a handful of pins, adjusting and readjusting. We recycled our cosplays on and off for several subsequent cons before retiring them the year the series finally concluded, and her Erza costume always caused her strife.

Part of it was the usual issues that come with costumes bought online: low-quality materials, inexact fit. But a large part of it was the impractical animated costume design to begin with. Though Erza is a powerful, autonomous female character—in fact, the leader of the team—she is still a victim of fan service. She's given several armors that appear designed to show off her cleavage rather than provide any real protection. In Erza we find an unstoppable warrior—nicknamed Titania, queen of the fairies—and yet she too is often reduced to a body to stare at.

We found this fan service disappointing, and it wore on our love for the show over the seasons. We'd text each other about the latest developments in the series, but the tone of those texts went from unbridled optimism to annoyance and disillusionment. We compared notes on when each of us felt like the show had gone too far. For her it was an arc when the guild goes on a journey to an island. (Island episodes and beach episodes in most anime series, especially shonen and shojo, are inevitably rife with fan service.) For me it was an arc during which the guild participates in a magic tournament; a battle between two female mages turns into an episode-long pinup competition. The female characters change into bikinis and pose with their breasts pushed together or backs arched while the men in the crowd cheer and sweat and drool.

This kind of use of fan service in shonen in particular assumes the worst of both sexes. Even when women occupy positions of power, they cannot do so without baring their cleavage or butts. But even the male viewers, at whom the fan service is targeted, are underestimated, because the assumption is that the show won't be able to hold their attention without frequent eye candy.

Sometimes fan service is built into the DNA of the show too, as an intentional part of the story. Another one of my favorite shonen in recent years, *Food Wars! Shokugeki no Soma*, blatantly uses fan service as part of the show's central joke. In the series an imaginative and innovative teenage chef named Soma Yukihira attends a top culinary high school in the hopes that he'll be able to take over his father's small local diner, where he's worked since he was a child. But the high school is full of talented chefs from all backgrounds, who display their dominance over their peers in high-stakes culinary battles called shokugeki. Soma aims to become the best chef, but he faces challenges thrown at him from the school and its governing body, the Elite Ten Council, the top-ranked student chefs.

The show follows the shonen formula—a talented underdog who wants to be number one, a cast of powerful characters, constant battles—but also provides a quality show about cooking as a passion and as an art form. The recipes are playful and inventive, and the show's dives into regional trends and its representation of innovative techniques like molecular gastronomy are as engrossing and informative as those of a live-action cooking show. And yet I only watched the first episode as a joke. The show looked ridiculous, and I assumed it would be completely inane. I was pleasantly surprised, though I was correct on the first account: in the world of *Shokugeki no Soma*, the characters' receptions of the dishes are represented via visual metaphors. Delicious dishes trigger dreamlike sequences in which the taster has a kind of orgasm; moans are uttered, clothes are torn from bodies by the mere force of the flavors. The ingredients dance around them, often wrapping them in an intimate embrace.

When convincing friends to watch it, I've had to tell them to push past the first few episodes and these blatant, bizarre displays of fan service. One friend stopped on the third episode, when Soma feeds his meek female classmate, Megumi Tadokoro, one of his culinary experiments gone wrong, honey-pickled squid. Disgusted by the flavor, Megumi suddenly appears attacked by honey-dripping squid tentacles, screaming as the tentacles grope her and tear her clothes. The rape implication, and the nod to tentacle porn, understandably turned my friend off the show, and though she eventually gave it another shot and came to love it, her admiration of it always came with qualifiers: that tentacle scene was gross; it was too much, and the fan service is funny but eventually gets old.

However, even when these scenes get too egregious, we can't disregard the show's modus operandi; it very knowingly uses fan service to deliver its comedy. In fact, the food orgasms are funnier when they happen to the male characters. It plays as a subversion of the theme; the fact that most of the sexual scenes involve female characters reflects the show's (and perhaps the industry's) views of gender. Female sexuality is depicted more often, so it appears as though it is more unbridled, perhaps more promiscuous. At the very least it is a spectacle meant to be enjoyed. In the instances when the men are stripped and romanced by their food, they are feminized, made vulnerable by their desire. The juxtaposition of a stern, über-masculine character and a fluffy fantasy sequence is hilarious because it presents a wildly unexpected contrast. In one episode, several chefs try a dish that makes surprising use of its vegetables and praise the "legume magic," which, in an explicit parody of *Sailor Moon*, transforms them all—including one very burly, masculine chef—into cabbage-costumed Sailor Scouts.

So the problem is not simply a show's use of fan service but also the intention behind it, and how it's divided among genders. The vast gulf between the amounts of female character fan service versus male character fan service that are found in anime shows how narrow the creators' scope of their audiences are. Like video games, anime is a realm of fandom that has been perceived as being only for boys, and it seems that, at least to some measure, that belief remains, as shows so often play to their straight male fans as though that's the only de-mographic that's watching.

This is why I no longer watch shows that I feel are doing me that disservice. In the Netflix anime series *Seven Deadly Sins*, a flimsy plot, poorly written characters, and dull dialogue are bolstered by nothing but the misogyny throughout. Ten minutes into the very first episode, a young man gropes the breast of a large-chested, small-waisted girl in a unitard as she's unconscious, then tells her when she wakes that he was just checking her heartbeat. She believes him, because she is painfully naive and helpless—a princess, in fact, a literal damsel in distress. He saves her multiple times in the episode, as she cries and thinks about how she's so helpless. And of course while she's being saved, her outfit gets torn up. I quickly gave up on the series; any show that normalizes sexual harassment and makes it the source of its comedy is disrespecting me as a fan.

Another central problem of fan service is that it often appears in a genre of shows that are in the uneasy space between children's entertainment and adult entertainment. Fan service in shonen is odd because those shows are aimed for young male viewers, usually of prepubescent age, but the sexual jokes and the constant breast and panty shots seem geared toward older audiences.

And these portrayals of sexuality hint at sex but rarely ever go so far as to openly speak of it or depict it. Part of the reason is the age of the characters; the main characters in shonen and shojo are often underage, in middle school or high school. But even in the cases when the characters are older, even modest expressions of love or romance are often just hinted at. The focus is the fight, not the feelings of the characters. In many cases, despite how flirtatious and daring a shonen or shojo might be, in the end the main character and the love interest still never give us any concrete closure. (One notable exception is the final episode of *Fairy Tail*, when two characters who've had a long-running flirtation are overheard talking about a baby, and when another character who spends the whole series putting off his lovestruck admirer's advances makes a risqué claim on her body. The central male-female protagonist relationship, however, remains vague; the show inches toward a concrete romantic resolution before quickly backing away.)

Sexuality, ironically, is both desired and avoided in nearly equal degrees. And of course there are whole shows that are built off fan service, like *Shokugeki no Soma*, as well as *Free! Eternal Summer*, about a male swim team, and *Keijo!!!!!!!!*, about a fictional sport in which women in swimsuits balance on floating platforms and use their breasts and butts to knock their opponents off. But fan service itself is still like a flirtation without any actual consummation.

After all, fan service isn't porn. "Hentai," which roughly translates to "pervert," is also the name for adult anime. Fan service is too meek to be pornography; it flaunts its assets but doesn't dare take things beyond tasteless boob shots and ripped clothing. And yet, there is still often a conflation of hentai with other forms of anime, particularly by American audiences.

In 2014 I came across a CNN article that was laced with this sense of skepticism of and unfamiliarity with the art form. The headline was "Sexually Explicit Japan Manga Evades New Laws on Child Pornography," about a new Japanese law designed to crack down on child porn excluding sexually explicit depictions of children in anime and manga. Though my own initial knee-jerk reaction is to agree with the idea that hentai featuring children could fall into the troubling category of child porn, it's a more nuanced issue. Anime and manga that portray child characters engaged in sexual acts are unacceptable, and, as the article suggests, could hypothetically be used by pedophiles to convince children that acting in such a manner is okay. However, one may also imagine these fictional stories being used by people predisposed to pedophilia and other taboo sexual inclinations as a safe outlet so they don't actually engage in any criminal activity in real life. The article itself does claim that "no link has been made between anime, manga and child abuse,"* which isn't to dismiss these anime and manga as acceptable but rather to give the issue a proper frame of reference in terms of the real-world effects and implications of these works.

Still, the tone of the piece struck me; I'd heard it before. Suspicion, and a Western sense of discovery, as though anime and manga represent foreign, unknown territory. The piece describes how CNN went to a shop in Tokyo with a hidden camera to find the "shocking" hentai, as though the news org was on a secret mission to infiltrate enemy lines. The whole affair reeks of othering, making something so mundane to Japanese culture—shops for anime and manga where, yes, there are often adult sections for hentai—seem alien.

But the most important takeaway of the piece was a quote by Dr. Mio Bryce, an expert on Japanese language, literature, manga and anime, who says, "Very often people think manga equals sexual or manga equals violence. But it's only a part of manga . . . there are some very poetic, very beautiful ones."†

Someone unfamiliar with anime and manga might encounter

---

* Will Ripley, Hilary Whiteman, Edmund Henry. "Sexually Explicit Japan Manga Evades New Laws on Child Pornography," CNN, June 18, 2014, https://www.cnn .com/2014/06/18/world/asia/japan-manga-anime-pornography/index.html.
† Ibid.

such a piece and still conclude that the whole art form, and perhaps even the larger culture, is perverse, as though one can't find adult sections with questionable material in American shops, or find the same issue of explicit, problematic material peddled in our sex industry. But this is the American habit of throwing stones from our fragile glass house. It is America projecting its own complicated relationship to sexuality: we're tethered to a puritanical shame and prudishness and yet also love to capitalize on and commercialize sex. American sexuality is a paradox.

Ironically, some of Japan's relationship to sexuality and shame traces its roots back to America, when America occupied the country after World War II, from 1945 to 1952. Having already devastated the country with our despicable nuclear attacks, which had calamitous lasting effects on the economy and cultural psyche, America also crept into other facets of Japanese daily life during the occupation. American media introduced Western takes on sexuality and courtship, which were more demonstrative, stressing public shows of affection, like kissing. Expectations for the progression of physical intimacy during courtship—our "bases," and steps like holding hands, followed by kissing—also seeped into the culture. While many Japanese schools had often been divided by sex, American reforms made schools suddenly coeducational.

American soldiers brought with them their abject Western notions of Japanese women as sexual objects. The demure and formal kimono—which Japanese women originally wore with an undergarment called koshimaki, a "waist cloth" that covered their genitals but did not resemble Western underwear—was imagined as something sexual, with the false idea that the women were simply nude underneath.

There's the stereotype of the Japanese underwear fetish, but this, too, is linked to the American occupation. In the Meiji era (1868–1912), Western clothing, like undergarments, was worn only by the wealthy, but in the Taisho era (1912–1926), as uniforms became more common in girls' schools, Western clothes became a bit more popular as a sign of upward mobility among women. In 1939 monpe, or trousers, became popular, and since women could not wear koshimaki underneath, they had no choice but to wear drawers. But when Japan lost the war, the resulting economic depression yet again changed the context in which women wore this Western-style underwear. The only women who could afford them were prostitutes serving American occupation forces. Panties and drawers then became associated only with sex workers and sex itself, so they became linked to a sense of shame.

But either way, anime and manga become the targets of cultural bias. An art form from another culture becomes, in the Western view, representative of moral ills, despite America's similar flaws—the ever-present use of sex as a marketing tool, the sexualization of youth, the misogyny rampant in media depictions of sex, the fetishization of women, the stigmas around and lack of protections provided to sex-industry workers, the intolerance of media against LGBTQIA+ characters and nontraditional relationships, among many, many others. Even when an anime fails, perhaps because of its use of fan service, there is still *Fairy Tail*, which I shared with my friend for years, and *Shokugeki no Soma*, which inspired me to cook, and *Sailor Moon*, which delivered strong women—straight and queer—for me to look up to as a child. Anime is, and always has been, more than cute girls, beefy guys, and panty shots.

When I was younger, I fantasized about visiting Japan. I felt that I already knew Tokyo; though I'd never seen it in person, Shibuya Crossing felt as much home to me as my New York. I saw it brought to life in so many anime, and it always caught my eye—the massive intersection with overwhelming hordes of people crossing in all directions, the bright lights of the billboards all around them. It looked like a sibling to my Times Square. But I also imagined the homes and tea shops, the fashion and life of Harajuku, the cherry blossoms, the stores full of endless anime and manga.

I knew some small phrases from anime—usually useless exclamations—but imagined that someday the tiny bits and pieces I picked up would suddenly coalesce into a fluency that I would use on my journey. I knew some customs—again, what I picked up from anime—and pictured the little I knew being enough for me to fit in in Japan.

But I've never been to Japan. In fact, the closest I've come to the land of the rising sun was in Disney World, where I went with my family and best friend for my sixteenth birthday. In the miniature Japan at Epcot's World Showcase, I gushed about the architecture— the pagoda, the torii gate—and tittered in excitement as I explored the gift shop, where I looked at scrolls, chopsticks, traditional Japanese clothes, and more, debating what to pick. (My parents got me a rising sun handkerchief, a royal-blue kimono-style robe, a tiger scroll, and—I kid you not—a katana.) It was one of my favorite parts of the trip, and though Japan was the largest "country" included in the showcase, I recall walking out and feeling as though it was entirely too small. I wanted so much more. But this was what I got: a country and culture narrowed down to an overpriced tasting-plate version of itself for tourists.

My own understanding of Japan wasn't so different. It, too, was scaled down; I knew the country only through the limited lens of anime and manga. I was wildly ignorant, and though I knew anime didn't make me an expert on Japan, it wasn't until I was older that I truly understood that my familiarity with one small genre of fiction could not give me a real sense of the country as a whole.

And yet my love for anime did give me something surprising and personal: an alternative insight into my Blackness. I clung to and relished Japanese culture in a way that I didn't with my African American culture. Having grown up in environments where I was always one of a handful of Black people, and having internalized many of the hateful stereotypes against Black people, I felt challenged by the very fact of my skin color. But Japanese culture and African American culture intersect in a few surprising ways.

As in our own American culture, there are several examples of fetishized and appropriated Blackness in Japanese culture. Black fashion and Black hairstyles have appeared in Japan, and Black music has been a particular point of interest. Unfortunately, tributes to Black music have sometimes come in the form of blackface, from bands like Momoiro Clover Z and Rats & Star.

In anime and manga, Blackness often feels out of place. As a kid, I looked for Black characters in anime. After all, I had wanted to be a Sailor Scout but couldn't place myself in that world, even in a fantasy, because I didn't quite fit; there were no Black people.

When I first ventured into cosplay, married to the idea of authenticity, I tried to think of "Black options." There weren't many that came to mind. Brock, from *Pokémon*; Aisha, from *Outlaw Star*; Yoruichi and Tōsen from *Bleach*. More often I found racist depictions of Black characters: Mr. Popo, *Dragon Ball Z*'s short, plump genie, whose skin is a midnight black and whose features are rounded and exaggerated. Between his Black skin, red lips, and simple, accommodating expression, Mr. Popo looks like an animated depiction of blackface. *Pokémon*'s Jynx could be his relative; her skin is also frequently depicted as Black, and, wearing a dress and long blond hair parted down the center, she appears oddly humanoid but also completely wrong. Her attacks take advantage of her large pink lips. Even in more recent series, like *One-Punch Man*, one may still find gross renderings of Black characters, like the hero Superalloy Darkshine, a shiny-skinned muscular Black man with a vacant appearance and large light-brown lips. The difference in the way so many animators draw Black characters can be subtle but clear: you can often catch it in the face, exaggerated features that emphasize how they are fundamentally unlike the Asian characters, whose features are often homogenized.

And yet despite the general dearth of Black characters in anime, there were shows that were rooted in Black culture. Shinichirō Watanabe is famous for creating works that cross genres and often reveal his deep appreciation for Black music and culture. *Cowboy Bebop*, from 1998, one of the first adult anime series I encountered as a teen, after years of shonen and shojo, mixed themes from film noir with those of spaghetti Westerns, and set it all in space. However, it was Watanabe's marriage of the tone, visuals, and music that really differentiated *Cowboy Bebop* and made it the influential series that it was. Black music was in the DNA of the show, which had one of the most memorable themes of any anime series in existence. "Tank!" by Seatbelts begins with an attack of trumpets, in a stuttering Morse code. It's followed by a tumbling pronunciation of drums, then a hustling bass rhythm—low, cool, and effortless. As the song builds, a voice counts us in as though we're part of the band, hanging out in a New York City jazz club, gins and tonics at the ready as he says, "Three, two, one, let's jam!" I never cared for jazz, its wild obtrusiveness. If only I could have heard "Tank!" as a kid, and seen it paired with the stylish color-blocked opening credits of *Cowboy Bebop*, I would have fallen in love with jazz immediately.

Though *Bebop* is so often praised as Watanabe's most influential work, it was his 2004 follow-up, *Samurai Champloo*, that resonated with me even more. There was the setting—Edo Japan, the inspiration for countless anime and films that have romanticized the era of the samurai. And then there was the music, beginning with the opening theme, the hip-hop song "Battlecry" by Nujabes. But Watanabe went even further, incorporating hip-hop throughout the whole show, making a seemingly incongruous pair of the music genre and the Edo era. The action of the episodes is interrupted by the sound of record scratches; characters get into tagging battles; and there are even beatboxers.

In the series, a girl named Fuu recruits two very different swordsmen, Mugen and Jin, to help her track down a samurai who smells like sunflowers. Unlike the stoic and polished Jin, Mugen isn't the typical anime samurai but a gruff, lovable rogue. And his hair, like that of Spike Spiegel, the cool-guy bounty hunter of *Cowboy Bebop*, is a messy mass of thick strands—notably Afro-like—framing his face. (When my friend and I discussed our possibly doing a *Champloo* cosplay, I proudly claimed Mugen, saying that my hair, then an untamed Afro that hadn't seen a salon in years, looked like his.)

Mugen fights wildly, though artfully. He's acrobatic, dropping to the ground for windmills and back spins. His fighting style is break dancing, and he's the equal of almost every samurai he meets. Even in America, where hip-hop was born, and where it is so prominent, it is still often disregarded as a crude art form. And of course hip-hop became synonymous with an "urban" culture that became coded for a poor, Black cross-section of America. And that, in turn, was associated with drug use, gang activity, and other kinds of crime.

In 2005 Watanabe told the *New York Times* in an interview, "I've been interested in hip-hop since it first appeared: the fact that it was born not in the music industry but on the street, the idea of using a turntable as an instrument, singing vividly about reality instead of typical love songs, and its links to graffiti and dance." He continued, "I believe samurai in the Edo period and modern hip-hop artists have something in common. Rappers open the way to their future with one microphone; samurai decided their fate with one sword."* Watanabe's incorporation of Black culture into his show normalizes and recontextualizes it; it subverts some of the stereotypes about Blackness by honoring it alongside classic Japanese traditions and customs.

---

* Charles Solomon, "The Manga Version of Hip-Hop," *New York Times*, July 26, 2005, https://www.nytimes.com/2005/07/26/arts/the-manga-version-of-hiphop .html.

Similarly, *Afro Samurai*, which came out in 2007, paired feudal Japan with Black culture. The show's protagonist had a mighty Afro that seemed to be its own character, the way it moved, cloudlike, as he fought. And in 2021, Netflix introduced a new Black samurai series, *Yasuke*, about a real African immigrant who became a samurai—and wears not an Afro but dreads.

But whether appropriation or appreciation, this works both ways: there's a similar fetishization of Japanese culture, anime in particular, that shows up in the works of Black musical artists too. Soulja Boy has studded his music with various references to the genre. He has a mixtape named after *Death Note*, and in his song "Anime" he begins, "Anime swag, I'm flying like Goku," then throws out reference after reference to other shows, including *Case Closed*, *Pokémon*, and *Inuyasha*. In his song "Pink Matter," Frank Ocean casually drops a reference to the bright pink villain of *Dragon Ball Z*: "That soft pink matter / Cotton candy, Majin Buu."*

In his song "My Shine," Childish Gambino, aka Donald Glover, playfully raps, "Everything I'm sayin', I'm super sayin' like Goku,"† and in "Gold Watch," Lupe Fiasco declares, "I am American mentally with Japanese tendencies," before later rolling out a list of things he likes, including "*Monocle* Magazine and Japanese manga."‡ (In 2013 the two nerdy rappers had a back-and-forth on Twitter that included this kicker by Lupe: "Oh and I watch more anime than you.")

But many Black artists seem to especially fixate on shonen, in particular Goku and the Z Fighters of *Dragon Ball Z*. In his book *The Tao of Wu*, RZA writes that the show "represents the journey of the Black man in America." He argues that Son Goku—extraordinary and fierce, from a noble ancient race—has abilities he doesn't immediately realize because he's lost his memory of his people and been

---

* Frank Ocean, "Pink Matter," *Channel Orange*, 2012, Def Jam Recordings, Compact Disc.

† Childish Gambino, "My Shine," *EP*, 2011, Glassnote, Compact Disc.

‡ Lupe Fiasco, "Gold Watch," *The Cool*, 2007, Atlantic Records, Compact Disc.

"robbed his knowledge of self." But when he's pushed beyond his limits, he transforms into a Super Saiyan, which RZA calls "a nigga with dreadlocks."

"So I say *we* are the Saiyans," RZA continues. "I even use the name Goku as a tag when I write. And when my hair is in an Afro? Word up: I'm Super Saiyan."*

Though I didn't see my Blackness translated in Goku, I understand how he may be adopted as a representative figure of the Black experience in America. One may read Goku's time on Earth and removal from his people as a kind of diaspora. One may read his lost heritage as analogous to the way America stripped the Black man of his history the minute he was shipped over the Atlantic like chattel. And one may read his Saiyan hair, which is part of his identity and an indicator of his strength, as natural Black hair, free from white beauty standards.

But this metaphor breaks down upon further scrutiny. Goku doesn't arrive on Earth enslaved but as the opposite: a would-be conqueror, a colonizer. He doesn't return to his planet but rather battles his people, instead fighting on behalf of humanity, as one of their number. And Saiyans transform into wild giant apes—and so finding a link to Blackness in that is problematic, to say the least. But the temptation is to take an underdog, an outsider, and see Blackness in that, because, at its root, the story of Blackness in America is one of exclusion and displacement—and resiliency. And for Black men in particular, Goku represents a classic standard of masculinity often lauded in Black culture. Goku is beaten down repeatedly but rises again and again to fight for his family and friends. At the heart of the show—as is true of many shonen—there is a sense of community, of friends having your back, even at the end of the world.

Goku hasn't been the only character to receive this treatment. Black fans often claim anime characters of alternate or ambiguous

---

* The RZA, *The Tao of Wu* (New York: Penguin, 2009).

ethnicity as one of their own. Another member of the Z Fighters, Piccolo, is often referred to in internet fan discourse as Black too. However, these conversations and adoptions of anime characters into Blackness again point to the fact that there aren't many Black characters in the genre to begin with, and when there are, they often embody stereotypes.

Inversely, one of TV's most intelligent satires of race and Black culture in America, *The Boondocks*, dipped into anime style and tropes to pay homage to the genre. The series creator, Aaron McGruder, has been open about the influence of anime on the show. In an interview with Moviefone, he said that the series was "our attempt at anime, but it's very, very black."*

I adored *The Boondocks*, having read the newspaper comic strip as a kid. But while the comic strips were flat and two-dimensional, and their satirical tone muted and less resonant on the page (especially to a child), the show was vivid and daring, clutch-your-gut funny and smart, even when it was pushing buttons. The show was about a Black family—the greedy, misogynistic Robert "Granddad" Freeman, and his two grandchildren, the ornery, foul-mouthed Riley and the mature, observant Huey—living in a primarily white suburban neighborhood and interacting with white and Black people alike.

The first episode I recall watching was ". . . Or Die Trying," the first one of the second season, when the Freemans and their neighbor, Jazmine, try to sneak into a movie theater. But there, they're confronted by Ruckus, an Uncle Tom who worships white people. Huey and Ruckus battle with nunchucks and a makeshift bo staff. In another episode, Robert's date with a woman from a dating site turns dangerous when she's revealed to be a deadly kung fu expert. And occasionally we encounter the *Afro Samurai*–esque martial arts

---

* Eric Larnick, "Aaron McGruder of 'Boondocks' on Working with George Lucas and His Future in Comics," *Comics Alliance*, January 20, 2012, https://comicsalliance.com/aaron-mcgruder-george-lucas-interview-red-tails.

master Bushido Brown. One of my favorite episodes, about a kickball game with substantial stakes, unrepentantly draws from an episode of *Samurai Champloo*.

The Boondocks always had its absurd moments, when the show went all out in its satire. But the scenes that were loving homages to old kung fu flicks and anime gave me a sense of glee. My Blackness was not separate from my nerdy identity; anime, I realized, could be a lens through which I could see my Blackness anew.

For so long I couldn't reconcile the two. When I watched anime, which either didn't contain Black characters or included only racist Black stereotypes, I saw myself—my Black self—missing from a fandom that has meant so much to me.

But through the works of creators like Watanabe and McGruder, I was able to see two cultural experiences coalescing in a way that demonstrated the value and beauty of each. My Blackness didn't have to be something odd or unfamiliar; it could be the bass line of a jazz number as the *Bebop* ventures through space or the way Mugen twists and turns his body in a fight, making dance into a defense. It could be Huey quoting Malcolm X and doing gravity-defying flips during fights.

A common stereotype of the anime fan is one who fetishizes Japanese culture through the fandom, and who may conceive of a whole history and culture as being captured through one very small medium of entertainment. Anime has shaped me in so many ways: my views of gender and sexuality, my understanding of power and strength, my access to my own cultural experience.

I've been a Sailor Scout, a Pokémon Master, and a Super Saiyan, but most importantly, I have been and continue to be a Black female fan who has understood herself inside and outside of the spaces my fandoms have built.

IV.
The Birth of a Black Hero

On Black tropes and heroism

It was opening weekend, so, predictably, the theater was full. We had driven thirty minutes to get to the multiplex, a cinema with a mini arcade, a bar and grill, Ben & Jerry's, Nathan's Famous hot dogs, Famous Famiglia pizza, and, most notably, "ultra-plush, power-operated, fully reclining seats" that my mom and I, equally hobbit-sized, sank into, legs dangling over the edge, as though we were toddlers sitting in big kids' chairs. This—the drive several towns over to the "fancy" theater; my mom's insistence that we order way too much at the concession counter; my insistence that we see one movie over another because I had researched each option—was our usual routine, since I was a kid. We went to the movies together.

The movies of my childhood, however—the movies I picked—were so often shades from the same palette. Whiteness. White heroes: I loved them. Towering on the big screen. Blond-haired or brown-haired or red-haired. Blue or green or brown eyes. Lean and trim or muscular. Almost exclusively beautiful. Michael Keaton and Val Kilmer and George Clooney as Batmen—I loved them years before Christian Bale could even muster up his growl. Nevertheless, the worlds of these heroes were mine, but only in the same sense that this America is mine: I live here, I belong here, but, by the same token,

I'm also excluded by that world's limited scope, its inability to see me and my Blackness.

This, of course, wasn't something that struck me as a kid, as I sat alongside my parents, shoveling oversalted popcorn and palmfuls of Buncha Crunch into my mouth. I was simply there to receive the story, however it was delivered, in whatever shade.

But on this day, when we sat down in this multiplex, just the two of us, surrounded by an audience of white Long Islanders, our paired seats forming an ultra-plush, power-operated, fully reclining island along the walkway dividing the lower and upper levels of the theater, I suspected I would be seeing something new.

A prince, a warrior, and a spy fly a ship into the dusk, returning from a mission. The camera focuses on the warrior, piloting the ship, as she takes in the sight in front of her, mouth set in a tight, proud smile, saying to her passengers and, it seems, to the audience, "We are home." The camera flies over the African landscape, practically two-toned in the light of the late afternoon, the terrain an eye-catching mix of rocky heights, wooded lows, and dusty plains. But it's not until the ship seems to aim right for a crash landing that the drums kick in on the soundtrack and we're finally introduced to Wakanda, the utopian home of the Black Panther.

At a theater in Long Island full of white people silently, attentively watching a film about a Black hero in a mystical Black country, my mother, a casual onlooker to my fandoms, and I, a fan who had grown up seeing white heroes, saw a powerful and multifaceted depiction of Blackness. It felt like a homecoming.

Black Panther's influence—and, of course, its financial and critical success—is an incontrovertible fact. But its most important contribution was its delivery of a well-crafted Hollywood blockbuster explicitly about Blackness.

Though the film was novel and groundbreaking, it would be wrong to think that 2018's *Black Panther* was the *actual* first of its kind. T'Challa has been kicking around since 1961, when he appeared on the cover of *Fantastic Four* No. 52, leaping through the air above the foursome, a caped figure all in black, his right hand clawed, reaching out before him, ready to attack. In this first issue, he's introduced as a smug antagonist to the white heroes; he reveals himself and the secret world of Wakanda so that he can bait them into being his prey in a superheroic hunt, thereby exhibiting his skills and dominance. This hero was definitely not the one Black fans deserved at the time. The presentation of an exclusively Black society so much richer and more technologically advanced than a white one was undermined by the racist othering in the writing—jungle jokes, expressions of shock and awe about tribal traditions, the politically incorrect villain Man-Ape (thankfully revised by Disney for the 2018 film, which refers to him only by his name, M'Baku).

But Black Panther, though mentioned to me at some point in passing by my father, was virtually unknown to me, and many others, until he graced the big screen. There were other Black heroes who surfaced during my childhood in the '90s and early aughts: Wesley Snipes's Blade, armed with bone-crushing martial arts skills and a katana; Spawn, dressed in gothic underworld chic; John Stewart, DC's first Black superhero, the paragon of reason and order, and my father's favorite Green Lantern; Storm, the veteran X-Man from the comics and the popular '90s animated series; and Virgil Hawkins, the hero of the WB animated show *Static Shock*. John Stewart, despite being a stately Black hero character well worthy of mention, served as more of a supporting player on Cartoon Network's animated series *Justice League*, standing alongside some bigger profile capesters like Superman and Batman; the show didn't belong to him. The same with Storm, an African mutant with earthshaking powers (and, briefly, the partner of Black Panther). The Blade movies and the generally panned *Spawn* served complex Black protagonists standing on the line between two worlds. Those films also set the stage very early on for darker, more serious takes on the superhero genre that we'd encounter in Christopher Nolan's Batman movies, *Logan*, and others.

And though a somewhat cheesy—and fun-loving—show geared toward kids and preteens, *Static Shock* seamlessly delivered a story about a hero dealing with superpowered villains, the typical trials and tribulations of adolescence, and the social and racial challenges that come with being a young Black man in America.

Though John, Blade, Spawn, Storm, and Static were some of *Black Panther*'s predecessors on TV and in movies when I was growing up, they felt disconnected to me—disconnected from one another, preventing my conception of a larger, consistent trend toward a prominent show of Blackness in comic book stories, and disconnected from me and my own perception of my Black identity.

Having grown up in suburbs unofficially segregated by race and economic levels, and having attended private schools where I was one of maybe a handful, at best, of Black kids, I couldn't imagine what a Black hero would look like—not cartoony and overblown but real and relatable to me. What so many TV shows and movies often missed, and continue to miss today, is a complex depiction of Blackness delivered front and center, not on the sidelines—something a fan can carry with her beyond the movie theater or TV screen.

What my mother and I carried with us that day after seeing *Black Panther* was a world rich with resources, its main export being Black ingenuity, a Blackness that lived in the vision of a queen, a whiz-kid princess, a female spy, a superhero king, an army of female warriors, and a villain motivated by his sense of birthright and the injuries caused by systemic racism in a so-called country of opportunity. *Black Panther* achieved a Blackness that was not monolithic—the Black hero as the quintessence of all Blackness in America, a capital-B Blackness that is simplified and stereotyped, undercutting the point of diverse representation in the first place. To serve media supposedly representative of Blackness but that fails to capture the complexity of Black identity is to subscribe to another kind of racism and fail the Black audiences that such media is, in theory, meant to serve.

Black Panther brought us to the brilliant fantasy world of Wakanda, but not before grounding us in the real world of Oakland, California, the home of our young to-be villain, Killmonger. When Killmonger, son to a royal Wakandan, returns to his father's home country and claims the throne from T'Challa, the two face off in a battle that is rooted in opposing political responses to institutionalized racism against Black people. T'Challa has grown up in a kind of paradise, sheltered from the troubles that Black Americans, or even other Black Africans, face. Hidden and thereby protected against the threat of colonialism (with the exception of the sneaky dealings of Ulysses Klaue, who aims to profit from Wakanda's priceless resource, vibranium), Wakanda exists outside of history, in a space where Blackness has been allowed to thrive, unperturbed by systemic oppression. The irony of *Black Panther* is a hero who shares his name with a group of 1960s Black militant revolutionaries but touts a politics of isolationism to the detriment of other countries and communities, particularly Black ones, that could benefit from Wakanda's resources. Killmonger demands revolution, albeit with questionable motives and execution, but his mixed inheritance—a strong, rich Africa and a disadvantaged America—creates a complex character, steeped in a fatalistic, gladiatorial approach to change, rather than the arch-eyebrowed, chin-stroking antagonists of more thinly written stories. ("Just bury me in the ocean with my ancestors that jumped from the ships, because they knew death was better than bondage,"* he declares at the end of the movie, somehow impressively managing to romanticize drowned slaves; implicitly critique the slaves who withstood bondage, torture, and abuse to survive; and die before a Wakandan sunset, all in the span of approximately fifteen seconds.)

Thankfully, T'Challa and company haven't been the only Black heroes to step up in the pop culture world in the last few years. In fact, as nerd culture has ballooned, there has also been a steady increase

---

* Ryan Coogler, *Black Panther* (Walt Disney Studios, 2019).

of Black heroes in the spotlight. In 2015 Luke Cage, aka Power Man, appeared as a secondary character on Netflix's Marvel TV series *Jessica Jones*, and then headlined his own series the next year. Two years later, *Black Lightning* joined the Arrowverse. The latter, based on the DC Comics, featured a retired vigilante hero who has reluctantly decided to don the mask once again, to protect his family. Here, too, was a depiction of Blackness that ducked racist stereotypes—a smart, responsible Black family with supernatural abilities and a sense for justice. But far from the idyllic setting—no Wakanda for the Pierce family here—they live in a contemporary urban community ravaged by social problems: racism, gang violence, corruption.

Luke Cage struggled more with its conception of a contemporary Black hero. The original character first premiered in the comic *Luke Cage: Hero for Hire*, in 1972, and the comic drew inspiration from a prominent trend in Black entertainment of the decade, blaxploitation films. Thankfully, Netflix and Marvel left that behind and brought out a modern-day Luke Cage, one I was tentatively excited to see. The season one premieres of the Netflix Marvel series *Daredevil* and *Jessica Jones* in 2015 proved that the team could produce a new spate of successful superhero TV shows. (And, sure, the Arrowverse had already been kicking around for a few years at that point. But, despite the early *Dark Knight*-esque appeal of *Arrow* and the lighthearted preciousness of *The Flash*, the shows, with their seemingly endless seasons and increasingly outlandish and unoriginal plot lines, couldn't match the deft fight choreography, distinct visual aesthetic, and inviting narrative maneuvers of *Daredevil* and *Jessica Jones*.)

The hero who waltzed into the world of *Jessica Jones* provided the season and, more importantly, its main character with a yang to an already electrifying yin. Mike Colter's smooth, calm, and grounded Luke served as a counterpoint to Krysten Ritter's abrasive, traumatized, and heavy-drinking Jessica. Luke broke into the bubble of *Jessica Jones*, providing a different tonal accent to the grim, hard-nosed noir that so influenced the show.

But Luke, of course, was never anything other than a secondary character in the story, popping in during the first season to serve as a love interest and vehicle to present the narrative complication of Reva, his deceased wife, who was killed by Jessica. The announcement of his own show seemed to promise a well-drawn Black hero finally rooted at the center of the story.

The opening credits of *Luke Cage* are awash in yellow, showing scenes from around Harlem—the Harlem-125th Street stop, the Lenox Avenue/Malcolm X Boulevard street signs, the Apollo—with a funky instrumental playing in the background. It's modern-day Harlem, but the show still demonstrates that it knows its roots: the first scene, opening in front of Pop's Barber Shop, rolls out to the sounds of "Dap Walk" by Ernie and the Top Notes, released in 1972—the same year the comic book hero Luke Cage was born on the page. The setting and tone of *Luke Cage* feels familiar, the particular comfort of a barbershop where people hang and trash-talk, the everywhere uninterrupted Blackness. It's a kind of Harlem I've seen, though only as a visitor, passing through the neighborhood or when I trekked there and back from Brooklyn on the A train for a year, working at the historic Black paper the *New York Amsterdam News,* just a stone's throw from the Apollo and across the street from a soul-food restaurant with mouthwatering baked mac and cheese. The show captures something intimate and homegrown, matching the mood to the protagonist's disposition. But this Luke Cage—unlike his comic book counterpart, who immediately declares himself a "hero for hire"—is a hero wary of the spotlight. The show, then, invents a series of false obstacles to make the plot move forward, maneuvering its circumstances around a hero who isn't so convinced he wants to be a hero. The other interesting figures in his life—mostly the villains, Cottonmouth, Diamondback, Black Mariah, Shades, and later Bushmaster, each portrayed by stylish, charismatic actors—effortlessly grab the camera's attention. The result is a show with a protagonist who somehow still seems like he's a side character in the story.

Where *Luke Cage* makes its biggest mistake is in the very approach that could have made the revived and restyled Power Man into a great, sophisticated Black hero for a new generation. In *Luke Cage*, Netflix created a hero with a muted personality who was best defined by his background—his home in Harlem, his pride in his Black identity. Of course, any contemporary Black hero written today must be drawn with some sense of how the racial politics of our country shape how he or she acts, talks, and moves through America. But every strong depiction of Blackness must aim for characters and stories that feel true to the Black experience without nearing minstrelsy, a performance of race. *Luke Cage*, at its worst moments, dipped into the latter, falling into the trap that many media-makers do when they finally get around to capturing Blackness onscreen: writing Blackness as though that, in itself, can be a personality. At times Luke Cage would be the Black protagonist and at others he would be idealized as the epitome of Blackness, an unfortunate, blown-out example of tokenism—reactionary political correctness working only in service of a limited and outdated idea of what representation looks like.

Luke waxes poetic about Harlem and Black history, name-dropping figures from African American History 101. In one scene, Luke confronts an armed man who, like countless other characters, has the shocking realization that this Black man is bulletproof. As Luke lifts him into the air to question and intimidate him, he pauses to also reprimand him in the name of Black community:

"Think about where you are. It's hallowed ground, this park, named for Jackie Robinson. It's here, it's all around you, if you respect yourself enough to take a look."

"At what?"

"Our legacy."*

As a Black born-and-bred New Yorker with family spread throughout the boroughs, I wondered to whom Luke's words were

---

* Marc Jobst, "Just to Get a Rep," *Luke Cage*, September 30, 2016.

targeted. "*Our* legacy" felt like a leap to me as I watched the scene, questioning if "our" included me, all of Black New York. Or perhaps it was more specific to someone born and bred in Black Harlem? But there's something amiss with this too; he's speaking of an older, idealized Harlem perhaps, one untouched by gentrification. Though the *Luke Cage* series opted for a modern-day setting rather than the 1970s, the show still had a nostalgic sense of its setting.

Of course, one shouldn't lay the onus on a single show to lead the way for all future movies and series featuring Black heroes. And the argument of authentic Blackness—how much is too much, how much is appropriately addressing race and how much is teetering into the realm of racial performance—gets as sticky in conversations about fictional characters as it does when it comes up in reference to real-life people. Perhaps this Luke Cage, had I met him when I was a child, would have been the Black hero to have opened my mind to the possibility of heroic, invincible Blackness with the same ease with which I accepted white heroes powerful enough to fly, lift trucks, and speed through cities.

At the end of the day, you might say, they're all just stories, so what difference may it have made if I traded one fiction for another? Because I should have a right, as should everyone, to enjoy the privilege of seeing myself in my fiction. Because, for a Black girl aware of how she stood out in white spaces and how ill at ease she felt in Black spaces, any kind of narrative that refused to take for granted my identity and perspective would have been a story that rang true for me.

I watched *Black Panther* with my mother that day understanding that the source of utter joy I felt as the credits started playing was the feeling that a beautiful story belonged to me in a way others hadn't, despite my uncompromising love for them as a fan.

Fortunately, *Black Panther* wasn't the last Black-hero story that resonated with me in recent years. In 2019, Damon Lindelof brought back Alan Moore's seminal graphic novel *Watchmen* in the form of a TV sequel. The original, though incisive and sharply aware of the politics and landscape of America in the 1980s, was notably absent of any mention of race, or even any major Black characters. Even in a satire of modern-day politics and pop culture tropes, white characters stood at the fore. Lindelof's HBO series served as a correction to this major oversight in the otherwise stunning original text, bringing racial politics to the heart of the story and making two of its heroes Black.

The show opens with the 1921 Tulsa Race Massacre before jumping to the current day, when a Black cop nervously pulls over a white driver. It's an inversion of a situation that happens in America daily: police harassment and brutality against Black people. Even while facing an officer of the law, the white man is still the predator, a member of a pseudo-KKK group called the Seventh Kavalry. By the end of the first episode, the season's many mysteries begin with a lynched white man, and the elderly Black man found waiting calmly next to the body.

It has taken so long for a Black woman to be the hero of her own story, but here we're treated to Angela Abar, aka Sister Night, a no-nonsense detective with a cosplay-worthy costume and a mean hook. Standing at the center of a disaster, with a group of white supremacists on one side and a scheming megalomaniac on the other, Angela is a Black hero who does not fall into any stereotypes and whose racial and cultural identity is apropos to the narrative but not the whole of her personality.

The show presents Black heroes with a sense of the real dangers, traumas, and injustices Black people face every day. Angela stumbles upon the white supremacist group and finds people she trusted and cared for among their ranks. And when she discovers, firsthand, the secret behind her family's history—her grandfather being the mysterious hero Hooded Justice, from the Minutemen—the show goes into a beautiful, heartbreaking alternative history on a minor figure in the graphic novel. Hooded Justice, a queer Black man who was nearly lynched, takes a symbol of Black oppression (the rope he was almost lynched with) and incorporates it into his superhero guise, which also includes a touch of whiteface so that no one will guess that the masked hero is actually a Black man.

Watchmen achieves a complex vision of the Black hero—valiant and strong and smart but nevertheless fighting an uphill battle not just against crime but a whole tradition of systemic inequality. Not only does *Watchmen* retroactively change the story of Hooded Justice, but it also introduces a new Dr. Manhattan, this time reimagined as a Black man. The result is contradictory and twofold: we're presented with another Black hero—a Black man with the power of a god and all the infinite possibilities that come with that—but that very rendering is what makes the series' ending exponentially more tragic. We're introduced to a nearly invincible Black man just long enough to see him sacrificed. It's an unfortunate irony for that character in particular: a white-turned-blue man who became disconnected from his humanity has to transform into a Black man to become more empathetic, more human, and finally save the world. We're faced with the Black man as the noble sacrifice, and only in the season's final scene, with its suggestion of Angela's newfound godhood, do we receive some consolation.

The scene—her moment of realization as she sees a miraculously uncracked egg (presumably invested with Dr. Manhattan's powers) still in the carton dropped on the floor, her slow walk around the backyard pool, her swallowing the egg, the deep breath, her foot hovering over the water's surface as the music kicks in and the screen turns to black—is electrifying in all its possibilities. Angela was heroic in her own right, even without god powers, and was the rightful hero of the story. But we may now imagine her as something more—a Black superheroine, a breed in such short supply in our culture. The show's final cut to black could be seen as an act of courtesy or a disservice to its implied deification of our Black female protagonist. Does that final suspense-building shot treat us to the pleasure of our imagination, allowing us our own rendering of a Black female superhero? Or does it shortchange Angela, feeding into the idea that a

Black female superhero who was the star of her own story is still, for some reason, unimaginable, unfilmable?

I was torn, wanting to see this heroic Black female with my own two eyes but also wanting her for myself, safe in my imagination, where she can't be defeated or contradicted. After all, even in our stories, the real world, with all its ills, always filters in.

I was pleasantly surprised to find this theme explicitly spelled out in the 2021 Disney+ series *The Falcon and the Winter Soldier*. Throughout the series, which takes place after the events of *Avengers: Endgame*, Sam Wilson, the Falcon, has many different kinds of interactions that call back to his race. Other Black people recognize him immediately and goof with him with the casual familiarity of family. Several white people, on the other hand, fail to recognize this famous hero, racially profiling him as just another threatening Black man. In one scene he is even stopped by the police before they recognize who he is. And yet, he is one of America's heroes, like Steve Rogers.

One of the major threads of the series regards who will carry Captain America's shield now that Steve is gone. Bucky, Steve's best friend and the traumatized former Winter Soldier, pushes for Sam to become the new Captain; he tells Sam that Steve left the shield for him. But Sam struggles to accept the title of Captain America and all that comes with it: There's the question of whether he's ready to take on Steve's legacy, but there's also his identity as a Black man in America.

I never warmed to Captain America because of his explicitly patriotic persona. Even when Steve broke the rules—as he did in *Captain America: Civil War*—the franchise granted him impunity. He and many other heroes in the MCU are glorified law enforcement figures until they are glorified vigilantes. They are either the institution itself or free to act outside of it. This is the power a white male hero—or any powerful white man in America, actually—wields.

The series introduces John Walker—another white war hero—as the next Captain America, though he's quickly perverted by the power and responsibility. What's unclear is how aware the MCU is of the fact that John is not so ridiculous or outlandish of a foil; he's not the opposite of Steve. In fact, they wear the same white male entitlement. It just looks uglier on John.

Even before the premiere of *The Falcon and the Winter Soldier*, it had occurred to me that a Black Captain America would be an issue in the MCU. A Black Captain America who is granted the same privileges, power, and respect as a white Cap would be utterly unrealistic; it would just be the franchise skipping over the complicated and very real politics that come with a Black man wearing that title. And what Black American would even want to wear the Stars and Stripes? I certainly wouldn't.

A character in the series expresses the same sentiment. In the second episode, Sam and Bucky talk to another super soldier—a Black man named Isaiah who didn't get to be the same hero-savior that Steve was. "You know what they did to me for being a hero? They put my ass in jail for thirty years. People running tests, taking my blood, coming into my cell," he tells Sam.[*] Tuskegee-style testing on a Black man in a Disney show? I was surprised by this twist in the narrative, which is perhaps the most historically realistic story I'd seen in the MCU. After all, there's a whole history of experimentation on Black people that, to make terrible matters already worse, often benefits white people most. There wouldn't be any Captain America without Isaiah.

And yet, by the end of the series, Sam still decides to claim Steve's shield as his own. When he visits Isaiah again, three episodes later, the elder super soldier refuses to even look at it, saying, "Them stars and stripes don't mean nothing good to me."[†]

Isaiah scoffs at Sam's idealism, especially in the face of America's history of systematic oppression of Black people. "They erased me, my history, but they been doing that for five hundred years," Isaiah

---

[*] Malcolm Spellman, "The Star-Spangled Man," *The Falcon and the Winter Soldier*, Disney+, March 26, 2021.

[†] Malcolm Spellman, "Truth," *The Falcon and the Winter Soldier*, Disney+, April 16, 2021.

says with a grim chuckle. "Pledge allegiance to that, my brother. They will never let a Black man be Captain America. And even if they did, no self-respecting Black man would ever want to be." Sam persists, saying he knows it'll be an uphill battle.

This scene also recalls Disney's own delayed inclusion and centering of Black heroes in the MCU. Surely this is a question the company asked in planning its various movie phases and, later, forays into TV: Is the world ready for Black heroes to lead the charge? For the first decade of the MCU, from *Iron Man* in 2008 until *Black Panther* in 2018, the answer they arrived at seemed to have been no.

What this new guard of Black heroes—some of many more to come, I hope—represents is a media newly awakening to the reality that there is a market in Black fandom, that there is a community of Black fans yearning to see themselves represented, and that Black heroes need not be "exclusively" Black in any sense: they need not be paragons of Blackness, and, in fact, shouldn't be, and they need not be bait aimed only toward Black audiences, as though the Black experience is so exotic that it cannot be fathomed by audiences of other races. But, more importantly, I'm certain that these Black heroes represent for so many people what they represent to me: a way of thinking about Blackness that isn't incompatible with power or strength or victory, as it so often seems in this country.

What a world it would be to live in if a young Black girl could, with no huge leap of her imagination, dream herself a Misty Knight or a Sister Night, an Anissa Pierce or a Shuri. What a fantasy to imagine my foot hovering over the water and for the scene not to cut to black but to continue into another season, or a full film, an infinite reel that begins with one thought: *I, too, am super. I, too, am heroic.*

The second time I saw *Black Panther*, it was in Brooklyn. I saw it with a friend at the Brooklyn Academy of Music in Fort Greene.

As soon as we walked into the building, the energy was markedly different from what I'd found with my mom in Long Island. For one, the space was more crowded with people, talking and moving in clusters, and around me weren't just white people but Black and brown people of all ages and backgrounds. They were in groups of families and friends, dressed in kente cloth and other African garb: men with stoles draped around their necks and women with their hair in updos under crisscrossing swaths of brightly patterned fabric.

This audience was here for Wakanda, and the whole experience felt immersive, the way people whooped and clapped and gasped and chortled along with the action. There was no shushing, no reverent silence. The noise signaled approval and love and belonging to a community that understood that owning this film, with its Black heroes and beautiful Black world, meant saying so out loud. The cross-armed greeting of "Wakanda Forever" became omnipresent among Black fans, and everywhere I spotted claims to Wakanda: T-shirts, hats, social media profiles all seemed to declare Wakandan citizenship. In 2018 *Saturday Night Live* did a sketch about the salute: When a screening of the movie lets out, three Black fans (including Chadwick Boseman, wearing a large Africa necklace) discuss whether two white fans are allowed to do the Wakanda salute like they are. The white guys spastically fling their arms up and out, and one enunciates the country's second syllable with a nasal, flat *a*: "Wa-can-da." The guys ask the Black fans why they can't have the salute, and one responds that once white people borrow something, they don't usually give it back.

Being the kind of fan I am, I have long held many fandoms as my own. I'm possessive and jealous with my love, ready with an "I liked this back when it was cool" brand of response. But I had never before encountered a fictional world that I felt such a claim to because of my Blackness. And I didn't just feel like it belonged to me; it felt like it belonged to the whole tribe of us Black fans, like the ones I saw the film with in that Brooklyn theater.

Though I have friends who grew up spending all their time venturing through mystical faraway worlds, I have never been more than an occasional guest in the fantasy genre. When I was eight, I discovered Middle-earth. My father had spoken to me of *The Hobbit* and the majesty and intricacies of J. R. R. Tolkien's world-building. Before I was even old enough to tackle books with complex and compound sentences, I had a collection of picture books with read-along records that I would play on a little red record player. One I played again and again was a picture-book version of *The Hobbit*.

I read it in full years later, carrying the fat, squat book with me everywhere in elementary school. I struggled with it; Tolkien's language was dense, his descriptions painstakingly detailed, so I would catch myself getting lost in long passages of greenery and trees and pastures. But I was dedicated to the story and to the world, which was verdant and magical in the way that dreams often are. On a school field day, while the other kids ran around in the sun, I found a tree, sat down cross-legged in the shade, and opened *The Hobbit*, preferring to parse through Tolkien's prose to get to the rich adventure underpinning it all. From my picture book, I already knew the broad strokes of the story, but still desperately awaited the appearance of Smaug and Gollum and Bilbo's first use of the ring. (That day while I was reading, the principal snapped a picture of me and had it blown up and hung in the halls; when I graduated in eighth grade and for years afterward, my picture was still there, me intently reading while the other kids played, *The Hobbit* in my hands.)

In my other encounters with fantasy, I was always more resistant. I took *The Hobbit* on my father's recommendation; he'd shown me *Star Wars* and superheroes, so when it came to fandoms, he could do no wrong. I had always loved fairy tales, and *The Hobbit* seemed like just that: magic, treasure, a dragon, all the familiar trappings of storybook narratives.

Mrs. B., who I had as a homeroom teacher twice in elementary school, introduced me to Narnia and Hogwarts. I disliked her, found her too boisterous and blunt, but she was a reader. She hosted a book club, hyped up the Scholastic Book Fair days, and read us fairy tales and fantasy stories. (Thank you, Mrs. B.) I was unimpressed by C. S. Lewis at first, with his bland English children in their big, fancy house. But I was drawn in by the world on the other side of the wardrobe, where there were magical creatures and witches and battles to fight. And when she first read us *Harry Potter and the Sorcerer's Stone*, I zoned out for much of the first chapter or so, obstinately resolving not to fall under the spell of a book that I knew was already becoming rapidly popular. But I couldn't help myself, of course, especially once Harry found his passageway into the magical world. The way it appeared like the flip side of a coin, in the shadow of the real London, behind platform walls, in fireplaces, in phone booths, in bathroom stalls, made the fantasy appear so close, as though it were right around the corner.

It wasn't, though. The fantasy was in a primarily white world of magic. There were the occasional Black magicians peppered in: a Dean Thomas here, an Angelina Johnson there, a Kingsley Shacklebolt for good measure. In my brief forays into fantasy, I never found people who looked like me. In my mind, then, Blackness couldn't coexist in the same space as did magic and dragons. Blackness had limits on the imagination, limits that didn't seem to affect white imaginary worlds.

Middle-earth, Narnia, Westeros—in these worlds Black people are the exception, rarely seen, if visible at all. But these worlds also function with a degree of narrative freedom not usually seen in their Black siblings. From the Shire to Rivendell, the Vale of Arryn to the Crownlands, the reach and the breadth of these worlds seem infinite. And the protagonists journey and embark on quests, encountering new allies, villains, magical creatures, and landscapes along the way. These fictional worlds exist independently from the real world; they work within their own rules and logic, and the characters need only concern themselves with conflicts that are particular to those worlds.

These worlds come from the white imagination, and so are spaces of privilege, where whiteness can be the default without question, and conflicts may be more dreamed-up than mined from real-life issues. Politics, of course, may appear: Rowling alludes to Nazism and genocide with Voldemort, his Death Eaters, and his pure-blood ideology, and James Cameron openly embraced a white colonialist narrative in *Avatar*. But even these metaphorical renderings of real-world politics reflect the privilege of the white imagination, which may choose to engage with the world or wholly depart from it.

Black imaginary worlds are rare in the mainstream, and when they appear, they are largely rooted in the real world. Some degree of social and racial politics seems to be an unspoken prerequisite for Black worlds.

Though set in the fictional Freeland, *Black Lightning* still bases its Black heroes in a realistic urban setting, facing systemic racism. Nisi Shawl's novel *Everfair* roots its fictional setting in the history of African colonization and slavery by Europeans. And then there are the fantastical realms of Octavia Butler. Those fictional locales may not always explicitly reflect the politics of the real world but build on themes of prejudice, segregation, slavery, racism, and classism in ways that are clearly rooted in a historical context—and a Black historical context at that.

And then there's Wakanda, a fictional country in northeast Africa. The imaginary world of *Black Panther* isn't strictly autonomous; Wakanda is inspired by the real geography and customs of the continent. It has a geographic identity, and its language, fashion, and aesthetic in the film are all influenced by those of various African countries and cultures. The characters' accents, and some of the dialogue, are Xhosa, and costume designer Ruth E. Carter based the costuming on African fashion from tribes across the continent.

Wakanda was fully built in and around Africa. "We wanted to

honor and have reverence for the continent, and bring it to the screen in a way that you haven't seen before, as being a prosperous place," production designer Hannah Beachler told *Nerdist*.*

But even in its isolation, Wakanda, which represents Black resilience and success, is still tethered to real-world politics. Wakanda hasn't been colonized, but it's still at risk of a kind of retroactive colonization of its resources; a white man, Ulysses Klaue, aims to exploit the country's priceless natural resource, vibranium. (It's notable, too, that in the comics Klaue is the son of a Nazi.) And the central conflict in the film, between T'Challa and Killmonger, reflects the rift between the African experience and the African American experience.

The message, then, becomes that Blackness is generally politicized, tethered to its history, its current politics, and thus the real world, even in its imagined worlds. There is no purely escapist fantasy for Blackness. Narnia is not for us.

There is a side route, however: African science fiction and fantasy. Though still political, this kind of fantasy imagines the continent as a place where mythology and whimsy can thrive. In Marlon James's *Black Leopard, Red Wolf*, a skilled hunter searches for a boy who's disappeared, and on his travels he encounters strange characters and mystical creatures like demons and shape-shifters and finds himself in odd, dreamlike lands. In her debut novel *Children of Blood and Bone*, Tomi Adeyemi, who was inspired to write the book by the Black Lives Matter movement, presents the West African kingdom of Orïsha, which is full of magic. Other authors, like Amos Tutuola, Nnedi Okorafor, Tade Thompson, and N. K. Jemisin, similarly re-create Africa or African-inspired fantasy worlds, where we find magic and myths.

This repositions Africa as a home for imagination and epic ad-

---

* Victoria McNally, "6 Things We Learned About Wakanda from the Black Panther Set," *Nerdist*, January 24, 2018, https://archive.nerdist.com/black-panther-6-things-wakanda-marvel/.

venture and frees the continent of some of the racist and political associations it bears from a white Western perspective, instead opening it up as a place full of infinite possibilities, like Middle-earth or Westeros.

African fantasy then functions as an alternate take on Black Zionism, the idea that Black Americans of the diaspora would need to return to Africa to reconnect with their ancestry and free themselves of the aftereffects of white colonialism, including systemic inequality.

When I was young, my paternal grandmother kept her house decorated with African decor, mostly in the living room and in the den. Masks, artwork, ankhs—I didn't understand why everywhere there seemed to be Africa. My grandmother and one of her sisters, my great-aunt, gave me illustrated books targeted toward Black children; some of them were about Kwanzaa, a holiday that confused me. But Africa can be a haven in the Black imagination, especially when a country where you were born, where you are a citizen, still disregards and brutalizes you.

I understand this impulse to reach back toward Africa. When I encountered Wakanda, I had not yet found a place for my Blackness. In many ways I'm still looking, even now. Because of how even geographies are politicized along the lines of race and class, Black communities are often called the "projects" or the "ghetto" until gentrification magically renews value in the neighborhood and drives the original residents out with higher rents and property rates. In my own suburban hometown, full of Black and Latinx people, my parents cautioned me against walking around on my own and complained how the neighborhood was nicer when they first bought the house. My block was solely occupied by Black public school kids, who played with each other but who I mostly avoided. At the edge of my town, a few blocks past the library where I spent so much time as a kid, the houses became smaller, packed together, with multiple Black and Latinx families crowded inside. The yards were tiny; the grass was always a sickly jaundiced yellow, as though it was constantly dying. But I vividly remember the intersection right at the end of these houses where, just a few feet away, on the other side of the street, the next village—an affluent, mostly white neighborhood—sprawled out with large, beautiful homes and lush, green, well-kept yards. My mother admired them as we passed. I thought of my white classmates in my mostly white private school, many of whom lived there. I especially thought of the residents of the first houses after that intersection, if they thought of the smaller houses just across the street, with their Black and brown residents, and if they considered how that proximity affected their homes' property value.

Of course I had no way of imagining a world of magic and possibilities and Blackness. The Blackness I saw in the world was stigmatized and segregated. Wakanda was beautiful, of course, but what really stayed with me was the community that rallied around the idea of it and that cheering audience at BAM. Sometime between me and my friend taking our seats and SZA coming in with the chorus to "All the Stars" during the end credits, among the Black people in kente cloth applauding with their family and friends, I found something that looked like Wakanda to me.

Just as it can be difficult to find Black spaces in fantasy, sci-fi—in particular sci-fi that uses time travel narratives—often chooses to skip past the issue of race.

My mother loves Jane Austen adaptations, the 2005 *Pride & Prejudice* being her favorite, followed by Emma Thompson's *Sense and Sensibility*. She loves Regency-era England, with its pastoral scenes and romantic trifles and town dramas and discourteous breaches of etiquette and social protocol. She will repeat a snappy line of dialogue in an astoundingly poor English accent and then say, "I was meant to be born back then." But my reply is always, "No, because you'd be a slave," and she pauses comically before saying, "Oh, yeah."

My mother also loves the movie *Kate & Leopold*, mostly because she loves Meg Ryan and especially Hugh Jackman. Though I'd seen it on the TV in her room more than once, I never stayed around to watch more than a few minutes of the movie. I adored Meg Ryan (and found Hugh Jackman moderately tolerable), but the stuck-across-time romantic premise bugged me. It seemed impractical, and her final choice in the end (perhaps the only part of the movie I have seen) was *inconceivable*, as a certain short Sicilian outlaw would say. Hugh Jackman was attractive, sure, but was he worth a lifetime without tampons, proper plumbing, antidepressants, equal rights for women, and Ben & Jerry's? Even if I were willing to part with the internet and a whole world of modern medicine for a lifetime supply of Hugh Jackman's classic leading-man charm, as a Black woman, I would have no place in that time period.

Unlike Kate, who's free to slough off the modern times to live in an earlier era and be with her beau, I would not be able to move so seamlessly through time. History would hook its thumbs into my side and drag me away from that happy ending.

Time travel stories make use of an infinitely flexible conceit, limited only by their own pseudoscientific rules of causality. But one of the most prominent flaws of the genre is the racial privilege baked into these stories, or the dangers of time-traveling while Black.

Marty McFly. James Cole, from *12 Monkeys*. Wolverine. Time travelers are almost always white and often male. It's an easy, practical choice for a writer of such time travel stories to make. Post-Reconstruction? No problem. Colonial times? Sure, let's go. When the protagonist is white, the issue of his displacement becomes less of a substantial knot in the narrative; in fact, cultural discrepancies between the protagonist's time and the time he has been transported to may serve for moments of comedy, like Marty baffling an auditorium of 1950s teenagers with a lively rock 'n' roll performance. (The fact that Marty, a suburban white boy, plays "white" music historically appropriated from a Black musical tradition and, in the movie's universe, inspires the famous Black musician Chuck Berry, who will go on to create the very music that will be adopted by white musicians and many members of Marty's generation, creates an ironic chicken-and-egg paradox. Though a harmless time travel joke, it comes at the expense of a history of Black ingenuity; the white kid who goes back in time gets to look cool and wholly original, with his skateboarding and rock 'n' roll. If Marty were Black, the story would have looked much different.)

Time travel shows and movies tend to fall into one of two categories: quaint personal journeys and heroic quests. In stories like *Back to the Future*, *The Time Traveler's Wife*, and *The Butterfly Effect*, the scale is that of a personal narrative, with a white protagonist comfortably insulated from a larger racial history. In the latter category, which includes films like *12 Monkeys*, *The Terminator*, and *Timecop*, the central conflict is so large—apocalypses, dystopias, national or global disasters—that the narrative can easily sweep past issues of race. As for forward time-traveling, the future is often surprisingly post-racial, as in *Star Trek* and *Doctor Who*, with the introduction of alien species who can shift the focus away from the now-irrelevant racial prejudices of the human race.

Many shows have tried to address time-traveling while Black, with different degrees of success. In the painfully juvenile, short-lived Fox comedy *Making History*, a Black character who travels to 1775 is mistaken for a slave, but it's played like a one-off joke. In the NBC series *Timeless*, a Black programmer, a white historian, and a white soldier form a team of time-hoppers pursuing a "time terrorist" who's out to hijack history. In the first episode, the programmer, Rufus, protests, "I am Black. There is literally no place in American history that'll be awesome for me."[*] His discomfort is always apparent. At one

---

[*] Eric Kripke and Shawn Ryan, "Pilot," *Timeless*, October 3, 2016.

point, he delivers a triumphant speech about future Black American leaders, including President Barack Obama, to a racist cop—but all it does is incite the cop to pounce on him, creating a distraction so that his white colleagues can break out of prison. In *Timeless*, the woe of time-traveling while Black is a detail, a hiccup, sometimes a plot exigency, but never a big theme unto itself, and so Rufus always exists in a secondary position to the show's two white protagonists.

I found my favorite time traveler in 2013. I'd heard of *Doctor Who* before but knew little about it other than the fact that it was an old British sci-fi show about space and aliens. One of my roommates in my sophomore year of college, a goth girl obsessed with H. P. Lovecraft, Tegan and Sara, Muse, vegan baked goods, and hair dye, spoke incessantly about the series, usually in a dopey attempt at a British accent. She adored David Tennant, who was starring as the Tenth Doctor at the time, but I was less than impressed by the seemingly foppish protagonist, with his pin-striped suit, Converse sneakers, and artfully tousled hair. And the show—it seemed cheesy and ridiculous. When I saw a poorly written episode one day at the apartment of friends, during Matt Smith's tenure as the Eleventh Doctor, I was turned off to the show for another year.

In the summer of 2013, though, a year out of college and on my own in my first apartment in Brooklyn, I began the show in earnest, starting with Christopher Eccleston's tenure as the titular character, an alien who travels through time and space in a blue police call box called the TARDIS. Though the show has the Doctor and his companions resolving strange happenings in the past, present, and future, it is more focused on adventures out in space, whether that be in the present or future, than it is in venturing to the past. That's not particularly surprising from the purview of the writers' room; travels to a future version of Earth or a distant planet give the writer full creative agency. They aren't beholden to the particulars of the past, needing to keep things factual or address particular cultural mores or politics. But in recent years the show has made some strides in addressing race in its narrative. For decades, one white man after another starred as the Doctor. Of the Doctor's travel companions, too, there have been only a couple of people of color, and the show has handled the issue awkwardly. In season three of the rebooted series, Martha Jones, the Tenth Doctor's Black companion, asks him how her race will be addressed in seventeenth-century England; he brushes her concerns off, saying that she should do as he does and walk around like she owns the place. Race, he suggests, is an inconsequential construct, except when it isn't—when they meet Shakespeare, the bard fetishizes her Blackness as he hits on her, raining down so many unintentionally racist sentiments that the Doctor winces, saying it's "political correctness gone mad."*

In another two-part episode that takes place in the past, the Doctor and Martha go on an undercover mission in which his memory of his real identity is erased. They work at a boys' boarding school, the Doctor as a normal human teacher, and Martha as a maid who is disrespected and looked down on because of her racial identity. Martha's nevertheless saddled with the responsibility of keeping track of the Doctor and carrying out the mission while being treated like a lesser human being.

The series got bolder a few seasons later, when the Twelfth Doctor (played by Peter Capaldi) brings his Black companion, Bill, to 1814 London to investigate a giant monster living beneath the Thames. When they step out of the TARDIS, they have an exchange that mirrors the one the Tenth Doctor and Martha had when they stepped out into Shakespearean England, though it seems the Doctor has learned to be less flippant when considering his companion's identity and how it will play out in the circumstances.

"Wait, you wanna go out there?" Bill asks.

"You don't?" the Docter replies.

"Well, it's 1814. Melanin."

---

* Steven Moffat, "The Shakespeare Code," *Doctor Who*, April 7, 2007.

"Yes."

"Slavery is still totally a thing."

"... Yes, it is."*

Capaldi delivers the last line perfectly, with a pregnant pause, a weary intake of breath. It's a show of disappointment. And yet, the writers once again failed to let the writing linger on the issue any longer than necessary; on the page, the dialogue plays as dismissive, as though the Doctor, an alien who presents as a cis white male, recognizes the issue but decides it is not worth any further concern. The subject is changed to one of costuming, as though Bill dressing up for the period should be enough to make up for the fact that she is a Black woman in a time when she would have otherwise been enslaved.

The episode does redeem itself somewhat when it reveals its villain. Before encountering the episode's antagonist, the Doctor tells Bill that he will do the talking because he knows her temper and he believes the situation calls for diplomacy and tact. (This in itself is troubling, that the Doctor clearly fears the complications that could be wrought by the angry Black woman, though her rage is certainly warranted.) And yet, when the antagonist walks in and, after seeing Bill, barks, "Who let this creature in here?"† the Doctor loses his temper, punching him in the face. He's disgusted; this villain isn't some scheming alien, just a regular racist human being with no regard for the lives of others.

But it was an episode of season eleven of the series, starring the actress Jodie Whittaker as the first female Doctor, that signaled a more fearless and nuanced—though ultimately still flawed—approach to time-traveling while Black. In season eleven, episode three, titled "Rosa," the Doctor and her three companions, Graham, a white man, Yasmin, a Pakistani woman, and Ryan, a Black man,

---

* Chris Chibnall, "Thin Ice," *Doctor Who*, April 29, 2017.
† Chibnall, "Thin Ice."

have to ensure that Rosa Parks incites the US civil rights movement as planned. The episode poignantly addresses each character's specific experience during this moment in history: Yasmin and Ryan encounter people who are either confounded by or openly hostile toward them, and they trade stories about how they still face racism in the present day. Meanwhile, the Doctor and Graham are forced to act complicit in the practice of segregation in order to make sure that history proceeds as it should. The episode's climactic scene, right before Parks refuses to give up her seat, is so affecting because Graham must confront the racial privilege he was born with, being a white man, and a history of injustice that precedes him.

The ending of the episode, however, is hokey; turns out the bad guy's motives weren't anything novel, just regular ole racism. "This happened in the past, kids, but racism is still very much prevalent" is the message of the episode, which is so busy being didactic that it fails to be imaginative. It's a problem that has plagued the Thirteenth Doctor, as the new writers' room attempted to fix all the show's diversity and gender problems at once, without subtlety.

There have been movies and TV shows in recent years that have handled the issue with more finesse. In the second season of the Netflix series *The Umbrella Academy*, adapted from the comic book series by Gerard Way, the protagonists, a family of misfit superheroes, having brought about the apocalypse, jump back in time and are scattered in and around Dallas, Texas, in the 1960s, around the time of President John F. Kennedy's assassination. The siblings are separated and find vastly different ways to deal with their circumstances. From the jump, the show demonstrates how the characters of color are treated differently in the South in the 1960s. Diego, a Hispanic man with knife-throwing abilities to match Bullseye's, immediately helps a woman getting mugged but is promptly imprisoned in a mental ward.

And in one of the most interesting story lines of the season, Allison, a Black woman with the power to force people to do what she wants by saying, "I heard a rumor . . . ," gets drawn into the civil rights movement.

Watching Diego and Allison land in the past gave me a familiar sensation of dread. Particularly Allison, as she walks into a whites-only diner, trying to figure things out. But her power was a comfort; I thought, seeing her face off against a couple of racist white guys, that she could take them. In fact, she could take on all the racists in the state. I had forgotten that season one had ended with her getting injured in the neck, meaning that she could not speak and could certainly not use her powers. She runs fearfully into the night, trying to evade the white boys, because she knows that the fact that she's from the future and the fact that she's a superhero don't amount to anything at the moment; she is simply another Black woman.

Allison becomes an activist and marries another organizer. But even when Allison regains her voice and can use her powers, she still struggles to keep other Black people safe. Her husband is beaten and arrested by a policeman before her eyes.

But even here, *The Umbrella Academy* halfway falls into the pattern of many other time travel stories: the main issue is the apocalypse, and though all the siblings are misplaced in time, since most of them are white, they conveniently have no interaction with the contentious racial circumstances of Dallas, Texas, in the 1960s. Their movement isn't restricted—conveniently, because that would slow down the narrative and distract from the larger conflict. Only Allison is consistently drawn into the civil rights movement. Klaus, the hedonistic hot mess of a necromancer, is the only other Hargreeves sibling who observes it—Black men jailed for no reason, Black men getting pummeled in the street by police—and, in his signature breezy manner, expresses some surprise but then floats along.

The 2019 Netflix movie *See You Yesterday*, which was produced by Spike Lee, took a different approach. Its protagonists, C.J. and Sebastian, are Black teenage geniuses who figure out the secret to time travel for a science expo at school. When C.J.'s older brother is shot dead by the police, she decides to go back in time to prevent his murder. Though the movie encounters some of the usual pitfalls of time travel plots (predictability, muddled rules) and features some cheesy '80s-style special effects, what it offers in terms of diversity and its themes is a treasure.

As C.J. and Sebastian work out the fantastical science of time travel in a garage, it feels practical, grounded in the reality of Black American life. The two don't set out to change the world or alter their own lives, nor do they jump far into the past or future for an excellent Bill-and-Ted-style adventure. They're not thrilled to have one-upped Einstein; they just want to get scholarships to college so they can leave their neighborhood. And C.J. just wants her brother back. Their actions and motivations are contained to this one very real instance of police brutality, so the plot never loses its footing in the real world.

When *See You Yesterday* opens, in C.J. and Sebastian's classroom, their teacher—played by Marty McFly himself, Michael J. Fox—is reading Octavia Butler's novel *Kindred* at his desk. In Butler's book, a Black woman living in Los Angeles in 1976 is repeatedly transported back to pre–Civil War Maryland, to a plantation where her ancestors lived. She tries to protect her lineage while also trying to stay alive, in a time when she's deemed a slave. She's literally beaten down by the past—whipped and nearly raped—and, after she time-travels for the last time, one of her arms is left behind, in the past. History has taken a part of her, and she will never be whole in the present. In *Kindred*, as in *See You Yesterday*, history is never just relegated to the past for Black people. It's living.

Though I found places I'd love to explore in fantasy worlds, I never found anything to love in time travel. Even if one forgets the headaches of time paradoxes and the dreaded butterfly effect, I had no interest in facing the unknown threats of the future or the familiar challenges of the past. Right now, our identity politics are better than ever, which isn't to say they are great; Black people are still getting killed by the police, women are still victims of inequality, and queer and trans lives are still overlooked or ignored completely.

A few years ago, on a weekday night in Midtown, I was walking down Seventh Avenue on my own. I was in a great mood; I had just had a date with my new boyfriend and walked him to his bus at Port Authority. I was happily recalling my evening on my walk to Penn Station to catch my train when I was interrupted by a bitter call of *nigger*. The word was spat out into the air, and it caught me as I crossed one empty intersection. I paused at the street corner, unsure where the word had come from and where its target had been. An old white man, scraggly and unkempt, had said it, and the word didn't even slow his gait. He shot it out like a drive-by, and I realized the word had been gift-wrapped for me; there was no one else around. And yet I was still confused. For all the times the word had been volleyed around me, it had never been spiked directly at me, and so my reaction was that surely this must have been a mistake, that this man could somehow see me—a twentysomething Black woman, a journalist and poet of upper-middle-class upbringing, of private schools and a college education—and just see a nigger. I thought my gender, my class, all my privilege had shielded me from such a word, and yet I saw it made no difference.

But still I have undoubtedly heard the word less than my parents and my grandparents did. In the past and present, white America has always kept its foot on Black America's throat.

See You Yesterday ends uncertainly, on a long shot of C.J. Her determined expression, as she runs toward the past again, could indicate hopeful resolve or plain foolishness. But in every version of the story, there's injustice and a Black person inevitably hurt or dead. This cyclical sorrow, the movie seems to say, is the state and cost of institutional racism in America. Though time travel narratives so often allow white protagonists to freely jump the timeline, there's an open field of possibilities for the genre to look at history through the eyes of the oppressed, forgotten, and marginalized. What *See*

You Yesterday asserts is that, for a people hindered by prejudice and police brutality, the future is a privilege. "See you yesterday," C.J.'s brother tells her solemnly, near the end of the film.* For these Black travelers, there are only yesterdays to contend with; tomorrow is just out of reach.

In the past few years, we haven't just gotten Black people traveling in time; we've gotten Black people transforming into horses, Black people inhabited by white people, Black people seeing talking cartoons. Things have been getting weird—or, to be precise, surreal.

I've always been a fan of the surreal. As a kid, I knew of Salvador Dalí's melting clocks and liked the implication of distorted time. In college I had a poster of his *Meditative Rose*. The bright red flower, with its petals perfectly fanned out, one drop of water perched on the nearest one, floats in the sky above a sandy landscape, large and imposing, like a UFO. Suddenly the beautiful seems monstrous. In college, too, René Magritte became my favorite; I adored his obsession with things seen and obscured.

My love of the surreal came with some qualifiers, however. When I looked closely at *The Persistence of Memory*, beyond the melting clocks that so caught my attention, I found elements of the artwork inexplicably disturbing: I never truly considered the fleshy mass at the center of the piece, always thinking it was some fabric or an animal, not a cut of a human face, the eyelashes curved like insect legs. And I never noticed that what always seemed like just a pattern on the pocket watch in the left corner of the canvas was actually a cluster of black ants. What bothered me was not the nature of these

---

* Stefon Bristol, *See You Yesterday*, 2019.

reveals themselves but the fact that these sights weren't immediately apparent; I felt as though I had been tricked into seeing something grotesque.

Of course, that is simply one execution of surrealism. Another is to bludgeon the viewer with the full force of the uncanny, as Dalí does in the horrific mangle of limbs in *Soft Construction with Boiled Beans*. And then there is the surreal that is so close to the normal, except for the artist's radical juxtaposition of incongruous elements. In Magritte's *Empire of Light* series, the houses in a neighborhood sit darkened in the nighttime, only their windows lit, a single lamppost providing a bit of soft illumination to the street. And yet, above the line of shadowy treetops, the sky is a milky blue, with perfect, pillowy white clouds. The painting can't hold both truths—the nighttime and the daytime—at once. It's an impossibility, and so it appears strange.

A recent wave of Black-written, -directed, and -acted movies and TV shows take these different surreal approaches to talk about race, particularly matters of racial injustice and racial performance.

In the first episode of Terence Nance's 2018 HBO show *Random Acts of Flyness*, Nance introduces his show, filming himself as he bikes down the street. Almost immediately, a police car flags him down, and he gets into an altercation with a white policeman. It's unclear whether this is real or a scripted scene. The blurred line between what could be documentary filmmaking and a contrived representation of police brutality is unnerving, not just because of the subject matter, but also because Nance puts us in a position where we aren't sure how to react as viewers: Should we feel fearful and tense, anticipating a real depiction of the type of exchange that happens every day between white police officers and Black citizens, or should we watch with some measure of incredulity, waiting for the punch line?

The show maintains this discomfort, branching off into interconnected segments: a ghastly '70s-style game show called *Everybody Dies*, hosted by a woman named Ripa the Reaper with her trusty scythe and "Murder Map" of America, riddled with light-up bullet holes; an infomercial featuring the *Mad Men* star Jon Hamm, as himself, selling a product to help white people fight their "acute viral perceptive albinitis'"*; and a talk show called *The Sexual Proclivities of the Black Community*, featuring an interview with a nonbinary Black person on their experiences with dating and relationships.

Nance uses various modes of filmmaking, from animation to urban musical-themed updates of classic fairy tales to documentary-style found footage, refusing to adhere to strictly surreal or satirical modes, and his relationship to fiction is just as flexible. Instead, he incorporates vérité documentary with interviews that are jarring not just for their proximity to his parody videos and infomercials but also for their naked sincerity.

But Nance uses his unique hodgepodge approach to tackle topics not frequently addressed in the Black community, like queerness, homophobia, and toxic masculinity. In one of my favorite segments, a first-person-shooter game is reimagined as a game in which a Black woman takes down catcallers with a frown. By using humor and a mash-up of media styles, the show was able to tap into something I've known since I first began to be sexualized by random men I encountered in the street—that catcalls, seen by the men as just compliments, were menacing, ways for them to try to exercise some power over my body. If I frowned in response, I risked the catcaller becoming belligerent. I still remember walking through the Lower East Side one summer day and frowning at a man who'd tossed off some comment about my appearance; he became enraged and hurled curses at me as I continued down the block. I tensed up and kept my head facing forward. I thought of this as I watched the woman shooting frowns in Nance's show, how this bit of comedic fiction so easily subverted exchanges like the one I had with the man in the Lower East Side.

* Terence Nance, "What are your thoughts on raising free black children?" *Random Acts of Flyness*, August 3, 2018.

But the project Nance undertakes in *Random Acts of Flyness* is one of subversions. Yes, he indulges in parodies and toys with realism, but he also often uses surrealism as a way to depict the terrors of the real world—and provide a fantastical escape from them. At the end of the first skit, with the realistic exchange between Nance and the cop, Nance runs away, the cop chasing behind him, but then suddenly Nance lifts off and flies away, no longer trapped in the reality of the circumstance.

The term "Afro-Surreal" was coined in the introduction to Henry Dumas's 1974 book *Ark of Bones and Other Stories* by the writer and activist Amiri Baraka, who used it to describe Dumas's "skill at creating an entirely different world organically connected to this one . . . the Black aesthetic in its actual contemporary and lived life."* In 2009 the writer D. Scot Miller published his "Afrosurreal Manifesto," defining the genre in detail, in the *San Francisco Bay Guardian*. Linked in its dreamlike aesthetic to the larger surrealist movement in visual art, Afro-surrealism was nevertheless its own separate beast, with deeper ties to the Négritude and, later, Black Arts movements. Both movements were incited by a desire on the part of Black artists to define their own identities, rights, and cultures in spite of the influence of colonialism and the injustices addressed by the civil rights and Black Power activism of the '60s and '70s.

"With Afro-surreal, it allows us to address the absurdity head-on," D. Scot Miller told Ytasha Womack in her book *Afrofuturism: The World of Black Sci-Fi and Fantasy Culture*. "Sometimes you have to be irreverent. Sometimes the situation is so absurd that the only way to address it is to be absurd."† Afro-surrealism is as fluid and true as a dream—art that, in its fluidity, can transcend genre. Is it horror? Is it comedy? Is it a thriller? It's every element of every genre that can

---

* Henry Dumas, *Ark of Bones and Other Stories* (Carbondale: Southern Illinois University Press, 1970).

† Ytasha L. Womack, *Afrofuturism: The World of Black Sci-Fi and Fantasy Culture* (Chicago: Lawrence Hill Books, 2013).

be collaged into a picture of contemporary Black life. Ralph Ellison's *Invisible Man*, Toni Morrison's *Beloved*, the works of Bob Kaufman, and the visual art of Kara Walker—all combine the real with the mystical or fantastical to create their portraits of Blackness in America.

In Boots Riley's cartoonish, anti-capitalist drug trip of a movie, *Sorry to Bother You*, the protagonist, a Black telemarketer named Cassius "Cash" Green, is at a bar with friends when he discovers his "white voice." The nasal, nebbish caricature of whiteness comes out of Cassius's mouth like a bad dub on an anime, and it unsettles everyone at the table; his racial ventriloquism is, as Cassius's friend describes it, "some *Puppet Master* shit."* Riley's version of Oakland, California, starts off grounded in reality, but Cash's seamless code-switching is one of the increasingly outlandish signs that things are just *off*.

Riley could have stopped there: the combination of the movie's loud aesthetic and his literalization of the act of code-switching rendered Cassius's world surreal enough. But for Riley to really tackle the scourge of capitalism with the sense of urgency that the film requires—he needs a more dramatic swerve into the surreal. Cassius discovers that Steve Lift , the immoral white CEO of Cassius's evil corporation, is using a cocaine-like drug to transform his workers into obedient "equisapiens," human-horse hybrids. The departure makes Cassius's code-switching more than just a punch line; the equisapiens are disturbing because they reflect the reality of how capitalism works in this country, and how employees are just treated as workhorses, exploited at the expense of their health, well-being, and humanity.

The film plays out like a fever dream, the term director Hiro Murai has used to describe the surreal tone of the show *Atlanta*, created by and starring Donald Glover. The show is about an intelligent but consistently irresponsible slouch named Earnest "Earn" Marks, his cousin Alfred "Paper Boi" Miles, and Paper Boi's friend Darius

---

* Boots Riley, *Sorry to Bother You* (Annapurna Pictures, 2018).

trying to launch Paper Boi's career as a rap star. "We're always looking for what we call 'dream logic,' something that feels right, but doesn't necessarily have a logical throughline," Murai told the *New York Times* in an interview.[*] So when, in the fifth episode of the first season, we're introduced to a Justin Bieber who is played by a Black man, we're meant to understand, within the dream logic of the show, that the Canadian pop star is, quite simply, Black. No gestures or mentions are made toward the race-bent Bieber, but the very existence of Black Bieber calls into question the real privilege of white celebrities, whose transgressions and hijinks are easily forgiven and forgotten.

Like *Sorry to Bother You*, *Atlanta* often uses surrealism as a way to talk about racial performance. Racial performance in *Atlanta* is sometimes used as a means of survival. The appearance of a Black student named Tobias in whiteface in the season one episode "Value," right after Earn's on-and-off girlfriend Van, a grade-school teacher, fails a drug test and loses her job, speaks to a Black student's poor prospects in the education system. The show positions Tobias, sitting there eerily silent and still in the back of the classroom, as a grim and disconcerting representation of the reality of racial inequity in schools. Perhaps the student imagines that borrowed whiteness will grant him the privilege of a better education, and thus a brighter future. After all, we see throughout the show how the education system fails the children, particularly children of color. Even Van's boss, a school administrator, shrugs the matter off, saying, "The system isn't made for these kids to succeed."[†]

Not unlike Tobias is the young, Patagonia-wearing, farmers' market frequenter Harrison Booth, who makes an appearance in the following episode as the subject of a segment on the fictional *Montague* show. Though not literally in chalky whiteface like Tobias,

---

[*] Leigh-Ann Jackson, "Dream Logic: Hiro Murai on the Look of 'Atlanta,' " *New York Times*, May 9, 2018, https://www.nytimes.com/2018/05/09/arts/television/atlanta-director-hiro-murai-donald-glover.html.

[†] Donald Glover, "Value," *Atlanta*, October 6, 2016.

Harrison wears a blond wig and acts the part of a "trans-racial" white man because he's unwilling or unable to cope with the injustices of Blackness and his own internalized racism.

And in some instances, an exaggerated performance of Blackness is necessary, as in the "Juneteenth" episode of *Atlanta*, which finds Earn and Van trying to schmooze with people at a party whose white host quotes Malcolm X, performs slam poems about Jim Crow, and talks about the "plight of the contemporary Black man."* Negro spirituals and other plantation-themed party accents entertained by a coterie of supposedly elite, sophisticated guests emphasize the ridiculousness of the whole affair.

Though *Atlanta* often maintains this tone—fairly realistic but occasionally absurd in its satires—it does sometimes dip into a surreal tone that draws the show closer to the genre of horror. In the season two episode "Woods," Paper Boi gets lost in a seemingly endless stretch of woods, where he encounters a destroyed deer carcass and a threatening old man. We're meant to understand the whole sequence as something dreamt up from Paper Boi's subconscious; he is stagnant in his life and indecisive about his career. And yet, even if the scenario is just a fantasy, the episode is fashioned in such a way—through its eerie tone and lighting, and Brian Tyree Henry's performance—that the stakes feel real.

The show goes even further in its infamous "Teddy Perkins" episode, when the title character (captured in nightmarish whiteface by Glover) blatantly recalls Michael Jackson and the story of his childhood abuse and celebrity. To say that particular thirty-five-minute commercial-free exercise in terror served as a cautionary tale would be too glib, but Teddy also represents how a Black man striving for success in a world that defines it by white standards may transform himself in order to adapt.

These episodes made me uncomfortable in the same way horror

---

* Janicza Bravo, "Juneteenth," *Atlanta*, October 25, 2016.

movies do; by departing from the grounding of the real world, the show opens up the possibility that anything can happen. Suddenly *Atlanta* may become a world of monsters and ghosts—fantastical threats on top of the everyday threats that come with being Black in America. It makes me think of the classic horror movie trope about the Black person in the movie dying first. I was aware of it from pretty early on. In fact, I remember exactly when: in 2001, when I went to see the science-fiction comedy film *Evolution*, starring David Duchovny, Julianne Moore, Orlando Jones, and Seann William Scott. I have completely forgotten the film except for one scene, when Jones's character refuses to investigate something or another because he's seen movies and so knows what comes next: the Black guy dies first. This revelation left me enraged, and not just because of the implicit racism of the trope but because even in these fictional universes, after presumably living lives where they have been marginalized, oppressed, and/or prejudiced against, these Black characters can't even cut a break when it comes down to the horrific and supernatural. That means we're not safe anywhere: even if I choose not to explore the haunted house or wander into the ominous woods alone at night, I may still be a victim because of my Blackness. But when am I not?

The crossover of the new Black surrealism with horror makes sense for the way that horror has traditionally used its frights as ways to talk about matters of gender, sexuality, race, and class.

In comedian and writer Jordan Peele's films, scares and strange occurrences are explicitly tied to the horrors of race in America.

"Black is in fashion,"* a white man says about halfway through Peele's 2017 horror-comedy *Get Out*. The line is laughably absurd, to think that Blackness can be a wearable trend like rompers or acid-washed jeans. And yet it's perfectly appropriate within the logic of the movie, where the man is a member of a cult of white people who literally auction off Black bodies and inhabit them.

---

* Jordan Peele, *Get Out*, Blumhouse Productions, 2017.

The auction of *Get Out*'s doomed protagonist, Chris (Daniel Kaluuya), is a blatant callback to slave auctions, and the white antagonists' assumptions about Chris's talents and abilities are taken from persisting racist stereotypes. Chris is fetishized, admired for his (assumed) sexual virility and natural athleticism, and envied for his skills, like his photographer's "eyes," to which they feel entitled. (We are left to imagine the terms under which a Black woman would be auctioned, likely as a docile Mammy, fiery Sapphire, or sexualized Jezebel. The Black female experience in Afro-Surrealism, as in many movements, is typically subordinated to that of the male.)

More disturbing than the sale of these Black bodies is the way that their white purchasers psychologically supplant their victims. These victims' consciousnesses still exist, and they're still aware, in whatever distant way, of what's happening as they're trapped in a kind of mental purgatory called the Sunken Place—but the Black victims are only meant to serve as grotesque costumes for these white people to wear.

In Peele's movies—*Get Out*, but also *Us* and *Candyman*—there's a broad, almost mythic sense of mysterious and disturbing wrongs passed down through the generations, and it is meant to replicate the horrors of slavery and the inheritance of racial injustice that Black people are given.

Just as I admire certain surreal paintings—like Salvador Dalí's *The Persistence of Memory*—until I take a closer look and discover the abject imagery that was there all along, Black movies and TV shows may get horrific and weird to inspire this same kind of awakening in their audiences.

In the 2020 Hulu series *Woke*, a Black cartoonist named Keef, whose career is just about to take off, encounters a woman who questions the politics of his work—which he then challenges. "Why is it that us people of color are always having to stand for something or, you know, say something in our work?" he asks. "I keep it light."[*]

---

[*] Keith Knight, "Rhymes with Broke," *Woke*, September 9, 2020.

But when he becomes a victim of police brutality for allegedly fitting the description of a Black man who actually looks nothing like him, he has a mental break, and all around him, his cartoons come to life, many goading him to stop trying to be blind to the issue of race in America and use his talents to get political.

While watching the show, I was struck by my similarity to Keef. Before Donald Trump, before the pandemic, before Black Lives Matter, before all these surreal Black TV shows and movies, and before I sat in that Brooklyn theater to watch *Black Panther*, I also resisted getting political. My Blackness was something fearful, and I was afraid to call attention to it. When that man in Midtown called me a nigger, what stung most wasn't the word itself but the surrealness of it, how it was a word that I never thought someone could find in their vocabulary for me. I've had to have my bubble of privilege punctured again and again by the brutalities of the world, by the news every day, to become aware of the strangeness of being Black in America.

In *Woke*, Keef's Black roommate tells him that once he becomes woke, he can't just go back to being blind. Once you see it all, you can't unsee it. There's no rewinding—though, as the time travel stories have shown us, even going back in time makes no difference to a Black person. Your identity is always there, and the world will always react to it.

In the last few years, as America has continued to fall apart, seemingly with no end in sight, I have trained myself to keep my eyes open, to stay woke, to look for Black art and the ways it reflects our reality—or distorts it. I'm looking for definitions of my Blackness, for reflections, and for hints of a community of people who look like me and value what our Blackness means. I'm looking for my Black heroes, for Wakanda, for Black journeyers into lands and times unknown, and for narratives that capture my fears and anxieties as a Black person in America.

In 2016, at the Television Critics Association tour, Donald Glover discussed his choice to tackle the absurd in *Atlanta*: "I feel like the absurdity of the world . . . is more interesting. I mean, like, Donald Trump is running for president right now. When I was eight, I saw him in a Pizza Hut commercial. Like, that's fucking weird."* And it's not just Trump; it has never been just about the figure in the White House at any given time. According to Boots Riley, "There was Occupy. There is Black Lives Matter. All of these things are happening in the world: forces pushing people to make other choices, and art in the industry around it tries to respond to that."†

As a critic and fan, I'd like to live in those artworks where my Blackness is whole and represented, as opposed to just a stereotype or a sketch, and where it is honored. Wakanda didn't begin in *Black Panther*; it has always been the space we—Black thinkers, Black artists, Black everyone, everywhere—have made for ourselves, a place beautiful, where we can live, not just survive.

* Tambay Obenson, "FX Releases a Second Promo for Donald Glover's 'Atlanta,'" *Shadow and Act*, June 8, 2016, https://shadowandact.com/fx-releases-a-second-promo-for-donald-glovers-atlanta.

† Alissa Wilkinson, "Why 'Sorry to Bother You' Director Boots Riley Thinks Artists Should Be Activists," *Vox*, July 6, 2018, https://www.vox.com/summer-movies/2018/7/6/17501500/boots-riley-interview-sorry-to-bother-you-coup-michel-gondry-activism.

V.

The Slytherin Fire-Bender of Sunagakure

Self-identification with fandom, racial and national identities in space Westerns, and the persistent fantasy of manifest destiny

I didn't understand the point of our Christian Existence class, but it was part of our four-year religion requirement at my private Catholic high school, and all I knew was that spending one class a day during senior year talking to Brother Mike about "existence" was easier than analyzing Bible verses or memorizing facts about the history of the Roman Catholic church.

That year Brother Mike introduced us to the enneagram, a pseudoscientific breakdown of personality types into nine main categories, numbered. He drew a circle on the board, then inside it a triangle and, overlaying it, a series of crisscrossing lines that created somewhat of a star pattern. He wrote numbers around the circle at the junctures where the lines met along the diameter, then later added in arrows at those junctures.

We had to memorize the drawing, re-create it ourselves on tests, and decipher what it meant. We studied the traits of every number until we became experts and took a lengthy test to determine what our numbers were. I was a four, aka "the artist" or "the individual-ist," my favorite of the nine types. At best, I was creative, sensitive, and introspective; at worst, I was moody and self-absorbed. I was thrilled even with the negative parts of the description, because it all rang true. After class I stopped by Brother Mike's desk and declared that I was a four but said it seemed I had more of the negative traits than the positive; I wasn't fully integrated or self-actualized (Brother Mike had also taught us about Maslow's hierarchy of needs). "Well, get integrating, girl!" he told me, a chipper tone in his voice. I was pleased; it was as though I had met the apparent exercise of the class: self-definition, self-awareness, then the achievement of a more wholesome, fulfilling Christian self.

By that point the Christian part of the equation had already lost my interest, but I hung on to the enneagram, seeking its revelations, ready to find some new gem of myself in its prescriptive outline of me. It was a new kind of astrology for me to become acquainted with. Though the old astrology still had its appeal: as a kid I enjoyed play-ing the contrary skeptic to my family's jokes about their star signs, but then I too was drawn in by it all. On a field trip in elementary school, I picked up *Astrostyle: Star-Studded Advice for Love, Life, and Looking Good,* by the so-called AstroTwins, Tali and Ophira Edut, and learned that mine is a fixed sign, I'm ruled by the sun, and I look good in yellows and golds. (For the record, I do look great in yellows and golds, though my wardrobe palette is limited to blacks and grays.)

This is all to say that I was primed for the era of the Hogwarts houses—and every other game of self-selecting fandom identity.

When *Harry Potter* was just beginning to get popular, we—the enthusiastic early fans—were all team Gryffindor. This was years before J. K. Rowling drew countless fans' ire with her transphobic comments and transparent attempts to slot in diversity into the world she'd created. Some have given up their associations with Hogwarts because of how its creator has tainted the fandom, while others have chosen to divorce the writer from the work. But in those early days, it was easier to get swept up in the fan frenzy and celebrate team Gryffindor.

Rowling has never been shy about her feelings toward her characters, and her prejudices toward her protagonists were apparent in her focus on their house, Gryffindor. (Rowling, a Leo, also made many of her main characters Leos, and Harry Potter even shares her birthday—a fact that would have annoyed me more as a kid if I wasn't also a Leo whose birthday is just four days earlier.) The breakdown of the houses in the wizarding school was clear: Gryffindor was for the brave heroes and always won the house cup at the end of the school year; Ravenclaws were smart but otherwise forgettable; Hufflepuffs were loyal do-gooders but even more forgettable; and Slytherins were villains, always second place to Gryffindors. Rowling barely spoke of any other house than Gryffindor. As a young fan, I didn't mind. I happily claimed Gryffindor, because there was no other choice. Even early merchandise from the series seemed to focus just on Gryffindor: I proudly sported the scarlet and gold.

It wasn't until a few years after the *Harry Potter* phenomenon took over pop culture that fans—myself included—began declaring their loyalties to other houses. The Sorting Hat became not just a fictional device in the book series but a real-life way for fans to imagine themselves into the world of their fandom. At the Warner Bros. Studio set, fans could get sorted into a house. When Rowling launched her fan site Pottermore, one of the big early draws was the Sorting Hat quiz. Though at that point I was already roughly a decade removed from my peak *Harry Potter* fandom, I immediately took the test—and then asked basically everyone I knew to do the same. I requested that my boyfriend at the time—who wasn't even a Potter fan—take it. At work, on a slow afternoon, I had my coworkers take the test and then find out their Patronuses, and we shouted the results at each other from over our desks.

When, on another afternoon, my coworker and I decided to rebrand our joint workspace, we designed a Hogwarts-inspired crest with our two house mascots on it: the snake and the badger.

I, of course, was the Slytherin. The house of the dark wizards suited my contrary temperament, and I am nothing if not ambitious. As for bravery, at some point during my fandom I stopped seeing Gryffindors as courageous and instead saw them as foolhardy; I didn't want to charge into battle but maneuver in a way that posed the least risk to myself. And I didn't want to be the hero; I wanted to rule the world.

While some of my friends were disappointed in their results (mostly the Hufflepuffs), I was proudly a Slytherin, as though it meant something real. When one of my friends declared, "Of course you're a Slytherin; you're the most Slytherin person I know!" I was flattered. I was pleased that a fictional system of categorization in which each house is distinguished by only two or three personality traits (and which could be easily upended by self-determination, as it was by Harry and Hermione in the first book, who chose Gryffindor rather than Slytherin and Ravenclaw, respectively) still validated my evaluation of myself. So I bought a Slytherin alumnus tee. I recast my view of the books and movies based on my newfound loyalty to Slytherin, complaining every time Gryffindor stole away the house cup or claimed the glory.

When a guy I was dating asked for my Hogwarts house and guessed Gryffindor, I took it as a grave offense. *He still doesn't know me at all*, I thought. As if I could bear the emblem of anything else but the snake.

For a fan, misidentification within a fandom is a unique insult. The Nickelodeon show *Avatar: The Last Airbender* imagined a world of four nations, each one connected to an element: air, water, earth, fire. Inspired by Eastern fashion, art, and martial arts, the creators gave each nation a unique character and political history. I was drawn to Fire, the fierce, combative nation that ruled over the others and was home to the series' big villains.

When a friend pegged me as a member of the Earth Kingdom, I shot him down, saying I was too passionate and intense to be Earth; I was ready to fight him right then. He quickly revised his assessment, saying that even if I was Fire, my *work ethic* was all Earth: steady and reliable? I let it go but was still annoyed at his transparent attempt at placation. A year or so later, I was at a tattoo shop getting some work done, and while talking about art and Comic Con, my tattooist showed me a piece of *Avatar* artwork he'd done. I told him about my friend's judgment of me being a member of the Earth Kingdom.

"Well, what sign are you?" he asked.

"Leo," I responded.

"Fire sign. Then you're totally Fire Nation," he said, matter-of-factly, with a shrug. Just like that—end of conversation. Though he was a stranger who knew nothing about me, this wasn't a question up for debate. It was absurd, and yet I found it comforting: *of course* I'm Fire Nation. Of course.

So many fandoms have these categories baked in: tribalism and the regional and class conflicts that result are popular themes, especially in fantasy, which often reimagines much more dated social systems like feudalism. I've seen *Game of Thrones* fans claim one house or another, and *Naruto* fans wear headbands from their adopted ninja village (my own pick being Sunagakure, the sand village). One friend has ranted at me more than once about the discrepancies in her Sorting Hat results, having been sorted into both Hufflepuff and Slytherin. Another also cited confusion when she got two different Sortings: Ravenclaw, then Hufflepuff. The sudden change disturbed me; if she was a Hufflepuff, then *did I really know her at all?* (The answer, of course, was yes, but for a second I did doubt myself.)

Fans will also try to reposition themselves and their friends as "types" based on their favorite groups of protagonists. Like every female New Yorker in the '90s had to, at some point in her adult life, decide that she was a Carrie, Charlotte, Samantha, or Miranda, in my sophomore year of college, after watching the extended cuts of the *Lord of the Rings* trilogy, my three roommates and I had to decide which one of us matched which hobbit. (Miranda and Frodo, by the way.)

One of my friends loves to scoff whenever I bring up my Hogwarts house or astrological sign or enneagram number or any fictional team I decide I'm on.

"I can't swipe anyone who puts their Hogwarts house," she's said when we've discussed dating profiles.

"Why?"

"Because we're *adults*, and *adults* shouldn't be talking about *Harry Potter*," she says contrarily, then also shoots down Myers-Briggs.

But every once in a while I get her to read about her Pisces traits. I've told her which is her Hogwarts house. I've told her about her enneagram number. Each time she dismisses the categories as arbitrary and self-serving, each system its own fiction. But then, after reading each description, she'll grouchily admit that the personality type does sound like her.

According to the Enneagram, as a four, I have an obsession with self-identification, but it's more than just me; fans love to connect to their fandoms in a way that says that they are actually part of the world. When they claim a house or tribe, they claim a whole community of characters and a whole culture and history.

It's the impulse of the fan who wants to interact with the fictional world, but it's also the impulse of many people who would like more control over how the world sees them. If I'm feeling isolated or othered as a Black woman in a society that sees its marginalized citizens as stereotypes rather than individuals, I cannot change how I appear in that society's imagination, but I can choose whatever house or nation or village or tribe that I decide suits me best. However, there are limits even to this, because fandoms so often find ways to exclude certain identities from their narratives or translate the stereotypes of our world into fictional ones. And no matter how a person may identify within the fandom—say, a cis man fully attired in a Wonder

Woman getup, or a Black Sailor Pluto—there is no guarantee that less open-minded fans will respect that choice.

There's freedom in being able to choose one's identity and place oneself in the context of a world where that only means something to a degree that one decides it does. It's, in many cases, a post-racial, post-class, post-nationalist fantasy. In many of these fandoms, there is no mention of race or class, because the real-life markers of identity are subordinated to the fictional divides in the story.

Each "sorting" is an act of self-discovery and self-identification, even on this small scale. When a guy I'm dating asks me if I'm a Gryffindor, I scoff and am insulted, as though any of this were real, but in that moment, I am trying to find a succinct way, a shared language to use to tell him who I am through the stories I love most.

When I was young, my family used to take vacations in Pennsylvania. Fernwood, the Poconos: I only remember the trips vaguely. There was the dreaded drive (I always got carsick), and between my mother's and my grandmother's travel provisions, the impossibly large stash of snacks. There was the road itself, the highway that stretched on and on, framed by trees, with nothing new to see until gradually the landscape changed shape around us to a wooded green that looked unfamiliar. It looked like the start of an adventure.

It felt something like journeying to the old West—or at least what I imagined pioneering out West was like, according to my grade-school history textbooks and the ever-popular *Oregon Trail* game. I remember grassy greens and dirt and a pony named Shevin; I was so small on his back and giggled as his flanks shifted when he walked, making me sway left and right in the saddle. I felt like I was sitting on top of a skyscraper, but I don't remember fear, just the animal beneath me, totally nonplussed about my presence as the trainer led him around in a circle in the dirt.

And after the horse, I remember the gift shop. I looked through an assortment of toy horses to find one that best resembled Shevin. But there were more foreign trinkets to admire. The shop screamed "Cowboys and Indians: Take the American West Home," with cheap souvenir replicas of American Indian favorites for non-Indians with money burning holes in their pockets. Consumer-driven appropriation way before Urban Outfitters could even say "Navajo Nation style." I got an "Indian" toy set, with a little plastic tomahawk, and a pink dream catcher that I kept hanging on my closet doorknob until I moved out. I'd touch the webbing sometimes, remembering how the shopkeeper told me my nightmares would get caught in those strands, and my good dreams would slide right through the center. I still got bad dreams.

Despite cosplaying as a cowgirl with my short pony ride and as an Indian with my tomahawk and dream catcher, I found no place for myself in the dream of the American West, where cowboys were valiant heroes and Indians were wild natives and rarely anything in between.

My generation seemed to skip the golden era of Western adventure. (Though we had *An American Tail: Fievel Goes West*, a '90s great, lest we forget.) My mom had *Little House on the Prairie* and *Kung Fu* when she was a kid. And my grandparents had actual Westerns from the genre's heyday in the '50s and '60s.

In the early aughts, my grandfather went through a Western phase. A lover of TV, my grandfather spent years in front of it—the remote always in his possession, the volume cranked up to an uncomfortable level, his place on the couch deflated into a sinkhole from which he could never rise without assistance. When I was a kid and he was still freshly retired, there were walks through the park, tennis matches, and band practice in addition to the trusty TV. But once he got to a certain age, he settled into the living room—my grandmother often puttering around in the kitchen or dining room, or contently sitting on the other end of the couch, paying little mind to what my grandfather had put on. Though my grandparents eventually got a cable package with over a hundred channels, my grandfather watched the same handful, switching between sports—tennis, football, and particularly baseball—sometimes using commercial breaks to ping-pong from one game to another.

But then at some point he became obsessed with Westerns. The Westerns Channel had a consistent stream of these old black-and-white movies. They all looked the same to me, with their poor production values and unsophisticated cinematography. The shots of the plains, the shoot-outs, one cowboy chasing another, urging his horse onward, the loop of the rein clutched in one hand and a gun in the other. The men who looked up from the shady corners of saloons, glancing up mysteriously from under the brims of their hats. They shot back pints and slammed them down on the bar. They delivered cryptic warnings to outsiders about how things work in "these parts," walked bowlegged, and rested a hand on their gun holster in case an outlaw or drunkard decided he was ready to rumble.

My grandfather switched between these Westerns and baseball, and when I think back to it now, the combination made sense. My grandparents were born and raised in the Caribbean, and though he lived in America for more than five decades, my grandfather loved critiquing America, going on long rants where he'd call it, to my mom and me, "*your* country" and "*your* president." He'd sound off on politics, getting so worked up that he'd trip over his words and spit out a stream of expletives while my mother interjected with a sharp, "Daddy!" and my grandmother made an indistinct noise of alarm (every Caribbean woman knows this noise, and its companion, the sucked teeth).

But America was his obsession, and baseball and Westerns were two representations of American values. The former became the country's pastime, heralded as a wholesome, family-friendly sport that could be played almost anywhere by anyone. The sport did not fully represent our country's diversity. And yet there was—and still remains—an aura of romanticism around the home run, the sight of the ball soaring out of the park, outside the bounds the game had set for it. This joyous reach out into the distance, and the running of the bases if they're loaded, the first, then second, then the third, all triumphantly following the same path to the win as the ball still flies off and out of sight, feels like it draws from the same place as the American love of exploration and conquest. That's certainly true of Westerns, which showed a pre-gentrified version of the American wilderness with all its dangers, outside the bounds of society, so the few who braved that wild unknown paved the way for their brothers: you hit a ball out of the park to clear a path to home base for your teammates.

The Western isn't the most adaptable of genres. It's founded on a series of dated, problematic tropes and a simplified vision of America that has long gone out of fashion. So when the Western has resurfaced in recent years, it has, more often than not, been broached ironically or at least with some self-conscious awareness that certain elements of the genre cannot be replicated in earnest. *Deadwood* dispelled the hokeyness of old Westerns and added the gloss and elevated style of contemporary prestige television. *Justified* and *Longmire* took a similar approach, steering the Western more into the territory of the modern crime drama. And then series like *Westworld* and *Wynonna Earp* contemporized the Western by pairing it with sci-fi and horror, respectively. The result is a form more dynamic and more critical of the colonialist fantasy and nationalism at the heart of the Western.

Though I never found anything of interest in the dusty trails of the shows my grandfather loved, I found a way into the genre through the places where it intersected with sci-fi: space Westerns. Of course one of the major examples of this is *the* sci-fi series of futuristic space-age exploration, *Star Trek*, which was first pitched by its creator, Gene Roddenberry, as a Western in space: "*Wagon Train* to the stars."* Never the Trekkie that many of my friends were, I've nevertheless seen enough of the series to recognize its pioneering attitude, with episodes about what lies at the far reaches of the universe.

When I was ten, I loved the anime series *Outlaw Star*, about a crew on a spaceship led by a lovable outlaw named Gene Starwind and his partner and travel companion, Jim Hawking. They pilot the ship with the help of an android girl named Melfina and pick up some questionable—though ultimately loyal—crewmates. Throughout the series, the crew takes on jobs and quests for a galactic treasure. And a few years later I discovered what would become one of my favorites, *Cowboy Bebop*, which was an enticing collage of genres and influences: Westerns, yes, but also sci-fi and noir. (Every episode of the series ended with a sign-off of "See you, Space Cowboy.") In both cases, the shows seemed to take place in specific time periods in the future, but the tropes and references to the past allowed the series to transcend any singular sense of setting; they were timeless. The Western is a great match for the space opera; they both share an exploratory spirit. And in the Wild West and the wilds of space alike, the politics of national and cultural identity—and how that clashes or meshes with what is usually some pseudofascist colonialist authority—are essential to the world-building of the narrative.

Two of my favorite fandoms—both in this genre and in general—are *Star Wars* and *Firefly*. In both universes, the good guys encounter various worlds during their adventures, maneuvering around an authoritarian body. But the differences in how the two function indicate differences in their approaches to the colonialist fantasy built into the Western genre.

---

* Newsweek Special Edition, "Gene Roddenberry's Wagon Train to 'Star Trek,'" *Newsweek*, January 3, 2016, https://www.newsweek.com/wagon-train-stars-410030.

"To me, Yoda is a Zen master," said Irvin Kirshner, the director of *The Empire Strikes Back*, during filming.* Indeed, perhaps the most foundational element of creator George Lucas's world-building in the franchise is its omnipresent adaptation of Eastern cultural norms and ideologies. The Force, with its focus on balance and spiritual connection, recalls yin and yang and the universal energy of chi. Jedi knights are the space equivalent of the samurai: their robes resemble kimonos, they bear not swords but lightsabers, and they follow a strict ascetic code based on standards of honor and justice.

Lucas used many different historical and political reference points: "stormtroopers" are an allusion to the World War II Nazi fighters, and the uniforms and helmets were also inspired by those of German Army members. The visuals of the masses of stormtroopers, arranged in their perfect lines, also recall marching droves of Nazis. And in 2005, Lucas, who was originally supposed to direct the famous Vietnam War film *Apocalypse Now*, told the *Chicago Tribune* that the conflict and President Nixon inspired the politics of the films. "It was really about the Vietnam War, and that was the period where Nixon was trying to run for a [second] term, which got me to thinking historically about how do democracies get turned into dictatorships?" Lucas said. "Because the democracies aren't overthrown; they're given away."† Lucas also said that the Vietcong inspired our rebel heroes' fight alongside the Ewoks in *Return of the Jedi*. In the book *Star Wars and History*, William J. Astore writes that the Vietcong and their furry fictional counterparts were both able to use their "superior knowledge of the local terrain and an ability to blend into that terrain" to their advantage.‡

---

* Matthew Bortolin, *The Dharma of Star Wars* (Somerville, MA: Wisdom Publications, 2005), XII.

† Mark Caro, "'Star Wars' Inadvertently Hits Too Close to U.S.'s Role," *Chicago Tribune*, May 18, 2005, https://www.chicagotribune.com/news/ct-xpm-2005-05-18-0505180309-story.html.

‡ William J. Astore, "Why Rebels Triumph," in *Star Wars and History*, ed. Janice Liedl and Nancy Reagin, (Hoboken, NJ: Wiley, 2012), 28.

Even if the films were inspired by the happenings in Vietnam and various tokens of Eastern culture, they still never take the next step in more explicitly implicating America as the analog for the Empire; America too is a colonialist superpower whose democracy has failed many times.

There is also a notable absence of Asian people—and people of color in general. The most prominent character of color in the original trilogy, Lando Calrissian, was a reluctant turncoat who, despite redeeming himself by helping the good guys in the end (and again in *The Rise of Skywalker*) was, for years, reviled by fans. *Star Wars* fell into the trap that many other space Westerns do, imagining a world of the future that inexplicably reflects traditions of the past—in particular the past of a different cultural persuasion, often Eastern—but neglecting to actually represent people of that cultural tradition. Instead, there are aliens—blue and green creatures, undersea creatures, creatures from other planets—who become stand-ins for racial diversity. In the prequels, George Lucas exacerbated this already problematic practice by including aliens that not just became stand-ins for racial diversity but representations of racial stereotypes. Fans rightly gave the movies flack for the inclusion of Jar Jar Binks, a lackadaisical Gungan with a broken-up West Indian accent, who falls into the troubling Uncle Tom stereotype. Ahmed Best, the Black actor who played Jar Jar, has spoken of how the swift and loud backlash against the character affected him personally and drew him to the point of depression. Then there were the Neimoidians, with their Eastern-inspired robes and headdresses and atrocious stereotypical Asian accents.

The sequels attempted to retroactively fix the franchise's race problem by introducing more people of color to the main cast, but still struggled through the writing. And to make matters worse, some of the new cast of color, like John Boyega and Kelly Marie Tran, as Finn and Rose Tico, respectively, faced racist backlash from fans.

One of my favorite parts of *Star Wars* was the journeys to different planets. The space battles were fine, but I most enjoyed watching our heroes when they had both feet on the ground, whether that ground be the sands of Tatooine or the beautiful, bright-green pastures of Naboo. For all the ways the *Star Wars* prequels were maligned, the world-building was exquisite. Though overdone with CGI, the prequels were nevertheless great works of imagination, not simply relying on space battles but building out the political context of the universe and giving us new worlds to explore. Even in their times of overindulgence, they were still visual feasts, especially for a kid who had grown up with the original movies.

The franchise introduced a boundless universe where nothing was off-limits. The Empire presented complications on that front, especially for our protagonists, who are usually on the side of an actual republic, but seminal to the protagonists' stories in *Star Wars* is a sense of entitlement to the full expanse of this universe. This bothered me less than the entitlement of white colonialist exploration and expansion that is found in Westerns, but only because in space Westerns it's less explicit and less feasible. In space Westerns, individual nations are often irrelevant, subordinated to planets. And while the Western frontier first and foremost belonged to American Indians, space is different: despite how desperately one people may try to claim it over another, as in the Space Race during the Cold War, we are always dwarfed by the enormity of it. Space cannot be owned.

In *A New Hope*, Luke Skywalker poses, one knee out, in the stance of an explorer, looking out at the horizon, imagining all the space and planets he's not able to see. Darth Vader and Emperor Palpatine—and the Empire at large—claim a right to power over the universe. This is a renewed version of manifest destiny.

Firefly faced a similar issue. I was introduced to the series via the film sequel, *Serenity*. Though neither of my parents knew the show, we all went to the theater to see it. I was stubbornly opposed to it, mostly because I was so used to picking the movies we saw and was insulted that I was going to see something that hadn't gotten my advance approval. But knowing nothing about the movie (I had never heard of *Firefly* and definitely didn't know that the show and movie were written by *Buffy* creator Joss Whedon), I imagined it would just be some weak sci-fi story that wouldn't be able to measure up to the glory of *Star Wars*. Resolved to be disinterested, I watched with resignation but then couldn't help but be drawn in. When it came out on DVD, my parents got it for me, and though I always liked the movie, it took me a few years to figure out that it was a sequel to a TV series. The story and characters had always felt incomplete in some way, as though the story was larger than what I'd seen, but it never occurred to me that there had, in fact, been more.

In college, my roommates and I watched *Firefly* together and shot references at each other constantly (Jayne's cunning hat; Jubal Early's go-to question, "Does that seem right to you?"; the line "I've seen so much death," followed by a dance, courtesy of Nathan Fillion in the *Serenity* blooper reel; and Wash's heartbreaking last line, "I'm a leaf on the wind."). In the series, a group of lovable rogues for hire take jobs in a transport ship and get into trouble. The ship is led by a Han Solo–esque captain, Mal Reynolds, who, with his badass first mate, Zoë, fought and lost in a war against an Empire-esque authoritarian body called the Alliance. They travel with the lovable pilot Wash; the selfish and brutish Jayne; Kaylee, the ship's sweetheart engineer; Inara, a respectable companion; a holy man named Shepherd; and two fresh additions to the crew who are being chased by the Alliance: Simon, a doctor, and his brilliant but unstable sister, River, who was the victim of inhumane experiments from the Alliance.

While "inner planets" ruled by the Alliance are more developed, "outer planets" are mostly forgotten by the government and look like the Wild West: dusty landscapes, saloons, lawlessness, guns in holsters, and cowboy hats. But the Western universe has an explicitly Chinese influence. Signs are in Chinese, the characters know Mandarin Chinese, and they wear Chinese fashion. In the first episode,

Kaylee appears in a powder-blue cheongsam top and wooden sandals and holds a parasol.

Though I didn't pick up on the show's relationship to race when I first watched it in college—and even thought the Eastern touches were cool—I later realized that the series' incorporation of Eastern culture was more for show than anything else. The crew of *Firefly* rarely spoke Mandarin except for when they were cursing. The idea, of course, was to have *Firefly* set in a more globalized human society, with the West adopting trends of the East. But the very way everyone in this universe spoke Mandarin showed how flippant the series was with the idea. The Chinese language was ornamental.

The lovable rogues of *Firefly* baldly fell in line with those of old Westerns. The show supported the notion that they had some more righteous sense of ownership to the universe. The show's opening theme, a slow country song written by Joss Whedon and performed by Sonny Rhodes, fits in with this theme; one of the lines of the chorus is "You can't take the sky from me."

At one point in the first episode, Mal looks out into space and declares that it's "getting awful crowded in my sky."* Though he is the tough captain character, Mal is also a romantic: the journeyman with his loyal crew, looking to travel the universe as he pleases, making a living as he can, and piss off the Alliance in the process. Just like in *Star Wars*, the series enjoys a setup that pits a small group of rebels against an oppressive governmental body that asserts an authoritarian control over space (which, like the Wild West in Westerns, is characterized as property that's open and free to everyone—except for the people of color who are chased away or not portrayed at all, of course) but doesn't contend with the fact that its cast of characters on both sides of the conflict are majorly white and certainly not Asian.

In the series, however, the mostly white space settlers and space explorers are often tailed and tracked by reavers, monstrous humans

---

* Joss Whedon, "The Train Job," *Firefly*, September 20, 2002.

gone mad, who are known for their senseless acts of violence—cannibalism, murder, rape, torture. The myth is that the reavers are men who traveled out to the ends of the universe and were driven crazy by the sight of nothingness. Manifest destiny, it seems, has a price. Becoming a reaver seems to be the moral cost of white exploration.

And yet, in *Serenity*, the movie reveals that the reavers were actually the results of an Alliance experiment gone bad, one meant to create a more peaceful society. The Alliance is therefore reestablished as the bad guy, not only for its crooked sanctions and inhumane exercise of authority, but also for attempting to force citizens to behave in a way that it believes will create a utopia—one likely more totalitarian. The film ends with the ship taking off again, and it's clear that for its pseudo-woke but really appropriative use of Asian identity and its playful use of Western tropes, *Firefly* is still in love with the Western genre, down to its white ethnocentric perspective.

It's a curious position to be placed in as a fan: to spend so much time in the worlds of the fandoms you love when what you see are identities that aren't yours. Even in fandoms that take you out to space, into fantastical futures with unique new species of animals and aliens, the post-racial approach—just like the realms of these worlds themselves, whether the wizarding world or the terraformed planets of *Firefly*, and just like the concept of manifest destiny itself—is a myth.

VI.

Espers and Anxiety, Mutants, Magic, and Mind Games

On mental illness, weirdness, and shows that revel in anxiety

When I was thirteen, I had a love-hate relationship with *Paranoia Agent*, the anime series created by Satoshi Kon, best known for his acclaimed anime films, including *Paprika* and *Millennium Actress*. The show, about two detectives who try to figure out the mystery behind a series of attacks by Lil' Slugger, a boy in a red cap and golden Rollerblades who wields a golden baseball bat, came on late at night on Adult Swim, and I watched it as part of my late-night anime lineup.

The plot was utterly intriguing; each episode seems to be written in an anthology format, with a new character who is attacked by Lil' Slugger. But the characters are related, if only in small ways, and the first victim of the attack, a character designer named Tsukiko Sagi, seems to be the center point from which the web of victims spreads. The central motif is characters who feel anxious, stressed—trapped in a corner. When they're at the pinnacle of their panic, Lil' Slugger suddenly appears.

I rarely rewatch shows or reread books—even the ones I'm in love with. As an arts critic, I compulsively consume new things, playing a constant game of catch-up. I love the excitement of encountering something new. *Paranoia Agent* is one of my few exceptions; I've watched the series at least three times since I first saw it at thirteen. There are some shows and movies that you find terrifying as a kid, but then the scares turn out to be unremarkable, even silly, when you encounter them again as an adult. *Paranoia Agent* always evokes the same feelings from me at any age.

At first glance, the show doesn't seem like it could be that scary: How frightening could a kid with Rollerblades be? And yet the series is shot through with an undercurrent of terror. I hated how anxious it made me, but I could never look away. The sight of Lil' Slugger was haunting—his face almost completely shadowed under his baseball cap, with the exception of a broad, sadistic grin. And the background animations throughout were similarly unnerving: dark neighborhoods, alleyways and side streets cloaked in shadow. And as with any successful horror series or movie, *Paranoia Agent* trains its audience to anticipate the coming horror via its use of music and sound effects. Before Lil' Slugger appears, a tense, fast-paced music plays, recalling a rapid heartbeat, and then there's the sound of the skates rolling along the concrete.

I've never been able to stomach horror very well—or anything even mildly suspenseful, for that matter—and went into *Paranoia Agent* having no clue what I was in for. The opening song, with its bouncy yodel, felt ironically light. The same was true for the opening sequence, which showed the characters laughing as the backgrounds changed behind them. But the laughter looked maniacal, unhinged even—their shoulders heaved a bit too heartily, and their grins stretched a bit too widely. And behind them, the scenes sometimes depicted disasters, and yet the characters laughed all the same.

I watched *Paranoia Agent* in the dark, late at night, sitting cross-legged on the floor of my room, looking up at my tiny TV. The sound of Lil' Slugger's skates in the distance, and the eerie music that was always the prologue to his appearance, was even more haunting when paired with the darkness of my room and the silence of the house in the evening. At the end of each episode, I would turn the TV off and the room would fall into a complete, uninterrupted darkness while I scrambled into bed.

When I first watched *Paranoia Agent*, I thought it was Lil' Slugger himself who frightened me, but when I revisited the series later, I gradually realized that it was the way the series depicted paranoia and anxiety that unnerved me, for all the ways it drew my attention to my own anxiety and the horror it could become.

Though I've had anxiety for as long as I can remember, my early anxiety felt amorphous and unnamed. Or perhaps it'd be more accurate to say that it was misnamed: I was *moody and pouty*. I was *shy and just a bit too hard on myself*. Now it's hard to tell how much of my dread—before gym class, on report card days, on the first day of school, before school concerts, before birthday parties, through the entirety of one summer I spent not in the cool silence of the library but among a crowd of unfamiliar kids at camp—could be chalked up to the typical insecurities of childhood or something more permanent in the way my body worked.

It was around the time that I first encountered *Paranoia Agent* that I started to become aware of my own anxiety. My adolescent hormones had just kicked into high gear, and I was still getting used to the unsettling fact that every few weeks my uterine lining would drop right out of my body. My face broke out with bad acne. I grew obsessed with my body shape, my weight, my body hair—everything about me suddenly seemed too prominent, exaggerated. The shyness I had always experienced as a child became laced with a more urgent sense of discomfort. And I was facing the gauntlet of adolescent life: high school was on the horizon, and I worried about which private school to attend and what embarrassing, life-changing experiences (according to what I'd seen in every teen TV show and movie ever) awaited me. Though I was already at the top of my class, I fretted about my grades constantly. The pressures mounted until I became swallowed by a constant fearfulness that underscored my everyday life.

Today I couldn't even tell you the particular shape or magnitude of my fears at that time—just the general feeling of suffocation. When I recall the specifics of that year, some parts of my memory fail, and I simply remember the times I was curled in a ball on the floor of my bedroom, with flash cards and notebooks sprawled around me.

When I watch *Paranoia Agent* now, it occurs to me that I would have been attacked by Lil' Slugger several times over in my life. The days when I've felt overwhelmed are impossible to count— sometimes they stack up like dominoes and fall one into another into the next until I'm just left with the feeling of something monumental having been collapsed.

What Kon achieved with *Paranoia Agent* was a series that embodied its psychological theme so deftly—through the story, the characters, the aesthetic, the music, and the overall mood—that it was able to take its viewer on a journey that elicited a similar reaction. Or at least it certainly did for me.

In the first episode, Tsukiko's anxiety is revealed slowly and quietly. Tsukiko barely speaks, but the stressors that are weighing on her are apparent everywhere: she sees her popular creation, the cute character Maromi, around the city, and at work, her boss pressures her for her next hit design while her coworkers jealously glare at her from the side. As the episode wears on, her anxiety becomes more visible. She takes shallow breaths, her chest heaving—something that happens to me when I'm at the start of a panic attack. As soon as the series branches out from Tsukiko's story, however, it becomes indicative of the ways panic can become contagious. The first scenes of the series show people on the streets and on the train, packed together, sweating, looking at their phones, and we hear excuses they give on calls as to why they're late or absent; everyone seems to be at the end of their rope. Once Lil' Slugger makes the news, the gossip of the city changes him as people use their imaginations and rumors to feed into the myth of him.

By the end of the series, we find out that Lil' Slugger is just a story brought to life and empowered by mass hysteria; the destruction he brings is the destruction these anxious, trapped people wish on themselves.

Though so much of the show scared me as a kid, I was also struck by some of its moments of humor. In one episode in particular, Kon's story and direction mimic what he had done in *Millennium Actress*, moving among nested narratives and taking up residence in a character's imagination and memories. When the cops apprehend a copycat Lil' Slugger, the episode spins out into a world made by the boy's delusions. We willingly follow the detectives interrogating him into the bizarre fantasy, letting that—even for a span of one episode— be the reality we subscribe to as viewers.

As the detectives get closer to—and ultimately figure out—the mystery of the case, this show about paranoia ends not with a whimper but a bang. A cataclysmic event destroys everything, and it becomes increasingly clear that the story of *Paranoia Agent* is explicitly informed by Japan's national psychology after World War II.

In the opening credits, one of the backgrounds shown is of a giant mushroom cloud rising in the distance, and the concluding disaster, and the wreckage it brings, is meant to recall the damages left by the war—and, in particular, the United States' attacks on Hiroshima and Nagasaki.

It's more than just stress and fear that feeds the creation of Lil' Slugger; there is guilt and shame and insecurity mixed up with the anxiety and paranoia.

Though it's grim, I find *Paranoia Agent* and other shows and movies like it—which build up and break down in surreal ways to show the illness, instability, and chaos of their characters' minds—to be a balm now.

At thirteen, I only knew that there were several mundane situations that made me nervous and that sometimes I got so panicked and sad that I found it impossible to function. I cried to myself that I was crazy, because I had no other word for it. I didn't know how else to define it but as something irregular. I hoped it made me more of an artist, but I knew it also dragged me down like stones in my shoes.

At some point I crawled through the worst of it and attributed it to just hormones and a tough year or so at school. But in high school it returned, especially in junior year, as I balanced doing my schoolwork with completing college applications, working my first job, and participating in a ridiculous number of extracurriculars. I pushed until I thought I would break down, and I spent the year physically and mentally exhausted. I settled into disordered eating patterns I'd dipped in and out of since my preteen years. I starved myself and worked out constantly, until my muscles burned.

And yet, again, I figured the problems were all circumstantial. When the anxiety flared up again, even more furiously, while I was in college, I ate only Cheerios, raw spinach, scrambled eggs, and rice, not because I couldn't afford groceries but because I feared spending money on food, thinking it pointless. I fretted about my career trajectory from the first moment I stepped onto campus. I worried about classes and internships. I rarely went to parties, because I worried about who would be there, what time they would end, and whether I could prepare an escape plan. I spent the first several weeks scared to take the train in a new city. By the time I neared the end of my undergraduate term, managing two theses, a full course load, a part-time job, extracurriculars, and multiple internships, I had developed a habit of spontaneously breaking down crying in public.

In the years that followed I realized this temperament wasn't going away. Though circumstances exacerbated it at times, it was permanent. In my years after college, it became more palpable: the panic attacks, the obsessive fixations on cleanliness or exercise, the spiraling thoughts. I cleaned for hours, was terrorized by lint and stray hairs, and at times I was unable to take care of my basic human needs: I skipped meals, forgot to drink water, and didn't get the sleep I needed. There were days when I wouldn't leave the bedroom. One day after a stressful job interview, I spiraled so badly that I stayed in bed for seven hours straight.

When I began going to therapy, and my therapist put a phrase to what I was experiencing—generalized anxiety disorder—I felt relieved at how the enormity of my emotions could fit into three small words. Those words alone, I knew, wouldn't be able to save me from a psychological menace dressed in shiny skates, or any of my literal fears and concerns. But therapy and a diagnosis—well, it was definitely a start.

Paranoia Agent, like countless other animated movies and series, followed the trail blazed by the 1988 anime film *Akira*. In the film, the leader of a teen biker gang, Kaneda, and his buddies, including a boy named Tetsuo, roam through a dystopian, cyberpunk version of Tokyo, fighting a rival gang. During an accident after a gang brawl, Tetsuo encounters an Esper and is injured, but is revealed to have his own psychic abilities. Taken to a government lab, Tetsuo becomes more powerful and erratic; he decides to exhume Akira, the most powerful Esper, whose remains are being cryogenically stored in a hidden facility. While Kaneda tries to stop him, Tetsuo loses control and is dispatched by the awakened Akira.

I came to *Akira* late, though of course I knew all about it. I had put off watching it, knowing how disturbing and grotesque the imagery would be. "Yeah, I watched *Akira way* too young," my convention friend told me once while we talked about it. I understood completely; I recalled watching *Vampire Hunter D*, with its nudity and profanity, as a kid, and also *Princess Mononoke*, which shocked me with its imagery. I knew *Akira* by sight: I'd seen the classic poster countless times, along with Kaneda's motorcycle jacket—usually worn by fans at Comic Con.

I loved the iconic look, and every once in a while, even now, I look up the jacket—brick red with a pill capsule on the back, surrounded by the motto "Good for Health, Bad for Education"—and consider buying one for myself, as though I, too, have just waltzed out of a dystopian Tokyo with bikers and psychics and drugs.

I never understood why Kaneda had a drug logo on his back, and even as I watched the film, the image commanded an inordinate amount of my attention as I took it all in. That's probably because the first time I watched *Akira* was during my first year on antidepressants for my anxiety.

The red pill or the blue pill? I always disliked the question, always thought that instead I would ideally like to opt for no pills at all. When I was a kid, my takeaway from medication commercials was that every pill comes with an intimidating roll call of possible side effects. Have you ever really tried to listen to the side effects listed at the end of a drug commercial? Or tried to read the scroll of conditions that inches up or down the screen? They're so normalized that often we don't even notice even the direst warnings (may cause death) or the most ironic (antidepressants that may cause suicidal thoughts or behaviors). And then there always seemed to be the specter of addiction.

My mother, who has always boasted about her high pain tolerance, having recovered from more than one major surgery with the use of little or no painkillers, passed on her reticence to using medication to me. But for me, even in the midst of my worst bouts of anxiety, when I've been too scared to eat, or when I've felt overwhelmed by a bit of dust on a counter, or when the simple matter of waking up on a Sunday morning would become an hour-long fit of weeping and panic, the damage I thought drugs could do seemed so much scarier—and, for all I knew, the side effects were not at all worth it.

I had seen so many movies and TV shows—especially in science fiction—that show drugs that cause pain and, often, trigger large existential breakdowns in the characters who take them. Who are we essentially? Can drugs quash or reveal our true selves? To what extent are our illnesses part of us? How have they shaped the way we define ourselves and how others define us?

In the *Akira* manga, there is a stronger emphasis on drug use than in the film. Neo-Tokyo is pumped full of drugs, and the government seeks out, kidnaps, experiments on, and tries to control people with psychic abilities. And the teens in the manga are explicitly addicted to drugs. It's Tetsuo, whose newfound psychic abilities sets off a cataclysmic chain of events, who is medicated to contain his unbridled telekinesis.

Tetsuo undergoes a frightening transformation in the movie. He begins as a sidekick character to the more dynamic Kaneda, but his awareness of his weakness and his insecurity about his status in relation to Kaneda exacerbate his already unstable state as his powers grow. He becomes obsessed with power and quickly determines that the people around him—even those trying to help him—are in his way.

As Tetsuo gets more and more out of control, the film implies that it is his psychic abilities that are driving him mad and changing his body. But of course Tetsuo had this hidden potential in the first place. In a classic question of "nature vs. nurture," the film has us wonder whether Tetsuo's megalomaniacal transformation was just a side effect of his psychic abilities being awoken, or whether he always had that quality in him and just needed the right trigger.

That was my most surprising reaction to the film, after avoiding it for years: though I found some of the scenes visually disturbing, it was really Tetsuo's psychological transformation that stuck with me.

Tetsuo undergoes something truly frightening, even outside of his eruption into a gross mass of psychic power; he encounters the scary situation of finding something new in yourself only to then have it completely overtake you.

I've felt this. Though I was surely always anxious to some degree or another, it wasn't until I hit my twenties that it seemed to become an overwhelming force in my life. The fact that I finally became aware of it and then found a name for it helped, but since then I have had to live with my anxiety in a new way, fully aware of my daily triggers and how my medication is performing. I was hesitant to begin taking antidepressants because I was afraid of how they might change me or what they might subdue or reveal in me. I'm not a doctor; I don't know what defines my body's chemistry, but I knew that this drug would change that for as long as I needed it to. And what about my temperament? I loved the romantic notion of the anxious, depressed artist, forever melancholy and plagued by her demons. One thing I'll say about my anxiety is that it is often productive—it pushes me to work. So I shape it into more useful forms, directing those times of panic and depression into poems and articles so I can focus on something I can control in those moments when I feel like I can't control what's happening in my body.

I feared my own Tetsuo moment of revelation—that I might find that even after the medication, I was fundamentally broken in some way. When I became aware of my anxiety, I thought of it as something I needed to explain to people. I offered it up to potential romantic interests and friends, warning them before I inevitably blew up into the wild, beast-like version of myself near the end of my own anime movie.

Akira casts a distrustful eye toward children throughout the film. Though the adults are the "bad guys"—the government goons and scientists who pull the strings—it is the kids who are the main movers in the story, and often the ones with the most power. Kaneda, Tetsuo, and their gang of teens get into mischief with other gangs in the streets. The Espers, all children with wrinkled faces (simultaneously young and old), have telekinetic abilities.

One of the most memorable scenes in the film is when the Espers attempt to attack Tetsuo while he's being held at the facility. The film's soundtrack, by Geinoh Yamashirogumi, was already a masterly work that paired brilliantly with the dark dystopian aesthetic of the movie. The especially dissonant number that accompanies this attack scene ties the sequence together. Toys come to life around Tetsuo—a tiny teddy bear, stuffed rabbit, and toy car awaken, playfully climbing up the side of Tetsuo's bed and marching to his pillow—and when he tries to grab them, they disappear. The toys reappear as massive, destructive Frankenstein-esque conglomerates of other toys. The teddy bear stands tall, its head crashing into the ceiling of Tetsuo's room, and suddenly milk pours from the gaps in his construction. Tetsuo runs into a wall, which breaks apart into building blocks. And yet, when Tetsuo stumbles and cuts himself on pieces of glass, the illusion breaks down, because the Esper children are scared away by the sight of his blood.

And in the end, Tetsuo himself mutates into a giant creature, beginning with his mechanical arm and expanding with the rest of his body. He seems to erupt from the inside out, the flesh bubbling and pulsing, in different shades of pink and nude, with pink and purple veins running through them. The amoeboid form that was once Tetsuo at times takes on a vaguely fetal appearance, as though he is reverting to an embryonic state or dying and being completely reborn. That is truly the scary heart of the film: What are we born with? What are our natural capabilities to cause pain and destruction in ourselves and others? For me, the film translated to the question of how much of me—my personality, my identity, my life—is defined by my anxiety. When I pull at the threads of my inner psychology, do I use them to build a stronger, better version of me, or do I unravel?

Akira literalized that question in its story and emphasized it with its frightening imagery. *Akira* intentionally offers an uncomfortable, disorienting experience for its audience in order to bring the story of Tetsuo's transformation more vividly to life. And even such a grossly visceral experience can feel refreshing. I found Tetsuo's final form grotesque, but there was also something perversely cathartic in the sight of a boy turned inside out by his demons. When I watched *Akira*, I was still adjusting to my meds, and so I was still being overcome with panic attacks and depressive bouts on a regular basis. Every time my anxiety hit, I felt like I was coming apart. But here's where Tetsuo's story diverged from mine: he couldn't put himself back together, but I did, and do so every day that I wake up to the nervous buzz of my brain and manage, even just slightly, to turn the volume down.

When the BBC show *Dirk Gently's Holistic Detective Agency* premiered in 2016, it was mostly dismissed by critics. There are a lot of threads throughout the first season: a missing girl, a dead millionaire, a curiously smart dog, a soul-swapping cult, a holistic detective, a holistic assassin, a gang of punk-rock energy vampires. Much of it can feel like sifting through the weeds, unable to fully make out what's around you. There's an insistent quirkiness to it that also straddles the line between "a uniquely entertaining, perhaps even innovative, example of television media" and "a precociously loony, nonsensical hot mess of a show." It's a series that expects you to trust it and to follow along on a journey that will at times be damn near incomprehensible but then ultimately be tied up at the end. The show excels at presenting fascinating, lively, and complex characters with enough heft and charisma to carry off the narrative in all its various directions.

In *Dirk Gently*, a broke hotel employee named Todd gets caught up in the mysterious murder of a millionaire at the hotel and the disappearance of the millionaire's teen daughter, Lydia Spring. While getting caught up in a series of strange, inexplicable events, Todd meets Dirk Gently, an eccentric, psychic British man who calls himself a "holistic detective," one who lets the universe lead him through mysteries until he is able to solve them. But Dirk has no control over when he'll encounter clues or when he'll find himself in danger; he stumbles through cases led just by his hunches, which always end up being right. He's a friend of coincidence, a believer in the dictum that everything is connected—something the show proves again and again as characters, moving in their seemingly separate circles, eventually intersect in surprising ways. Scenes are mirrored, dialogue is repeated, so there is always a sense of some grand design at work.

Todd is caught up in the middle of it all, and he spends much of the season resentful of the way Dirk drags him into deadly situations. Many of the show's characters, Todd included, could be identified as "freaks," as one character says. Todd's sister, Amanda, a punk drummer with pararibulitis, a fictional neurological disease that causes realistic and painful multisensory hallucinations, says it to Farah, a badass bodyguard who is trying to find Lydia Spring, and who denies being as weird as Dirk and the others. In addition to being a talented investigator and fighter, she is also remarkably anxious and paranoid. But ironically, these traits are also part of what makes her so formidable; she is cautious and incisive, the rock of the group, while Dirk and Todd bungle their way through situations with killer cult members, booby-trapped mazes, and even time travel.

This is also a larger theme in the show: to what extent the characters' illnesses and quirks are hindrances and to what extent they're boons—perhaps, one could even say, powers. After one too many close calls, Dirk becomes disillusioned with his psychic abilities. He tells Todd despairingly that he has no agency in his own life, no way of telling where the universe might take him and how dangerous each new case might be. But Dirk is also at the center of wild, imaginative adventures, with magic and alternate universes. And he is proof of a larger power, some kind of organizing principle in the universe that works through him. His psychic power, though something he has little control over, is still messianic, ultimately in service of a greater good, and a protective charm that keeps him safe. Bart, a gravel-voiced holistic assassin with a similar link to the universe, kills people when she feels like it and can't be trapped or get hurt. But all the people she kills are meant to be killed. Even so, she, like Dirk, also comes to resent being a pawn of the universe and doubts her ability, only to find that when she follows her instincts, the universe always takes care of her. Though she's an assassin who usually wanders around splattered with blood, she never wants for food or transportation or shelter. Everything is provided for her.

Even in the case of Amanda, whose illness causes her to actually feel the pain associated with her neurological hallucinations—knife cuts, burns, frostbite, and more—she finds out that she has a unique ability linked to her disease. Her pararibulitis attacks, which once stopped her from even venturing outside her house, attract a group of energy vampires called the Rowdy 3, psychic beings who feed off chaos and human emotions. They feast on the energy that emanates from her during her attacks and protect her, even make her their leader. And in season two, Amanda finds that her pararibulitis gives her psychic abilities; when she ventures to another world, she discovers that she is actually a powerful witch.

Todd considers himself a down-on-his-luck schmuck, irresponsible and selfish but otherwise unremarkable. When Dirk comes into his life, Todd eventually realizes that he also fits into the mysterious grand scheme. And in season two, when Todd and Dirk are separated, Todd realizes that the universe is still on his side. He's suddenly thrilled to realize that he's an essential part of the narrative and will be led along like Dirk is.

The show is constantly enacting this theme of madness belying order not just in the plot but also in the execution; what may seem like a world that's muddled and nonsensical is actually one that is controlled by a sometimes opaque but always intentional logic. The show's chaos may initially seem like an illness or flaw, but it is eventually revealed to be what makes it powerful.

There are days when my anxiety seems insurmountable and the urgent question "Why am I so crazy?" seems to knock around my skull incessantly. But my anxiety has also pushed me to set and manage new goals for myself, and more than once it has helped me prepare for tough situations. Anxiety constantly has you milling around in the past or living in an uncertain future. I wouldn't call this a superpower, but for all the stress and strife my disorder has caused, it has also led me to many successes and new relationships and opportunities. And at the end of the day, that, at least, is powerful.

Mental illness and power are also central themes in the FX series *Legion*, which lets the emotional and mental instability of its protagonist rule the show's aesthetic and perspective. When I began *Legion*, I wasn't sure what to expect. I vaguely knew the character from the *X-Men* comic universe—a powerful but unstable mutant with multiple personalities—but wasn't sure how much the show would intersect, either narratively or stylistically, with the other Marvel films and TV shows that had cropped up before it. *Legion* premiered in 2017, when the Netflix Marvel shows—*Daredevil, Jessica Jones, Luke Cage* (*Iron Fist* premiered around the same time as *Legion*)—were already in full swing.

But those Marvel TV shows, with their gritty style and traditional mode of TV storytelling, were no indication of what *Legion* would ultimately be. In *Legion*, a man named David finds himself in a mental institution after a suicide attempt; he's schizophrenic, getting regular doses of medication, alongside his addict friend Lenny. When a strange woman named Syd with an aversion to being touched is admitted and becomes David's new girlfriend, gradually things begin to unwind, starting with a devastating catastrophe in the hospital. David soon joins Syd at a home for mutants and learns of his true abilities.

Legion immediately distinguished itself from the other superhero fare of the time with its style and tone—off-kilter and modish, dedicated to the bright color-blocked hues and loud patterns of the '60s and '70s—but the series was also playfully vague in its setting. Though everywhere there are hints of the '60s, from the fashion and set design to the series' musical choices—the Who and the Rolling Stones, but also picks from subsequent decades, like Jane's Addiction and Radiohead—it never decisively settles itself in any one time period, creating a world packed with anachronisms. The effect is a show that never provides the viewer with any concrete grounding. *Legion* buffets its audience around in the same way David is buffeted by the strange sequence of events around him and by the powerful but contorted workings of his own mind. This is a logical—in fact, clever—approach to storytelling, because we so often underestimate how trapped we are in our own perceptions of the world around us. The ways we learn to communicate, the ways we see (or don't see) objects around us, the ways we respond to everyday stimuli and situations—they are all individual. There's no objective way to experience the world, and with a mental illness, it can be that much easier to become chained to the distorted mirror of one's perception. How many times have I worked myself into a panic over some perceived threat or emergency, just to have a friend or family member or my therapist say, "This isn't actually a problem. This is all in your head"? Too many to count. Of course David's world is full of strangeness and contradictions; mine would be too.

Season one journeyed through David's thoughts and memories, jumping back and forward in time, erasing facts, revealing details, ultimately guiding David—and the viewer—toward a more comprehensive view of his abilities and the powerful parasitic mutant, Farouk, the Shadow King, who has taken up residency in David's mind. The show never stays in the outside world, the "real world," for long; instead it bounds in and out of David's mind, where he encounters various incarnations of the Shadow King and where he himself, at one point in the series, is temporarily trapped. The extent to which David is confused or lost is the extent to which the show twists its aesthetic and narrative to create the same sensation in the audience.

We slip so easily into David's purview, seeing Farouk as the devil with the yellow eyes (a lumpy, ambiguous mass of a being with a menacing grin) or a frightening figure from a children's book, that our relationship to the narrative is skewed. Jeff Russo's score, full of eerie, dissonant strings, give the series a creeping tone, brewing the same kind of suspense one would get from a horror movie.

By season two, David has developed a better grasp of his abilities and uses them to have mental battles with the Shadow King: the two face off on a dance floor, have a tense mental tête-à-tête at a dinner table, and meet imagination to imagination on a constantly morphing battlefield. David ventures into the minds of his friends, who, while infected with a mental malady that draws them to retreat to a "mind maze" of their own making, reveal their deepest needs and vulnerabilities. All of this is meanwhile interrupted by classroom-style psychology lessons—narrated by Jon Hamm, via voice-over—on the workings of the human mind: how ideas are born, how reality is perceived.

"Who teaches us to be normal when we're one of a kind?" Syd asks more than once throughout the series. The answer is society—family and friends and neighbors, all the institutions that uphold certain standards of behavior and understandings about how people can and should relate to one another. Unfortunately, that often doesn't leave much room for individuals struggling with mental illnesses. It's why so many people with mental illnesses fall through the cracks in, say, the education system and job market, or are penalized without much thought, ending up in prison.

Syd supports and defends David, even as he falls apart. In one episode, when he's trapped in his mind by Farouk, in a kind of mental coffin, he talks to a version of himself—his rational mind, who, comically, speaks in a British accent. Even David doesn't know that he's created this illusion for himself. His rational mind explains that David's brain responded to the panic and created a way for David to figure out how to escape. His entrapment, David's rational self tells him, is an illusion. He is only trapped in his mind; he needs only to think his way out.

Thinking a way out is something that David must do repeatedly, and that act emphasizes his tenuous grasp on reality. "Reality is a choice," one character declares in season two. In one segment, about the nocebo effect, the show explains how the mind can create its own reality. But identity proves to be just as tricky a concept.

David—fragile, confused, trapped in a clinic and then later chased by people for reasons he doesn't understand—is our sympathetic protagonist. Early on we see flashes of him in the past, as a kid and teen always looking forlorn and running into trouble. In a flashback to the time right before he got to the hospital, he looks tired and clearly strung out on drugs in an attempt to remedy the overwhelming sound of voices in his mind.

Though, as Syd slowly realizes that David is not the person she thinks he is—or wants him to be—we too gradually see his transformation, and the series shifts the perspective, casting doubt on its hero and all the information it has offered us thus far.

After Farouk kills David's sister, David becomes obsessed with taking the Shadow King down, so much so that his behaviors become more erratic. Syd notices discrepancies in the things he tells her and the things he decides to do. She senses that David is keeping secrets and telling lies. In his rage he goes on a gleeful killing spree and even tortures a friend with seemingly no remorse. Syd sees David's "true face," as he chases Farouk down, declaring that he is a lunatic because of what the Shadow King did to him all his life.

After beginning the series with the idea that David was not actually ill, just gifted with abilities, *Legion* then circles back and has us reexamine that belief, which we may have blindly taken for fact. David's friends realize he is psychic *and also* ill, even dangerous, but by the time they do, he has already gotten too powerful. David transforms into a villain before our eyes. Farouk himself ruefully acknowledges the change, that he has suddenly become the hero, tasked to stop David, and David, whose powers may destroy the world, has become the villain.

The show's use of split screens and quirky (i.e., rotating, ping-ponging) camera angles should have warned us: no single perspective can be trusted. There is no such thing as objectivity, no such thing as the hero and the villain. At any given time, things can change, and everything we'd assumed was real could be fake. The most artful trick *Legion* accomplishes is creating a prestige television experience—with fantastic actors, high-quality cinematography, and stellar style—that completely commits (despite some questionable leaps of logic and various digressions) to an undertaking that has us question the limits of these characters' perspectives, and perhaps even our own. If certain truths of our existence are unknowable, since we're tethered to our subjective viewpoints, then concepts like time and space and morality and even the physical plane are all relative truths, compromises we make in order to understand our world and hold on to some notion of society and order.

David, a mutant with the ability to penetrate and influence minds, with the ability to craft new realities, breaks from those social contracts to become a villainous god, no longer the victim but the narcissist who only trusts the truth he creates himself.

But this is also an interesting way in which shows that feature characters with mental illness tend to shift—not only in terms of surreal effects but in terms of perspective, causing us to ask who gets to be the hero of the story. In the last episode of the second season of *Legion*, Syd points a gun at David. "Guess what? You're not the hero," she tells him. "Then who is?" David asks. "Me," Syd responds, before pulling the trigger.*

What I love about *Legion* is that David's mental illness doesn't define him in one singular, incontrovertible way. His illness isn't totally synonymous with his power. Neither is it the reason he turns into a villain. It is one facet of him that feeds into the whole of his identity, and while he is still accountable for his actions, he is more than his illness—and his powers, for that matter. Just as important is what he does with his ability and how he seeks help for his illness. And that, along with depictions of characters with mental illness who aren't villains, who live their lives with all the complications that come with their disease, is what I crave more of in movies and TV. Once again, I look for myself in my fandoms: Where is the depressed character, the anxious character who takes her meds in the morning? I want to see her struggle but thrive—and save the world.

In the TV series *The Magicians*, adapted from Lev Grossman's acclaimed fantasy trilogy, there is a similar—though less bleak—shift in perspective away from the mentally ill protagonist, having us question who is the reliable narrator and who is actually the hero of the story.

In *The Magicians*, a depressed loner named Quentin Coldwater, who is obsessed with a fantasy book series, finds out that magicians—and the world depicted in his books—are real. He goes to a magical grad school, a kind of Hogwarts University called Brakebills, to hone

---

* Noah Hawley, "Chapter 19," *Legion*, June 12, 2018.

his abilities, but gets caught up in a battle against a murderous villain called the Beast.

There are many things that are remarkable about the TV series, most notably the playfully meta ways it plucks from the plot, characters, and story structures of popular fantasy series like *Harry Potter* and *The Chronicles of Narnia*. But it also cleverly subverts the classic formula that these stories and so many others follow: that of the hero's journey.

Joseph Campbell, author of *The Hero with a Thousand Faces*, famously wrote that the hero's journey follows a distinct path, with familiar obstacles that the protagonist must overcome. This narrative framework—which contains steps like a call to action, a passage into an unknown world, a personal transformation, and the hero's eventual return—is omnipresent in TV shows, books, films, and more. What makes *The Magicians* different is that it establishes a hero just to have him dethroned by other characters in the story. It makes us reframe not only our understanding of the show's characters and their place in the story, but the very idea of a hero itself.

And that shift in the story is also linked to Quentin's portrayal as an outsider with clinical depression. *The Magicians*, like *Legion*, begins with its main character in a mental hospital. I immediately empathized with Quentin, who dressed in grays and blacks, hid behind a dramatic cascade of hair, and avoided people at parties, reading his fantasy books instead of socializing with others. He would be the kind of boy—intelligent but moody and self-involved—that I would have had a crush on as a teen. He falls so neatly into the type of character who we're taught to believe will lead the story: he is the outcast who won't grow up, still believing in fairy tales. I saw my disposition as a child—emotional, more invested in the fictions I read than in real life, more content reading in a corner than hanging out with my peers—in Quentin's.

Quentin is clearly the Harry Potter analog. It's immediately obvious that he's a magician—or at least will be, once he gets some training—and though he hasn't grown up abused and stowed away in a tiny broom closet under the stairs, he has the same sense of isolation because of his mental illness. And Quentin, like Harry, is presented as the chosen one. When we first meet the Beast, as he waltzes into a Brakebills classroom at the end of the first episode, he recognizes Quentin, saying, with a villainous purr, "Quentin Coldwater, there you are."* It's Quentin's Voldemort moment, one that signals to us that Quentin is the most essential character in this story. Though there are other worthy principal characters—Julia, Quentin's childhood friend, who, unlike Quentin, is rejected from Brakebills and has a hedge witch story line that runs parallel to Quentin's, and Alice, the Hermione Granger of the group, a brilliant and accomplished magician—Quentin is clearly the nexus of the action.

In one of my favorite episodes of the series, Quentin wakes up back at the mental hospital, and we're meant to see it as an "it was all a dream" plot twist. Julia, along with one of her hedge witch companions, has cast a spell on Quentin to trap him in a dream where he's meant to believe that magic doesn't exist and that he has dreamt up Brakebills and all the rest because he's mentally unstable. The aim of the episode isn't just to make us, even temporarily, doubt what has happened in the show thus far—because we already know it must be some spell or alternate reality we're seeing; it subtly causes us to question, however briefly, the perspective of our protagonist. We are often shackled to Quentin's purview, to his way of thinking and seeing, even outside of this episode; by beginning the show with Quentin and using Quentin as our way into the world of Brakebills, *The Magicians* coerces us into believing that he is the center of this universe, without which the story couldn't take place.

But once we near the end of the first season, *The Magicians* throws a wrench into its own narrative. Quentin realizes that he

---

* Sera Gamble and John McNamara, "Unauthorized Magic," *The Magicians*, December 16, 2015.

might not actually be the hero the story needs. "My entire life, ever since the first time I read *Fillory and Further*, I've been waiting for some powerful being to come down and say, 'Quentin Coldwater, you are the one,'" he tells Alice in the finale. "Every book, every movie, it's about one special guy. He's chosen. In real life, for every one guy, there are a billion people who aren't. Almost none of us are the one."* With that, Quentin passes on his hero duties to Alice, saying that she's a better magician and perhaps the true hero of the story—and she's ultimately the one to defeat the Beast.

It's a surprising, admirable move on the part of the show, like Harry Potter stepping aside to let the more capable Hermione defeat Voldemort instead. "The chosen one," the show implies, is usually just a product of chance and self-confidence rather than actual ability—it comes down to a privileged perspective. Exceptionalism becomes a self-fulfilling prophecy.

When I was younger, I didn't realize this. For years I didn't question the heroes of the stories I loved. I was invested in the myth of the chosen one. When I imagined my own fantasy worlds like the ones I read in books, I imagined myself as the chosen hero, selected by the universe for some hidden, innate quality that made me special above all others. Now I recognize this self-obsessed kind of thinking in the ways my mind moves through its anxieties: I am at the center of every awkward event or conversation. Everyone is watching and judging me—or at least my mind tricks me into thinking so. When I'm feeling socially anxious at, say, a party or a work meeting, I feel painfully visible, as though everyone's eyes are glued on me, as though I occupy all their thoughts. Some part of me wants the attention but then also resents it.

At worst this is a troubling brand of narcissism, to think that one is elevated on a higher plane than others. That is where David's

---

* Gamble and McNamara, "Have You Brought Me Little Cakes," *The Magicians*, April 11, 2016.

villainy started in *Legion*, but we've seen it elsewhere, too. In the film version of *Harry Potter and the Half-Blood Prince*, Hermione warns Harry about a peer who has a crush on him: "She's only interested in you because she thinks you're the chosen one." "But I am the chosen one!" Harry says, to which Hermione responds by smartly smacking him on the head.* In *Star Wars*, too, Anakin Skywalker is brought down at least in part by the myth of the chosen one; Obi-Wan Kenobi believes Anakin is the person fated to bring balance to the Force. Instead, Anakin, drawn in by his narcissism, intends to become so powerful that he can cheat death. He readily kills anyone whom he thinks isn't resolutely on his side.

It's important to note, too, that in these examples the chosen one is a man. Much of the long history of literature and storytelling is gendered in such a way, with the special male hero at the center. But women? Forgotten, with the exception of a still fairly recent wave of fiction—especially YA fiction, like *The Hunger Games* and the *Divergent* series, but also shows and movies like *Buffy the Vampire Slayer*—that has been retroactively correcting that unfortunate trend.

In *The Magicians*, Julia, the only other member of the main cast of players who we meet before we get to the university, doesn't fit the bill for the mold of "hero" that the show has established from the get-go. But she also comes to usurp Quentin's role as the hero figure. She's popular, unlike Quentin, and while Quentin has held on to his connection to the fantasy world of his youth, Julia has let that go. In fact, her story line in the first season, a kind of antihero's journey, is predicated on the fact that she is *not* the chosen one. Julia, unlike Quentin, is not accepted into the university, so her story line, as interesting as it is, is subordinated to the main one. Her path isn't as glamorous as Quentin's, and while Quentin, we may safely assume, is on the path to heroism, Julia is on the path to self-destruction.

The show mistreats the character in the most unsavory ways: she's

---

* David Yates, *Harry Potter and the Half-Blood Prince*, Warner Bros., 2009.

raped, then saddled with an unwanted pregnancy, and her abortion results in her losing part of her soul. But as a result of her rape, she gains the powers of a god. And, driven by revenge, she briefly teams up with the Beast, a murderer and pedophile. For the first two seasons, Julia is empowered only in circumstances where she's the victim or the villain. Then, at the end of season two, when magic disappears, Julia is the only one who can perform it, and she gets progressively more powerful over the course of season three.

Julia, not Quentin, is the exception this time, and she becomes the most powerful one of the group—an actual god. Suddenly it seems that perhaps Julia has always been the secret hero of the story.

But *The Magicians* gradually reveals that it isn't interested in the idea of the singular hero at all. The third season is premised on a quest involving seven keys, in which each of the main characters is called to play a vital role in getting the keys to bring magic back. Each key quest enables the characters to become the hero of that story, and one isn't subordinated to another; each key is essential, and so each character must play his or her part.

At the end of season four, *The Magicians* showed its commitment to dismantling the tropes of the fantasy genre and reconfiguring them in ways that are innovative and contemporary. Quentin sacrifices himself to save the world, and though the show takes the time to recognize his absence, both in the rest of the finale and in large parts of season five, it continues with the rest of the story.

I was surprised and heartbroken at this change—I ugly-cried at my laptop not simply because the character who I thought was the hero of the story gave up everything for his friends, but because he was a person who had spent all of the previous seasons dealing with his mental illness while still trying to save the world. With this move the show risked creating a tone of suicidal ideation, and I felt sympathy for Quentin, an outcast who struggled through depression and then dealt with all the strange events and traumas of this new magical world. He couldn't accept a version of the story where he wasn't tasked with being the chosen one but was just someone living in the world—magical or otherwise—and enjoying it with his family and friends. Because the show ultimately reveals that the story is larger than Quentin and what's happening in his head. He isn't the lone ranger who must save the day; there is a whole cast of heroes beside him, each powerful and flawed in equal measure.

In my own story, I'd like to think that I'm still the hero, but I hope never to become trapped in my own perspective. In real life, there are no easy narratives, no perfect heroes. Even on the days when I'm too anxious or depressed to function, when my internal world shifts and is cast in black, the world around me keeps moving, full of others who are also struggling and fighting and trying their best. Sick or not, we are all the heroes of this narrative, a strange reality we all inhabit together.

VII.

Do You Know Shinigami Love Apples?

Gods, faith, and belief systems in fandom

There was a long period in my life when Jesus was everywhere: hanging from the crucifix at church, of course, but also in all my classrooms, in courtyards, in paintings, in textbooks, even on my school papers. My elementary school was a private Catholic school that went from pre-K to eighth grade and sat next door to a church in the suburbs of Long Island. There we took classes taught by nuns and were instructed to write *JMJ* on top of every quiz, test, or essay: *Jesus Mary Joseph.* (The logic behind the rule was rooted in a long and well-established tradition of Catholic guilt: if we were forced to consider the Holy Family every time we scribbled *JMJ* with our No. 2 pencils, then hopefully we would be discouraged from cheating.)

Though the schools I attended were firm and vocal about how I was expected to engage with my beliefs—both religious and political—at home we were surprisingly agnostic. We went to church on Sundays when I was young, but our visits slowly tapered off. Gradually church just became something to go to on Easter and Christmas.

Faith was never a part of how we spoke, thought, or related to one another in our home. My father, when asked, was frustratingly oblique about the true nature of his faith, but it seemed clear to me as a child that he either didn't believe or didn't care much either way. His responses to my inquiries about his beliefs always felt like a closed door; I left it at that and didn't ask any other questions. My mother seemed ambivalent about Catholicism but had a God who felt both vague and yet specific in function. He would crop up in aphorisms: "God doesn't give you more than you can handle," "God works in mysterious ways," "Everything happens for a reason." Her God was an amalgamation of fate and karma, a sense of intuition and a benevolent something to thank when things ultimately worked out, even after hardship and struggle. Neither approach to faith made sense to me, unclear as both were, so I had only the version from my small, illustrated Bible that I was gifted as a child, and of course the version from school. But that God was so specific that I couldn't help but foster a growing doubt as I got older, that perhaps much of what I believed to be God was the church, and perhaps much of what I believed to be canon was simply narratives that, like poetry, held their own truths beneath the convenient fiction of metaphor.

When I was in eighth grade, in the midst of our preparations for graduation, we gathered in the church for the sacrament of confirmation—all of us in our nice clothes, standing and publicly declaring our dedication to the faith and the church, while our parents watched from the pews behind us. I think of this moment sometimes, when I consider how my relationship to faith has changed, and how guilty and fake I felt, silently mouthing the words but not speaking them aloud. I had become more decisive on the subject of my doubt and didn't know how to name it. Atheism was a term I knew but was too frightened to use—it was too self-consciously rebellious and too final: Nietzsche I was not. And yet my false participation in the sacrament made me feel cowardly. The sound of everyone speaking the pledge and praying together in unison was overwhelming. I kept looking up at the stained-glass windows and the Stations of the Cross as though they would suddenly speak my name and decide for me the particular shape my faith would take.

It didn't escape me that what I was considering was a modern-day mythology. I loved reading about mythology as a kid; my father started me off by telling me loose tidbits about Greek, Norse, and Arthurian myths, and I found my way to the rest. My aunt bought me a giant coffee-table book about ancient Egypt; my favorite parts were about the myths. In middle school I bought an encyclopedia of Greek, Celtic, and Norse mythology. They reminded me of the stories in my illustrated Bible but were divorced from the stodgy morals I was used to; these were stories about flawed, spiteful gods and the humans who were praised or punished according to their whims. It was a much more cynical—and thus, for me, more believable—view of omnipotence. I read and reread the book's entry on Ragnarok, the doomsday of the Norse gods. It seemed obvious to me that such a thing could happen in a mythology, because the thought of an omniscient, infallible consciousness struck me as curious and also frightening. No wonder the Old Testament was full of grim stories about punishment and fear. We love creating myths to fill the space where our deepest existential fears live. Perhaps a fear of God is preferable to the fear of total nothingness, of evil, of the absence of order.

A large reason for my father's interest in Norse myth—and thus my own—was Thor. Not the original Norse god, but the caped Marvel hero. He read *Thor* comics as a kid, and I remember one day him coming back from a visit to my grandmother's house with some old comics in tow. He dropped them on the carpet in front of him in the living room, and I picked up a *Thor* while he went on about the hero and his adventures.

I felt strange about the conflation of this old mythology with comic books. My defensiveness surprised me; suddenly I imagined the people for whom Thor and Loki and Odin were real. Until then it had never occurred to me that these gods were anything more than entertaining fictions. But the appearance of mythology in the world of comic books likely bothered me because it was one system of belief—one deemed archaic, with no one to claim blasphemy against it—positioned within another: my own, my realm of fandom. The collision revealed how our fandoms themselves replicate religions. In comic books, for example, some fans truly believe in the ethical themes represented in the stories (justice, heroism, right vs. wrong). Fandom, more than the Catholicism I grew up with, has always been a kind of church for me, where I could believe in integrity and magic and good guys always saving the day.

In many of my favorite anime that I encountered during that time, those series contained bold religious allusions and imagery, and possessed characters that were granted the power, will, smarts, or technology to combat gods—or become the equivalent of gods themselves.

In middle school I fell in love with *Fullmetal Alchemist* (*FMA*), which I still list among my favorite anime series of all time (though I say so with the qualifier that the more expansive, more coherently written remake, *Fullmetal Alchemist: Brotherhood*, which premiered a few years after the original, is what I now rank among my top picks, instead of the version I loved as a kid).

In the series, adapted from the manga of the same name, alchemy—the magic of transforming materials—is real, and considered an advanced science. In this steampunk world, in which colonialism, racism, and religious prejudice are rampant, and where the government licenses worthy alchemists but then enlists them to fight immoral wars in return, two bright young boys—Alphonse and Edward Elric—dream of learning alchemy. When their mother dies, however, they decide to break a forbidden rule of alchemy: human transmutation—trying to bring a human back from the dead. They follow the formula and do the math but underestimate alchemy's central tenet of equivalent exchange; one can't use alchemy to create something out of nothing—it's what distinguishes alchemy from magic. In the exchange, which results in not their resurrected mother but rather a mangled, zombielike animated corpse, Ed loses a leg and Al loses his entire body. In a last-ditch attempt to save his younger brother, Ed sacrifices his arm to bond Al's soul to a suit of armor. The rest of the plot follows from their attempts to find a way to get Al's body and Ed's missing limbs back somehow through alchemy. Ed becomes a state alchemist so he and Al can hunt down leads on a philosopher's stone, a powerful substance with alchemical abilities that could make such a goal possible. Along the way, though, Ed and Al get tangled up in mysteries about alchemy, the government, and their own lineage.

From the start, when Ed and Al try to bring their mother back from the dead, they choose to use alchemy knowing that it's a way of manipulating the natural world.

In one early episode of the series, the Elric brothers journey to a desert town, following rumors that a priest there, Father Cornello, is performing "miracles"—transmutations that the brothers surmise could only be performed with the help of a philosopher's stone. The townspeople, including a young woman named Rose, praise Cornello as a prophet and miracle worker and pray to his god. But when the brothers arrive, Ed is mercilessly reproachful about the people's faith, chastising Rose in particular for using her faith as a crutch. He speaks instead of the validity of science over blind faith.

When I watched the episode as a teen, I was as impatient with Rose and the others as Ed was. It was something I was facing in myself at the time, trying to figure out whether I believed in God, and, more importantly, why: Was it really faith or just a response to my fears about us being alone in a world that moves without logic or meaning? How much was my God just what I grabbed while reaching for straws, hoping for some answer to my life and the universe at large?

Though my schools never reinforced that dichotomy between science and religion, as in creationism vs. evolution, for some time in middle school I latched onto the idea that I could only believe in science—that I stood for logic instead of faith. I fancied myself a fresh, junior member of the rationalist movement.

But this dichotomy, at least as it's presented in *FMA*, isn't that simple. There are nuances to both, I realize now: the truths within faith, the miracles within science. One of the great ironies of *FMA* is how alchemy, which is in the real world considered a fake science, is in the series not only a legitimate field of science but a practice that is nevertheless marked by a large element of mysticism.

It's within the act of alchemical transmutation that the series opens up to a metaphysical plane: a white space with a mighty gate that, in the original series, opens to an alternate reality, and in the remake reflects ultimate knowledge. A plain white figure—featureless, appearing as only the outline of a person—who calls itself Truth is the guardian. And the gate that Ed encounters is etched with the Kabbalah Tree of Life. Somewhere between Truth and the gate of knowledge is the show's interpretation of God. Adam and Eve and the apple, Odin and his self-sacrifice at Yggdrasil, Prometheus and his gift of fire: several religions and mythologies contain versions of a story of knowledge acquired at a great cost. This is no different. The characters in *FMA* generally understand that alchemy is a Faustian gift. Seeing the young Elric brothers try to bring back their mother only to summon some misshapen creature horrified me; it was one of the scenes of the series that I still remember clearly today—the disconcerting array of ribs and other bones, the limbs splayed all in wrong directions, and the head, tilted backward and upside down, with the jaw open and the pupil-less eyes glowing. The same degree of horror met me when I got to a story line involving Ed and Al's visit to a researcher named Shou Tucker, a bio-alchemist known for creating a chimera who could speak.

In an episode that's notorious among anime fans, Ed and Al find that Tucker has created a new speaking chimera, only to discover that Tucker has transmuted his young daughter and dog together for the benefit of his research. Even more, they figure out that he had created his first chimera by transmuting his wife, who had supposedly left the family years earlier. In that traumatizing episode, Tucker epitomizes the immorality of science performed at the expense of human life. But as the Elric brothers marvel at him and his grotesque handiwork, Tucker doesn't relent; in fact, he suggests that Ed and Al aren't so different from him.

The central antagonists of the series, homunculi with devastating special abilities, are by-products of scientific probing gone bad. They are appropriately named after, and embody, the seven deadly sins.

But *FMA* was never just about characters who pervert the laws of nature to their whims; in *Brotherhood* especially, alchemy is a way to transform matter that's been translated and interpreted in different ways according to different cultures. In the places where the Elric brothers live and work, alchemy is a tool of the state, a military weapon. Out East, alchemy is used for healing. In the nation of Ishval, alchemy is rejected altogether as an abominable act against God. One indigenous Ishvalan, seeking revenge for his brother and his people, who had suffered in an unjust civil war during which they were almost entirely eradicated by state alchemists, uses the principles of alchemy to an opposite end: not to create but destroy alchemists. But this man, who the alchemists call Scar, isn't pardoned by the show's morality either, though many of the state alchemists willingly committed atrocities against the Ishvalan people; Scar is a religious zealot, a hypocrite who contorts his understanding of his faith and his people's history to fit his mission. He wants to stop alchemists from using the abilities that make them like gods, but he too claims a kind of godhood, using a form of alchemy to enact his revenge. He is simply the other side of the coin.

In this way Scar recalls Light Yagami, the sociopathic antihero of the anime *Death Note*, another one of my favorite series of all time. In the universe of *Death Note*, shinigami, or gods of death, decide who dies and when by writing names in their notebooks, called Death Notes. When one such book drops to Earth, Light, a brilliant but narcissistic young man who's bored with his life of success, finds it and tests it out. Once he realizes the book's power, he becomes a god of death himself, doling out fatal punishments to criminals at first but then, gradually, to anyone standing in his way. Hoping to stop Light is L, an eccentric and mysterious top detective who is able to match even Light's genius-level intelligence.

Light aims to create a new world, wiping out whoever he deems unworthy in his own personal rapture. He gains popularity and interest; he has disciples. And the heavy Christian imagery throughout, as in the exquisite opening credits to the show, emphasize *Death Note*'s fascination with the fall of man. Apples, fruit beloved by shinigami, repeatedly appear in the opening, recalling the apple of the biblical story of Adam and Eve. Many of the scenes in the opening theme are rendered in the style of religious Renaissance art. One of the most striking images is of Light and a shinigami named Ryuk. It's a reference to Michelangelo's *The Fall of Man*. Light is in the position of Adam, reaching from the left corner of the frame. Michelangelo's Adam, pitiful and laggard, his arm reaching out but his hand falling limp, has always drawn my attention more than God, effortlessly strong and resolute. In *Death Note*'s version Light doesn't have the slouch or weak reach of Adam but a strong, determined posture and firm extension of the arm. And he reaches not for Ryuk's hand but an apple, but there's a hindrance that's almost missable at first: a chain hangs from Light's wrist and falls across his body and leads out of the frame. He'll aspire to godhood, perhaps even be granted it, but will still ultimately be caught due to his pride. Thanks in part to

Death Note, I decided my view on capital punishment early on: that we have no right to determine who should live or die, because we are not gods.

In *Neon Genesis Evangelion,* too, the characters aim to outwit and overpower the heavens. *NGE* is perhaps best known for its vivid and omnipresent use of religious imagery and symbolism, taking from Christianity and Kabbalah, among others. Set after a worldwide disaster, *NGE* is about a Japanese boy named Shinji, whose genius father recruits him to pilot a special mecha called Evangelion with which to fight Angels, powerful but unpredictable alien creatures who threaten the Earth. NERV, the organization to which Shinji's father belongs, has trapped an Angel they call Adam, considering it the first of its kind.

NERV uses this Angel to develop its Evangelions, which are terrifying hybrids between animal and machine. By the end, Shinji discovers that one of his peers at NERV is actually the Angel Adam in human form—and the trapped Angel is Lilith, named after the original woman, the first wife of Adam, in Jewish mythology. Throughout the series, most of the Angels appear to be completely novel creatures, not the humanoid winged beings of various religions. And even though NERV attempts to close the gap between the Angels and humans by experimenting on the former to make the latter more powerful, the series soon reveals that Angels and humans weren't ever so different after all. But the implication there is cynical: that Angels have the fallibility of humans, and humans have the power of Angels. Both are equally capable of devastating acts of destruction.

NGE reminds me of the Book of Revelation: it's full of symbols and images all pointed in the direction of an apocalypse. That book always seemed more interesting to me, at least in theory. My first year of high school, our religious education requirement was a class of Bible studies. Our teacher, a young man with a doofy disposition and a love for Dante, would quiz us on the details and meanings of the parables. But the whole Bible was too big to cover in one school year, and in our sophomore year we moved on to a church history class instead. So we never focused on Revelation. Perhaps the thinking was that it was too blatantly allegorical, too difficult to parse, and too removed from the essential parts of my school's interpretation of the Catholic faith.

By then, however, my faith was faltering again. I had graduated middle school after that confirmation ceremony feeling cynical and unsure about not just Catholicism but also the existence of God. I understood the nature of belief but never felt it in my body as some of the people around me seemed to, speaking of God's presence, his intentions, his love. But for high school I was accepted to a private Catholic school with a substantial campus and many resources. The school was eccentric, almost cultlike, in its elitism and religious politics. It had dogs who were free to walk the halls with students; courtyards full of guinea fowl and peacocks, and pools of exotic fish; chapels and retreat rooms; a full lab; and a large, very vocal parrot who sat on a towering bird stand in the administrative office. Everywhere there was Jesus in some form or another: crucifixes, inspirational Christian posters in the classrooms and hallways, Jesus and Mary statues. We prayed before every class and watched religious music videos with the morning video announcements. We sat through assemblies with the school's version of sex ed: fearmongering experiences where C-list MTV stars and pro-life activists attempted to shame us out of having premarital sex and terrify us with vivid descriptions of STDs. My school proudly took students on field trips to pro-life marches but sent out pamphlets decrying Philip Pullman's *His Dark Materials* series for its apparent bastardization of Christianity and then, in a highly publicized move, canceled prom, claiming it encouraged sex and drinking and other reprehensible behavior.

Religion was so omnipresent, so in the air of my every day in high school, that it was overwhelming. I had been so thrilled to start high school but wasn't sure where to place my newly found skepticism in God and my religion. I attempted to swing in the opposite direction and lean into what my high school was offering. I tried on faith like a new pair of shoes: I accessorized with the little plastic rosaries we got and kept a prayer card in my pocket.

In my junior-year religion class, I found a new word for my status: agnostic. It seemed practical to me, balanced, somewhere between the total belief of the faithful and the total doubt of the atheist.

It was around that same time that I fell for the 2005 movie *Constantine*, based on the *Hellblazer* comics. I didn't see it in theaters but caught it when it came to cable. One of the channels loved playing it; it seemed like it was always on. My mother still jokes about my love for *Constantine*, even today, for several valid reasons: (1) I generally don't like movies that fall into the category of "thriller" or "horror," even if they're tame; (2) It took me several viewings to get past the smattering of cheap jump-scares in the film, and I still can't watch the scene when Constantine's partner is killed by a swarm of demon-bees; (3) I've never liked Keanu Reeves's acting, which, despite his natural charisma, always appeared flat and lifeless to me. But I could take him as this version of John Constantine, a gruff, chain-smoking detective who was born with the ability to see angels and demons. The cynical detective tries to do enough good deeds to buy his place in heaven, like a Boy Scout trying to get a badge.

A complete reimagining of the character and the original comic, *Constantine* took its cues from noir detective movies and set its protagonist in Los Angeles—what better location for a story about heavenly beings and a world of disillusionment and sin than the City of Angels? I remain awed at the movie's rendering of hell, the Upside Down before the Upside Down of *Stranger Things* even existed. In all my imaginings of the landscape of hell, from what I was offered in the Bible and Dante's *Inferno*, it never occurred to me to think that perhaps hell would be a more broken version of what we already know. Wrecked, as though by war, and swarming with hell creatures, but totally familiar, identifiable. It's a grim thought, that hell isn't that far away—though, as the movie suggests, neither is heaven, as Constantine nearly gets rewarded with a fast pass to eternal bliss in the clouds for selflessly sacrificing his life for another.

The religious logic of *Constantine* works like an algebraic equation. There's always an opposite side to one idea or reality, and both elements must be balanced for everyone to survive. In one scene, Constantine tells Detective Angela Dodson about the deal between God and Satan, that humans have free will, but demons and angels can influence them, like the old trope of the angel and devil on one's shoulders. "They call it the balance. I call it hypocritical bullshit," Constantine tells Angela with a scoff. Later Angela tries to reason this arrangement away with a platitude, shared with no small amount of irony: "I guess God has a plan for all of us." Constantine isn't having it: "God's a kid with an ant farm, lady. He's not planning anything."* I think about these lines often, and how the version of the universe they illustrate is one ruled by a petty, aloof deity. It makes sense to me: If we are made in the image of such a god, what else could we be but tiny creatures marching through our days, oblivious to the larger story happening around us? It's one of the grand paradoxes of humanity: we have remarkable power and ability, enough to change ecosystems and journey out into the stars—but we're insignificant in the grand scheme of the universe at large.

One of my religion teachers in high school, a charmingly offbeat Marianist brother with a droll sense of humor, made no effort to hide his judgment of the other forms of belief. He described agnostics derisively as being neither here nor there; I imagined them, in his flippant description, as eternal wafflers, too cowardly or lazy to interrogate the existential questions any further and arrive at a firm decision.

Even today my mind skirts around questions of faith but considers those definitions that were offered to us in that classroom: I doubt God exists, but I don't know for sure. I suspect if there is a God, he or

---

* Francis Lawrence, *Constantine*, Warner Bros., 2005.

she or they is so large and far removed from us—too overwhelming for us to even conceive—that it makes no real difference. In our lives of loves, friendships, careers, illnesses, health, wars, peace, griefs, and successes, we have a lot more immediate concerns, from the monumental task of our personal survival to the ways we build our relationships with those around us. The question of whether God actually exists is so much less interesting to me than the question of how I am to live in the world right now, with or without a God, and the question of what I choose to believe.

Because what those anime taught me also is the fearsome power of people, who create and destroy their own gods. This is something I encountered in the work of Neil Gaiman. Often combining real mythologies with his own whimsical fictions, Gaiman writes works that I've always felt probed the same areas where my mind loves to venture, with the same tone and macabre style that I identify in my own writing.

I love Neil Gaiman. But I will never forgive him for writing *American Gods*. Over a decade ago, I recall sitting in my roommates' room in college, telling them about my idea for a book: "I was thinking— what if the old gods, like all the gods from classic mythology—were still around today?" I wondered aloud. My friend said, "You mean like *American Gods*?" As disappointed as I was to discover that my great novel idea, held for all of a couple hours, was already taken by Gaiman, I still read *American Gods* immediately, with relish. That same year I also started Gaiman's *Sandman* series, courtesy of our punk vegan RA across the hall, who I had a crush on (thanks, Dave).

Gaiman's worlds, with all their mythology and literary references, felt inherently familiar to me. They also expanded my idea of what and who gods are and how religions and myths function in our society.

The graphic novel series *The Sandman* begins with the capture of its titular character, named Morpheus, a powerful entity in charge of the realm of dreams. Held hostage for decades, Morpheus finally escapes to find his kingdom destroyed and various elements of the world gone out of whack; he must regain his power and repair the damage left by his absence. *Sandman* continues on beyond this initial arc, tracking Morpheus's other journeys as well, and his relationship with his brothers and sisters, anthropomorphic beings known as the Endless: Death, Destiny, Desire, Despair, Delusion, Destruction, and, of course, Dream.

Sandman traverses the realms of comics, myths, literature, and more. Morpheus hops from dream to dream and speaks to the twisted brothers Cain and Abel, from the biblical story. He ventures to hell and back, requesting an audience with Lucifer. He encounters members of the Justice League and also the paranormal detective John Constantine. And in the stories of his brothers and sisters, we find their own mythologies—theirs and those of other characters, like the cats, who join together and tell old stories. All of these separate stories and realities are given the same weight, because in Gaiman's works, the fact that someone—anyone—believes a story is enough to make it real.

I discovered the same in *American Gods*, which finds its protagonist, Shadow Moon, upon his release from jail and his employment by the mysterious Mr. Wednesday. In a trip across America, Shadow encounters gods old and new: gods brought to America by immigrants carrying their beliefs with them, and gods created by our changing beliefs and values in contemporary America. The gods are at war, with Shadow caught up in the middle of it all.

"I can believe things that are true and things that aren't true and I can believe things where nobody knows if they're true or not," one character tells Shadow.* The war Shadow is witnessing is one for the faithful of America. These old and new gods are powerful, but only because of the people who believe in them; their belief is what keeps them alive and what enables their miracles. America has always

---

* Neil Gaiman, *American Gods* (New York: HarperCollins, 2002).

been a country of faith: We dreamt of liberty, we dreamt of Western expansion, we dreamt of glory and success. And today, we believe in the internet, the media, technology. To be human is to be constantly in the process of building and breaking down systems of belief, for ourselves individually and ourselves as a society, so we can survive without going mad. We have such enormous power as storytellers, something Shadow eventually figures out along the way: "People populate the darkness; with ghosts, with gods, with electrons, with tales. People imagine, and people believe; and it is that rock-solid belief, that makes things happen."*

In another Gaiman work I discovered in college, *Good Omens*, coauthored with Terry Pratchett, the Antichrist is a normal boy, and he and his friends, determined to stop the end of the world, fight against the Four Horsemen of the Apocalypse (well, in *Good Omens*, Four Bikers of the Apocalypse) and ultimately win.

Today I'm more at home with my personal rejection of religion and ambivalence toward the question of God. Some days I find no God to believe in, but then other days, when it's convenient, I consider the comforting thought of a universal order that's beyond my capacity to understand. At the end of the day, all we're talking about is concepts, just like one would in a classroom: life, death, heaven, hell, God or gods or the chaotic nothingness of the universe. And yet, as Gaiman says, that doesn't mean they're inconsequential. In fact, they are important because they take up real estate inside our minds. "It's all imaginary anyway. That's why it's important. People only fight over imaginary things," he writes.†

---

* Gaiman, *American Gods*.
† Gaiman, *American Gods*.

Fandoms, you could argue, are inherently vehicles for political belief systems and different worldviews as well. Even the nerdy TV shows and movies with the boldest political agendas that I was exposed to as a kid appealed to me without making me explicitly aware of what they were messaging.

When I was a toddler, I was a fan of the 1992 musical animated film *FernGully: The Last Rainforest*. In *FernGully*, a young logger discovers a community of magical fairies in the rain forest he's supposed to be tearing down and chooses to help them instead. But he's fighting against not just his logger friends but an evil force named Hexxus that feeds on smog, oil, and pollution.

I was entranced by the colors and music of the movie, and its dark implications flew right over my head. Robin Williams played a mentally unstable lab bat with clear PTSD from the experimentation he's endured—but I just found the bat funny. And Hexxus, voiced by Tim Curry, was frightening not just for his villainous nature, but for his protean form—bubbling and black like an oil spill—and his ravenous appetite. Curry's voice work was seductive, giving his antagonist another dimension of taboo. Even now, decades after the film was released, I still remember Hexxus's sensual Marilyn Manson–esque theme, "Toxic Love." I watched the movie thinking that of course the rain forests shouldn't be cut down, but didn't fully connect it to the fact that deforestation was a global issue that was happening not because of malevolent, sentient sludge, but because of human commerce.

I watched the show *Captain Planet* and, later, the early *Ice Age* movies, with the same reaction: I was intrigued and entertained by the action and characters enough to be vaguely aware that the Earth needed protection but not enough that I was nervous about global warming and endangered species.

And the shows and movies I watched that incorporated pacifist themes sometimes caused some confusion in me. For instance, I spent a good chunk of my elementary school years in love with *Gun-*

dam Wing and then bought the movie *Endless Waltz*. Throughout the series, the Gundam pilots are our protagonists who supposedly fight for peace, though the politics of the show were much more nuanced than that—more than I could understand with any depth as a child.

The main Gundam pilot, Heero Yuy, is a child assassin, and he and the other Gundam pilots are capable of being merciless killers. The characters in the series who rally for more peaceful methods, like Relena Peacecraft, a young diplomat and the love interest to Heero, and Quatre Raberba Winner, the most empathetic of the young Gundam pilots, are written for most of the series as cute idealists. I found both Relena and Quatre unbearably annoying, and despite my own personal distaste for war, I fell for the show's glorification of the fighters; I was obsessed with Heero and liked Duo Maxwell, a goofy pilot in a priest collar who ironically pilots a Gundam named Deathscythe and refers to himself as the god of death.

In the film *Endless Waltz*, the pilots plan to retire their Gundams, thinking they've achieved peace after all their killing in the series. But then a young girl named Mariemaia leads a rebellion and threatens to become the ruler of Earth. Chang Wufei, the only one of the pilots who holds on to his Gundam, and who joins Mariemaia's army, voices the ideological paradox of the whole series: "I need to determine for myself whether or not peace at the expense of lives can really be defined as peace . . . and I will become evil itself to find out."[*]

The quote brings to mind J. Robert Oppenheimer, the father of the atomic bomb, who, upon seeing the detonation of the devastating weapon, recalled a line from the Bhagavad Gita: "Now I am become Death, the destroyer of worlds." Wufei's choice confused and distressed me at the time. It seemed like an obvious betrayal; of course Mariemaia was the villain and so it followed that Wufei had turned to the dark side. It didn't occur to me—and wouldn't, until my late

---

[*] Yasunao Aoki, *Gundam Wing the Movie: Endless Waltz*, Sunrise, 1998.

teens—that ideologies are nice to claim in theory, but in practice so many prove impractical, or more complex than they seem.

My favorite line of the film actually belongs to Mariemaia, who says, "History is much like an endless waltz: the three beats of war, peace, and revolution continue on forever." So war is also a dance—refined, beautiful, and, of course, repetitive. What does absolute pacifism mean in that context? Is there such a thing? As a kid, I had hoped, but I was also the one rooting for the pilots when they got back into the cockpits for one last fight for peace.

As a teen I grew more skeptical of art with explicit political agendas. Though by high school I had already known I wanted to be a journalist, I hated politics, avoided the news. I preferred to remain blissfully oblivious about the problems of the world—it all seemed like too much of a burden. *Wall-E* I rejected for being too blatantly political. *Happy Feet*, too, enraged me for switching from its light, fleet-footed entertainment to activism. It didn't matter if I agreed with the message; a contrarian, I hated to be preached to.

As I've grown as a critic, so has my sensitivity to the politics of works of art. In two of my favorite series, for example, *Doctor Who* and *Avatar: The Last Airbender*, there are pacifist, environmentally conscious protagonists who often find themselves caught up in the middle of wars and other conflicts, and yet still refuse, even when their lives are at risk, to perpetuate a pattern of violence. The environment is also essential to both series, the former often warning about how our treatment of the planet is affecting our future, and the latter espousing an elemental oneness that connects humans to the natural world.

In *Doctor Who*, the regenerating alien who travels in time and space takes his companions with him to various strange planets—and often past, present, and future versions of Earth. In the second episode of the show's 2005 relaunch, the Ninth Doctor takes Rose to the end of the world; they crash a party where the attendees all view the Earth's destruction by the sun. Despite knowing that they are billions of years in the future, when humans no longer inhabit the planet, Rose is visibly distraught by the sight and the thought of her world dying. But the celebration is disrupted by a moneymaking hostage scheme led by Lady Cassandra, a piece of skin connected to a brain who calls herself the last human being. The episode has a bleak view of humanity, that even at the end of the world, the last human, no more than a vain, superficial extraction of what we'd consider a human to be, takes advantage of the situation for her own commercial benefit.

The series often includes plots in which the greed and economic interests of humans have larger, more dire consequences. In one of my favorite episodes of the show, "Midnight," from season four, the Tenth Doctor goes to a toxic planet called Midnight, which features a fancy spa and shuttle tours of the surface, which can't be explored on foot due to lethal radiation. When the shuttle malfunctions during the Doctor's tour and is attacked by an unseen creature who then possesses a passenger, the rest of the passengers panic and turn on one another until one sacrifices herself to save them all. The episode, written by one of the great scribes of *Doctor Who*, Russell T. Davies, feels like a descendant of the *Twilight Zone* episode "The Monsters Are Due on Maple Street." Humans' disruption of a natural environment for the sake of commerce ends up causing catastrophe. The same occurs in the season twelve episode "Orphan 55," in which the Thirteenth Doctor and her companions venture to a spa that is attacked by vicious creatures. Here the show gets explicit, tossing aside the metaphor, declaring that the planet is actually a future version of Earth, destroyed by global warming and war, and the creatures are mutated humans. The theme extends to the season eleven episode "Arachnids in the UK," though here at the expense of Americans in particular. Chris Noth guest stars as an immoral American businessman whose company's illegal dumping of toxic chemicals has created giant mutated spiders. But it's the businessman's eagerness to use firearms to resolve the situation in the end that disgusts the Doctor even more.

After all, the Doctor famously despises guns, often marching onto battlefields armed with nothing but a sonic screwdriver. So often war, as imagined in the universe of *Doctor Who*, is a conflict generated by greed. In the first season of the series reboot, an alien species called the Slitheen invades not because they want to rule Earth but because they want to sell it. And in the two-part episode "The Hungry Earth/ Cold Blood," a drilling operation awakens a civilization of aliens who are hibernating deep within the Earth, the Silurians, who claim the planet as their own native land and criticize the humans for overtaking it. The Doctor and his companions find themselves in the middle of tense negotiations, with hostages on both sides, trying to avoid the outbreak of a war between the Silurians and the humans, but nearly fail when individuals on both sides start to act out of personal interest.

Despite the stubborn idealism of the show, which, depending on the showrunner and writers, can veer into the territory of didactic moralism, *Doctor Who* also recognizes the limits of pacifism. The Time War, a long, vicious conflict between the Time Lords and their enemies the Daleks, occurs before the start of the 2005 series relaunch, and the event strongly influences the character of the Ninth Doctor and all the Doctors to follow. In the 2013 fiftieth anniversary special, "The Day of the Doctor," the show reveals that there was another, previously unaccounted for, incarnation of the Doctor: the War Doctor, played by John Hurt. Faced with the sight of countless casualties and unceasing violence and destruction, the Doctor was forced to decide whether to let the war go on or to wipe out both sides, including his own people. Having always believed that he destroyed his home planet of Gallifrey, the Doctor constantly referred to the fact that he was the last of his kind. He carried the guilt of how he massacred the Time Lords with him in his journeys through time and space, and it made him more empathetic but also bitter and cynical. But this War Doctor figures out an alternative: He locks the war—both sides, exactly as they are—in a single moment in time, in a pocket of an alternate universe. Ultimately the Doctor is saved from carrying the guilt of a genocide on his shoulders any longer. And the series is able to keep its pacifist hero, who is always granted leeway so he can continue to be as unyielding and wholesome as the show wants him to be.

In the animated series *Avatar: The Last Airbender*, the world is divided into four nations, each represented by an element: earth, fire, air, water. Certain members of each nation can manipulate, or "bend," their element, with the exception of one person, the avatar, who can control all four. Reborn as a different person from a different nation each generation, the avatar is meant to keep the peace among the nations and serve as a bridge between the world of the living and the spirit world. But Aang, the current avatar, a twelve-year-old Air Nomad boy who was frozen in ice for a hundred years, wakes up to find the world at war, as the Fire Nation has taken over, and his people, the Air Nomads, are extinct. He is tasked with finishing his avatar training so he can defeat the despotic Fire Lord and bring peace to the world.

The world of *Avatar* is marked by a connection to the elements and the balance among them. The avatar, who can use each one and also converse with the spirits, represents a communion with and respect for the natural world that isn't as explicit as the environmentalist messages espoused in *Doctor Who*. But Aang is as much of a pacifist as the Doctor. (Korra, Aang's brash and pugnacious avatar successor in the sequel series, *The Legend of Korra*, doesn't fall into this camp.) While determining how to defeat the Fire Lord without killing him, Aang connects to his previous lives, including a former avatar named Kyoshi, a mighty warrior who resolutely tells him that one man may need to be killed in order to save the lives of many others. Aang, however, is naive, fearful of his power and responsibility as the avatar. He hesitates to learn fire-bending because he fears its destructive power. And he fears going into the avatar state, a state of consciousness where he is able to access all his power, because he is more at risk of losing control and inadvertently hurting those around him. Ultimately, though, as in *Doctor Who*, the show grants him a loophole; in fighting the Fire Lord, Aang is able to defeat him not by killing him but by taking away his bending abilities, so he is able to stop the threat while remaining true to his ideals.

My issue with these shows doesn't have to do with the politics but the way the narratives give their protagonists easy outs. The creators want their stories to have believable stakes but don't want to sustain those stakes at the expense of their characters' moral superiority. But in a world full of cruelty and injustice and imperfections, there cannot be any perfect heroes, and any stories that try to say so are doing their fans a disservice.

In their messages of empathy and kindness, these shows are touched with a sense of wholehearted, childlike innocence. They want us to believe in our ultimate capacity for good, and the omnipresence of goodness in the world.

That's something that has also been the signature of the films of the celebrated director Hayao Miyazaki, whose work changed the world of animation. Miyazaki created lush, vivid illustrations and imaginative worlds full of magic and monsters and ghosts. He told modern-day fairy tales, morality stories where the politics aren't didactic but flawlessly incorporated into the stitching of the narratives.

My first Miyazaki film was *Princess Mononoke*, about a boy who searches for a cure to a fatal curse. Along the way he encounters San, a feral human girl who lives among the wolves in a forest, and who fights back against the industrialization of the land, which is affecting the natural ecosystem and angering the animal spirits who are losing their home.

Princess Mononoke frightened me at first. I was flipping channels and came across the sight of the blind boar god Okkoto being devoured by bloody, moving tendrils. It was a disgusting, horrifying sight, especially when taken out of context—as was Okkoto's boar army, whom he doesn't realize are actually humans in boar-skin disguises. They seem to glide across the forest floor with dark, pupil-less eyes.

Having grown up in the suburbs and lived in cities for all of my adult life, I have never felt any kind of affection toward or kinship with nature. The country and woods feel threatening; parks are okay as long as they aren't too large and wild. I have glared at too-vocal birds and gone to war with squirrels outside my window. The majesty of nature is wonderful—from a distance. So a film in which nature was fierce, mobilized even, was a subversion of the clichés I'd often encountered about nature, as picturesque and serene. I felt vindicated in my long-standing row with the natural world; nature could be as vicious and unkind as I had suspected.

We like to personify nature, give her a female face and share idioms about her temperament: "Mother Nature has a temper." These innocent turns of phrase reflect a misogynist gender stereotype of the hysterical, temperamental woman. And various mythologies have had their share of female gods of nature—the wolf goddess of *Princess Mononoke* recalls the wolf mother of Romulus and Remus, and San is reminiscent of the various wild maidens of the woods, like Artemis, from Greek myth, and Diana, from Roman myth.

Part of Miyazaki's allure, however, is how he doesn't let his stories fall into tropes or deliver easy messages. The women of *Princess Mononoke* are complex: San, who doesn't quite fit into either the natural world or the human world; her fierce yet loving and wise wolf mother, Moro; Lady Eboshi, the leader of the nearby Irontown, who employs a fleet of scrappy former prostitutes to mine the forest's resources in the service of a self-sufficient, women-led community.

Just as complex as his characters are his themes, which are always political without ever being preachy. The films contain nuanced narratives and character relationships that resist simple categorization. For as much as *Princess Mononoke* is about humans facing the consequences of their greed, it is also about different kinds of social structures, marginalized people, and how innovation can create opportunities for more equitable societies.

What sticks with me in *Princess Mononoke* isn't just the message but the images. The image of the boar god stuck with me for years, and though I've seen the film several times since, every time I see it, I'm freshly struck by the beauty of Miyazaki's animation—how nature is rendered, with the bright green grasses and trees and the chattering kodama forest spirits, and how it is destroyed, with the wave of death that runs over the land. Nature gives and it takes away, resisting the stubborn influence of humanity. When we encounter the Great Forest Spirit, a deerlike god who with an eerily humanoid face and a grand bounty of antlers on his head, vegetation blooms and then promptly dies beneath the touch of his hooved feet.

War and destruction of the natural world are linked in Miyazaki's films, despite the fact that when we speak of war in our casual conversations or in our books or shows or movies, we often speak only of the human casualties. Miyazaki never loses sight of the larger toll of war, how our lives are inextricably tied to the lives of the plants and animals and landscapes around us. In his 1984 film *Nausicaä of the Valley of the Wind*, a princess in a postapocalyptic world tries to stop humans from destroying a forest of giant insect creatures. But humans themselves are at fault for creating the so-called Toxic Jungle, as a result of their warring.

So much of the magic and power in Miyazaki's films comes from characters—often female characters—fully comprehending their connection to the natural world. In *Spirited Away*, the young Chihiro gets stuck working in the spirit world to save her parents after they're turned into pigs for eating the spirits' food. Chihiro is able to save her friend, a spirit named Haku, once she realizes her link to him: she recalls how she fell into a river as a child but safely washed ashore, and that Haku is the spirit of that very river. This recollection frees and empowers Haku, and the two of them are able to save Chihiro's parents and return Chihiro and her family to the world of the living again.

There is extraordinary magic in the simple act of respecting nature. This isn't just true in Miyazaki's films. In Makoto Shinkai's 2019 anime film *Weathering with You*, there is love and magic to be found even in a world ravaged by climate change. In the film, a high school student named Hodaka runs away from home to Tokyo, but the city is plagued by seemingly endless rain. Getting a job with a small publishing company that peddles conspiracy theories and stories about the occult, he learns about weather maidens, girls who have the ability to change the weather, and then meets one, a girl named Hina. Together, Hodaka and Hina form a business where they take requests from people who want the sunshine that Hina can summon—for weddings, parties, outdoor markets—for a fee. But when the two get tailed by cops and Hina reveals that her body is transforming as a result of her powers, the weather in Tokyo turns apocalyptic, and the teens struggle to find shelter from the authorities and the natural disaster brewing outside.

Though climate change is never explicitly mentioned in the film, the issue is unquestionably part of the story's DNA. Shinkai himself has stated that he created this film with our climate crisis in mind. But the film sticks to magic as the cause and resolution of the disaster. A priest reveals that the strange weather attacking the city is not as unique an occurrence as people would believe; it is perhaps a singular event in recorded history, but there exists a long history before that, when the weather would occasionally get catastrophically wild. In those instances, the priest reveals, weather maidens, who are linked to the skies, served as sacrifices, and the weather returned to normal. Later in the film, as the streets flood and it starts to snow—despite it being late summer—Hina decides to sacrifice herself to fix the weather, and the skies immediately clear, and the sun comes out. Magic is everywhere—not simply in the movie's narrative but in its design: drops of water glisten and sparkle, the sun breaks through the clouds with impossibly bright slivers of light, a prism of colors in brisk pinks, purples, and blues. And we see the realm of the sky, an inverse natural world of liquid sea creatures and a spring-green field of grass.

While films like *Princess Mononoke* and *Nausicaä* make clear links between human greed and conflict and the destruction of the natural world, the magical logic of *Weathering with You* posits that the disaster is connected to the utter beauty and fantasy of the sky world. Even more, the implication is that this crisis makes sense, and is even warranted, in the natural functioning of this sky world. Every once in a while, the film's mythology tells us, the sky opens up until a water maiden sacrifices herself, and then all is normal until the next time.

When Hodaka and Hina ultimately decide not to have Hina sacrifice herself (after Hina's initial attempt and a subsequent rescue by Hodaka), the story is valuing the preservation of the couple over the preservation of the world. The move isn't necessarily a negative one—in fact, it prevents the story from falling into the trope of having the magical girl selflessly sacrifice herself to save the day, a messianic figure erasing any culpability of the people around her. It also isn't the first time Shinkai has made this choice: in *Your Name*, his protagonists transcend time and space, in the face of a different natural disaster, to find and save each other. In that case, love easily skipped over the obstacle, but it's difficult to see the climate disaster in *Weathering with You*—one that's very real to us at the moment—in the same light, and thus more difficult to imagine how its protagonists can survive in such a world.

Shinkai's larger world takes a backseat to the world of Hodaka and Hina, who are together in the end, but Shinkai also doesn't let everything around them totally fall away. The movie ends three years after it began, and we see a Japan nearly sunken into the sea, the Rainbow Bridge almost completely submerged, while the sky above it is a murky gray. The image—and what it represents—is striking, but is then superseded by the last bit of plot. Hodaka and Hina joyously reunite, and the story ends with the two teenagers in love. The kids make the decision that they won't sacrifice their love to save the city—that's not their responsibility, and Hina has a right to live her own life—but neither they nor the film ask how they can go on. What kind of future can they have? The couple has their happy ending, but there's a cost in the form of this world in crisis, which isn't so far off from our own.

All these works, to whatever extent they may or may not assert certain ideologies, have something in common. In any fandom there's an essential quality of belief—in certain politics, sure, but also in characters, in worlds, in scenarios, as strange and fantastical and mystifying as they might be. Because even in worlds marked by death gods or time-traveling aliens or weather maidens, the very first step into each world is an act of faith, a moment of engagement with the logic and beliefs of a world whose fictions can reveal something real in the viewer.

In the 2019 anime film *Children of the Sea*, a teen girl named Ruka meets two brothers who were raised by sea creatures and who have odd aquatic abilities. Sea life is disappearing, and Ruka wades through many mysteries involving the changes in the ocean, a ghost whale, the brothers, and her own relationship to it all. The last third of the film cuts its tether to the narrative, and to reality, breaking off into a cosmic, existential query that considers the concept of ultimate knowledge. "Am I the universe?" Ruka asks, her mind and body suddenly part of a trippy transcendental awakening triggered by the transformations of the ocean.

I've found my own (albeit less psychedelic) awakenings through my fandoms, my own understanding of my world within the vast universes around me, full of such color and mystery and light.

VIII.

Con Crazy

How fandom and cons have changed;
authorship and the evolution of the canon

If fandoms can be religions or political ideologies or any systems of belief, then perhaps conventions—with their rites and rituals—are like church. I remember the moment I decided I should become a con-goer. I was sitting on my roommate's bed in our junior year of college, she at her writing desk, and we were talking about some nerdy thing or another. Then the thought occurred to me: Wasn't there a New York–based comic convention? I looked it up and found it, excitedly reading off the panel descriptions and celebrity guest names aloud. I was overwhelmed by the options—pages and pages of event listings, not just limited to comics but also books and anime and movies and TV shows and reunion panels for beloved fandoms.

I had only been to one comic convention before, also while in college—something small and local, more for actual comic collectors than anyone else. Though I found it underwhelming, I also got an immense satisfaction from just being there, surrounded by tables of comics, rows of boxes with people rifling through enthusiastically, talking to one another about the particulars of the trade with such a casual sense of expertise. But I've always had a love for fairs and conventions.

Perhaps it began with the Scholastic Book Fairs at school, when we would be walked downstairs by our teachers to browse the makeshift shelves suddenly set up in our auditorium, our small allowances in hand. But there were also the elementary school Christmas gift fairs, where we'd go to the same auditorium with our gift lists in hand and browse tables of little knickknacks for different prices. In high school, when I was just getting into martial arts, my dad took me and my friend to a martial arts convention, where we saw demonstrations and gear and practiced our wrist grabs and arm bars while waiting in line for an event. In college, it was the club fairs and the job fairs, then later literary conferences. My whole grad school experience—a low-residency program where students would visit campus twice a year for ten days—felt like a conference, with each day packed from morning to evening with lectures, workshops, and readings.

Despite my aversion to crowds of people and excessive noise, and my impatience with standing in lines, I am addicted to the very feel of conferences. I've defined myself by my passions my whole life, and I am immediately drawn to people who exhibit that same connection to their beloved hobbies and interests. There's something precious in this—the love itself but also the inclination to make that private love a public event. Conventions, specialty fairs, and conferences have enthusiasm in the air. It's intoxicating—breathing in the excitement of other people and letting it feed your own.

That year, however, we had just missed New York Comic Con. We vowed to catch it the following year. That next year, fall 2011, we made our plan, buying our tickets and arranging our travel. My roommate had already moved back home to Alabama at that point, having graduated a year early, but she flew up to New York to join me and our other friend, who took the bus with me. We were overwhelmed by the Javits Center, where the convention took place, far off in the westernmost part of midtown. We would lose each other in the crowds of the show floor, so we started linking ourselves to one another in single-file formation like kindergartners crossing the street. We were confused by the layout of the convention center, wandered around blindly while constantly distracted by the sights of our fellow nerds in cosplay. Our approach to panels was scattershot, and we were often too late to line up to get in to catch the events we wanted to see. We missed panel after panel, including a much-hyped *Avengers* one with the cast, but my friend was sunny about it all: "Well, now we know for next time," she'd say. We still enjoyed every part of it.

My mom and aunt packed us food to take with us for our long days out in Manhattan, and we found corners of the convention center to sit down and eat our room-temperature pasta. We found an airy atrium where the anime booths were sequestered and hung out there. It was our place of refuge from the busy show floor and panel rooms. We shopped together—I eagerly spent my convention allowance on a replica state alchemist pocket watch from *Fullmetal Alchemist*. And in one of my favorite events of all my con-going years, the three of us sat in on a late-night screening of a few episodes of *Revolutionary Girl Utena*. We weren't sure whether to stay for another event; we'd had a long day of queuing and standing and sitting and fighting through crowds, and this was one of the last panels of the day. But we agreed to just check it out for a second and found a community of nerds sitting in the dark, cheering and laughing and commenting aloud. It was my first prominent experience of communal fandom, something I would encounter again and again in subsequent cons and then, of course, while watching *Black Panther* in theaters.

When I think back to my young nerdy self, going to her first major convention and being totally overwhelmed and clueless about how it worked, I look back fondly on her innocence—to think, that little twenty-one-year-old nerd figured she could walk into the second largest comic convention in the US at the time and catch any ole panel she could! ("One does not simply walk into the

Javits Center," I imagine Boromir saying to me.) Though, to be fair
to her (and all other convention noobies), convention culture has
dramatically changed in the decade since I first started attending.

The onslaught of superhero media and a fresh interest in fandom
has meant that it has become a more profitable and visible industry.
Conventions moved further from their niches—slowly there became
less of a focus on the comics and art themselves. The Javits Center
used to host a whole wing just for the comics and art, but this shrank
and moved throughout the years. We began to notice the growing
presence of big franchises and moneymakers like Disney, the CW,
HBO, and more, dominating with hours-long blocks of content.
More interactive gaming and exclusive screeners—not just trailers
but full episodes and chunks of movies still in development. New
York, which was always second to San Diego, the oldest pop culture
convention in the world, in terms of its star appeal, suddenly started
getting more of its own big names on stages to promote their latest
projects. And with that, the air of exclusivity left the convention as
well; the growing popularity of nerd culture allowed casual consum-
ers of fandoms a gateway into convention culture. The definition
of what could be considered fandom similarly expanded, so mainstream sitcoms and dramas and comedies with none of the cult
appeal or traditionally nerdy elements (sci-fi, fantasy, etc.) of other
fandoms grew under the umbrella of convention culture too.

Ticketing quickly became its own adventure. Our first year we
purchased our passes fairly last-minute, with no problem. By our
second or third years, things had gotten more difficult. I recall going
to a comic book retailer in person a few weeks before the event. Then
finding a way to get to Comic Con steadily became a new source
of anxiety; my friend and I, who by now had a tradition of going
together every year, would team up and coordinate on buying the
passes. We both waited in virtual queues on sites that kept crashing,
praying that there would still be tickets left by the time we got to
checkout. One year I kept the tab open at work for hours and barely

moved from my desk, not even to pee, afraid that I would miss our shot. And one year, after me and my friend both failed to get badges, my saintly boyfriend at the time went to a little shop in Chinatown, one of the few retailers that was selling them, and waited hours in a long line just to ensure that we wouldn't miss a year of the con.

And it didn't end there. We became used to the advance planning necessary to win Comic Con and the utter exhaustion that came with it. With each year, we started our convention earlier. Every morning we caucused, negotiating what each of us wanted to see and how much time we would need to set aside to queue. We split up when necessary, one person heading off early to queue while the other caught the end of a panel, one person scoping out pairs of seats closer to the stage while the other hovered a few rows back, saving our place in case we couldn't find anything better. We even planned out our bathroom breaks, having learned that a bathroom queue could take as long as one for a panel, and bathroom breaks while cosplaying often required even more thinking ahead. We got used to the convention center, finding the fastest routes to where we needed to go and the best spots to relax away from crowds—as well as the less-frequented bathrooms. And when the convention expanded to include even more venues, we adjusted yet again. Each year we checked the new changes and modified our plan of attack. In addition to arming ourselves with programs, we relied on Twitter for last-minute updates on panel changes and lines. We became experts at navigating the con.

Fandom was already its own draw for the event, but a culture developed around the very idea of fandom itself. The chaos and noise and energy of a convention is infectious. My recollections of conventions past are always multisensory: I hear the roar of crowds echoing throughout the auditoriums, I see the show floor part to welcome a con-goer in jaw-dropping cosplay, I smell the buttery popcorn wafting from the snack vendors beyond the booths of comics and collectibles. So much of the excitement is driven simply by the idea of the excitement itself, the prospect of being a part of this fanatic group of people who will camp outside a convention center overnight just to see a panel on a TV show they love. It's being part of a movement, something larger than yourself.

Though I and most of my nerd friends know nothing about sports, and though sports and nerd culture are rarely spoken of in the same breath, the same principles of fandom apply. Consider the Super Bowl: you may be ambivalent about football, but you're still going to watch and cheer and drink beer with friends, because even more than the game itself, it's about the ceremony and the excitement around it.

In early 2020, I considered flying out to Comic-Con International in San Diego. For several of the previous years I had gotten press passes to New York Comic Con with my friend, who still flew up to New York every October to stay with me for our annual tradition.

But when I checked the site, I discovered that I had just missed the registration deadline by a day or two. *Oh well*, I thought. *That's too bad, but I can always go next year.* However, just a few weeks later, the country began shutting down due to the coronavirus pandemic. In those early days of lockdown in March, I held on to the hope that things would be recovered enough by the fall that me and my friend could go to New York Comic Con as usual. But as we got deeper into spring and then into the first warm days of summer, it became clear that even if conferences were to come back, they would still be unsafe to attend. That ended up not being an issue, because the live conventions announced their cancellations and many moved online instead.

San Diego in particular, which, for the previous years hosted more than 130,000 convention attendees, was supposed to celebrate its fiftieth anniversary. But the alternative was a disappointing experience: prerecorded panels on YouTube and a virtual exhibit hall. Amid a time of Zoom meetings and FaceTime and Google Hangouts from people's bedrooms and living rooms, Comic-Con had also opted in for a digital experience, called Comic-Con@Home.

Many fandoms have been born in and fostered by internet culture—fan fiction, chat rooms, online gaming, etc.—so it initially seemed as though an online convention could bring fandom back to its roots and open up opportunities for new kinds of fan interaction in an unprecedented time. But the virtual event only showed how Comic-Con failed to translate its most essential qualities to the new format. And it ultimately served as a lesson on fandom—how, even in times when industries and conventions are halted or threatened, fandoms will always continue to thrive and even drive the culture.

The digital convention, like the live one, still featured hundreds of panels, including ones on pop culture heavy hitters like *Star Trek* and *The Walking Dead*, as well as industry panels on publishing, designing, and cosplay, and panels on how to use comics in the classroom. The coronavirus also inspired a number of timely offerings, including a few panels on fictional portrayals of the apocalypse and other worldwide catastrophes.

The cosplay competition, which is always such a staple of my own convention experience—a relaxing final activity for Saturday, often our busiest convention day—moved to Tumblr. Usually a staged event full of wholesome competition, pageantry, gadgetry, intricate designs, and all the bells and whistles you could imagine—both figurative and literal—it was rendered unremarkable and utterly flat on screen. And screenings, like the one my friends and I went to that first convention, when we gathered to watch episodes of *Revolutionary Girl Utena*, were moved to Scener, a browser extension that created a "virtual movie theater" so viewers could watch a movie in sync while chatting in real time. I hopped into a watch party of *The Avengers* for a few minutes but was immediately bored; it simply wasn't the same.

The show floor always draws me in, despite how frustratingly packed it can be, and despite the fact that after years of our convention attendance, many of the vendors have become familiar to us.

My friend patiently tolerates the show floor as we wander through, but prefers when we have a purpose in mind: one year we searched for a Funko Pop of the Hulk from *Thor: Ragnarok*; other years we've searched for original artwork or accessories for our cosplay. And every year I search for a souvenir: a new T-shirt or hoodie or necklace to show off one of my fandoms. And when my friend and I would cosplay (always planned out together), the show floor was where we'd get the best response, with people complimenting us and stopping to ask us to pose for pictures. The digital show floor was a two-dimensional map of the exhibit hall where it would normally have been held, a flimsy facsimile meant to be interactive but not at all practical or user-friendly.

And as for the panels, which were all prerecorded, they felt cleaned up and sterilized, with no room for anything human or spontaneous. The editing of some videos was egregious, with blunt cuts, and comments were disabled, so there was no sense of the fan community. "Exclusive" reveals lost their buzz because can a trailer dropped in a public YouTube video still be considered exclusive?

This also recalls the shift I've seen in my con-going years overall. Convention culture is no longer niche, which has meant, for many cons, a shift from a more fan- and industry-forward approach to a focus on using conventions as publicity platforms for big moneymakers. More than the public, egalitarian experience that Comic-Con@Home presented itself to be, it came across as a vehicle for company-controlled marketing.

This neglects the irrepressible sense of intimacy that's at the heart of fandom: intimacy with a book or movie or TV show or game is then funneled into a sense of kinship with others who have that same relationship with it. Conventions should be the nexus of this communion: how two shinigami can pose for a serendipitous photo on the show floor; the way a casual private conversation between two people in a line can transform into a huge group debate; or the hush that falls over the audience before an advance screening of the widely anticipated new thing, when all the fans seem to lean in, ever so slightly, together.

But even in the face of a pandemic, fans aren't so easily stopped. During Comic-Con@Home fans waxed nostalgic on social media and consoled one another, sharing pictures of conventions past. Some posed in pictures taken in front of the empty convention center. Others took the convention home: would-be attendees shared pictures of themselves with their printout badges and cosplay; they set up their kitchen tables as concession stands; and instead of queuing up in a convention hall, they "queued up" in the hallways of their homes. And a few months later, seemingly having learned from the mistakes of its convention sibling, New York Comic Con went online too, but hosted live panels and enabled comments and chats so fans could interact in real time. And perhaps for many fans who have never felt comfortable at conventions, whether because of how a cosplayer chooses to identify a character (race-bent or gender-bent interpretations), or gendered harassment or a lack of accessibility, the online conventions allowed them a safe, comfortable way to be a part of the experience.

This is also to say that none of these events totally define fandom, which predates convention culture, when friends gathered to watch old episodes of *Buck Rogers in the 25th Century* or *Kung Fu*, or have Dungeons & Dragons gaming nights. Fandom has never been the point at which pop culture ends. Rather, fans give pop culture a longer, more complex life that is self-sustaining, long past the last season of *Game of Thrones* or the last *Avengers* film. Pop culture and conventions may have changed, but the fans—we'll always be here, deciding on the next big thing.

The list of losses and tragedies we faced in 2020 is too long for me to recount, but when I look back at the time through the lens of my fandoms, I recall a summer and fall without conventions or block-busters.

At our first Comic Con, the biggest event was the *Avengers* panel on the main stage. This was during Phase One of the Marvel Cinematic Universe, and the very first crossover film; we inched forward on a giant, unwieldy line with thousands of other eager fans for what seemed like forever. We couldn't know how that excitement would just be a harbinger of things to come, how for the next decade the MCU would rule the box office and define such a large chunk of our pop culture landscape.

Since then, franchises like the MCU have polarized audiences and especially critics, who have had to contend with these new cultural goliaths. The year before the pandemic would wipe out box offices, 2019 was also supposed to be the time of completion for many top pop culture franchises, including *Star Wars* and the MCU. And yet we've reached a point of mainstream, commercially successful fandoms in which narratives are extended, stretched in every direction—forward and backward in time, and diagonally with spin-offs and related content. In March 2019, Disney paid $71 billion for 21st Century Fox's entertainment business, ensuring that Marvel characters previously owned by Fox—including Deadpool, the X-Men, and the Fantastic Four—could appear as future additions to the MCU.

Some fans and critics complained about substandard, formulaic movies and ever-lengthening run times. That November, Martin Scorsese wrote a much-discussed opinion piece for the *New York Times* in which he declared that he didn't consider the MCU films artful cinema:

> Many of the elements that define cinema as I know it are there in Marvel pictures. What's not there is revelation, mystery or

genuine emotional danger. Nothing is at risk. The pictures are made to satisfy a specific set of demands, and they are designed as variations on a finite number of themes.*

And yet audiences remain invested, and so the films have kept making money. At the time *Avengers: Infinity War* came out, it was the fourth-highest-grossing movie of all time, closely followed by *The Avengers*, *Avengers: Age of Ultron*, and *Black Panther*, all in the top ten. The MCU seems never-ending, but that raises questions about how sustainable the franchise can be going forward, as it continues to expand. Can it actually keep expanding? Can it be extended indefinitely without becoming meaningless, or will it reach some natural limit? How infinite can a fictional world be?

Comic books, from which the MCU has descended, often have a nontraditional approach to story, with their long arcs, which intersect with those of other comics, for crossovers and team-ups like the Justice League and the Avengers, the latter of whom first appeared in September 1963.

But with these wide-ranging stories come inconsistencies that even the comic czar himself, Stan Lee, found hard to contend with while he was turning out stories. Built into this kind of narrative approach is something I've noticed in other long-standing fandoms I enjoy, like *Doctor Who*: a generative fountainhead of material birthed from those spaces where the story was inconsistent.

The filmmakers and producers behind the MCU couldn't have guessed the magnitude of what they were getting into from the onset. "At the time it was hard to understand the full scope of it," Jon Favreau, the director of *Iron Man* and *Iron Man 2*, told *Vanity Fair* in 2017. "By the time I saw *Avengers* I understood how sophisticated

---

* Martin Scorsese, "I Said Marvel Movies Aren't Cinema. Let Me Explain," *New York Times*, November 4, 2019, https://www.nytimes.com/2019/11/04/opinion/martin-scorsese-marvel.html.

the scope was. How difficult it is to juggle."** In theory, Favreau said, every MCU movie should stand on its own. But we know different: between the journey of the Tesseract and the appearances of Nick Fury and recurring characters like Red Skull and Ronan the Accuser from one MCU movie to the next, the franchise shows that it's as deeply invested in Easter eggs, in-jokes, and interconnections as it is in traditional plot.

As a fan who ran to the theater every time there was a new superhero movie, even before *Iron Man* kicked off the MCU, I began to notice my relationship to that particular genre of superhero fandom change early on. That first year I went to New York Comic Con and missed the *Avengers* panel, I was distraught. A few movies into the cinematic universe, and I was already hooked. I had seen the two *Iron Man* films, *The Incredible Hulk*, and *Thor*, and when *The Avengers* came out in 2012, I saw it twice in theaters, the second time with my cap and gown still on, just after my college graduation.

But I had made a notable exclusion in my early MCU days: I saw all the films in Phase One, which culminated in *The Avengers*, except for *Captain America: The First Avenger*. The declaration in the movie's title that Cap was "the first Avenger" left me unimpressed. I never cared for the brazen patriotism of this golden boy hero, and the genre of storytelling that he belonged to—American war narratives— was one I always found unappealing. And yet I, the MCU fan, had to make the choice of whether to skip a film I wasn't interested in and risk missing plot threads and character details in subsequent movies or watch it anyway just so I could remain informed. Despite my enthusiasm—my *fandom*—I resented it. I soon realized it would happen again. There would be films I wouldn't want to see, and yet each film would continue to build on one another, so any skipped one

---

* Joanna Robinson, "Marvel Looks Back at Iron Man—The Movie That Started It All," *Vanity Fair*, November 29, 2017. https://www.vanityfair.com/hollywood /2017/11/marvel-looks-back-at-iron-man-the-movie-that-started-it-all.

would be like a breach in the architecture of the franchise and, most importantly, in the narrative.

That architecture already felt shaky to me. Once we arrived at Phase Two, I found myself even more detached from the fandom. I hated the third *Iron Man* and snoozed through the second *Thor*. I skipped yet another *Captain America* but was delighted with *Guardians of the Galaxy*. I saw *Avengers: Age of Ultron* in a crowded, sticky-floored theater packed with families on opening weekend, and I left disappointed at the quality of the story. As the MCU expanded, the team-up movies in particular—*Avengers: Age of Ultron, Captain America: Civil War, Avengers: Infinity War, Avengers: Endgame*—have grown unwieldy. Some MCU films are so jam-packed that they feel airless and hollow; the most meaningful character interactions are limited to emotionally charged glances and insubstantial dialogue. Character development is put on hold until the heroes can retreat back to their individual properties, where they have more room to grow.

When I returned home after seeing *Age of Ultron* in 2015, I caught my roommate watching the Marvel TV series *Agents of S.H.I.E.L.D.* and noticed references that fit the series into the narrative of the cinematic universe, which I had thought were mostly unrelated. I told my roommate, who hadn't seen *Age of Ultron* and had little interest in the MCU films overall, about the links, which had completely flown over her head. But the thought nagged at me: What else was I, an MCU fan, missing in the narrative of *Agents of S.H.I.E.L.D.*? I thought the same thing when I caught my roommate watching *Agent Carter*. When I finally dipped into the *Captain America* movies (*Winter Soldier* being my favorite), the gaps in my knowledge became even more obvious.

Once Disney's streaming service, Disney+, launched in late 2019, with the promise of premiering original content, most notably new spin-off series from the MCU (*WandaVision, The Falcon and the Winter Soldier, Loki, Hawkeye*, etc.), I felt like I had lost the edge on my fandom; I no longer felt respected as a fan but poached as a consumer. Even in their most interesting moments, as in *WandaVision*, the crossovers and spin-offs didn't feel like they naturally evolved from the story but rather were sloppily manufactured and stretched as a means of convincing me to spend more money just to get the full picture of the narrative. I no longer find it worth it.

It's not just the MCU, either; I felt my undying love for *Star Wars* waver at some point during the sequels, which recycled the same old themes and story structures from the originals, were inconsistent across the different directors' approaches, prioritized the same unnecessary muddle of action scenes that I'd come to know from the MCU, and grossly pandered to old fans. I felt the universe become more diffuse with each new installment: in the films *Rogue One* and *Solo: A Star Wars Story*, and the TV series *The Mandalorian*. I'm haunted by the CGI rebirths of Leia and Grand Moff Tarkin. And though the prequel sequels always get the most flack for ruining *Star Wars*, I'd say the later movies commit a worse sin: they rely too heavily on the templates of the early films, diving back into the universe again and again in an act of self-cannibalization. Everything is picked apart and explained, even if those explanations are needlessly complicated and nonsensical; even if those explanations contradict the narrative already established.

Though even before Disney got ownership of the MCU and *Star Wars*, it was already well-acquainted with this approach to churning out creative content (as a child, I recall being disgusted by the sequels to *Pocahontas*, *The Little Mermaid*, and *The Lion King*, among many others). There's also the empire of *Harry Potter*, which began with seven books, which became eight movies, which then got a spin-off series based on a magical textbook within the original series, and then a sequel story to the original series that was turned into a stage play. And the DC Arrowverse, which began with *Arrow*, a show I watched for its Batman-esque overtones and never-ending drama (the number of times people get killed or stranded on islands just to miraculously reappear, alive or no longer on said islands, is astounding) but became too exhausted to continue. I watched the second entrant to the Arrowverse, *The Flash*, until that too felt endlessly repetitive (the number of times people travel in time just to figure out that traveling in time is a terrible idea is almost as astounding as *Arrow*'s aforementioned obsession with islands). Skipping *Supergirl*, I still caught some of the crossover events across the Arrowverse, which also came to include *Legends of Tomorrow*, *Black Lightning*, *Batwoman*, and *Superman & Lois*. Eventually, with this universe, as with so many others, when the narrative began to stretch and thin, I found the currency of my attention—as a consumer, as a fan, as a subscriber—too valuable to lay down for franchises that clearly had no interest in delivering the best stories and characters they could.

One imagines that, with time, the intricate web linking these movies and TV shows will get more frayed, and those subsequent films and series will seem increasingly inessential.

In 2019, despite my growing ambivalence to the MCU, I found myself excited to see *Avengers: Endgame*. I recruited my mother to see it with me—she didn't have a choice in the matter. But that wasn't even the full extent of this hostage situation. I decided to catch her up on the whole MCU. I gave her the SparkNotes versions of the movies she'd missed. For some, I just shared one or two essential details. Some I skipped altogether, declaring, "There's nothing really important you need to know about that one," hoping that I wouldn't miss something in my slapdash rundown. Then I had her watch *Infinity War*; we had a short break and then went to the theater to see *Endgame*. Today, she still complains about that time I had her "sit all those hours watching Avengers movies." I admit, I was tough on my hostage viewer, since altogether that amounted to nearly six hours of Avengers action in one day. I didn't care for the last couple of *Avengers* films, and despite my love for these characters and this fandom, I still approach the films warily, as a critic and as a fan, aware of how they may fail to meet my standards for good writing, directing, and overall storytelling.

And yet eventually, as Alex McLevy wrote in the AV Club after attending a twenty-plus-hour Marvel movie marathon, "the experience overtakes the nature of the content."* When watching any individual movie in the MCU, a kind of pattern recognition—an intellectual interest in how each new story evokes or departs from the others—may replace some, or all, narrative pleasure. The narrative worth caring about becomes the story of one's own interaction with the MCU.

When my mom and I sat in the theater at the end of *Endgame*, having already sat through more than five hours of MCU content, and Doctor Strange's portals opened to reveal T'Challa, Shuri, and Okoye—and then later all the other heroes—ready to join the battle and turn the tide against Thanos, the sight and sound of Cap's rallying cry ("Avengers"—then a pregnant pause—"assemble!") felt like electricity running through me. It was *the* comic book moment, staged with such a sense of finality and universal importance that I couldn't think of anything past it; how could the MCU continue after a battle like that, after those losses? But the very path that led us to that triumphant moment, of Cap calling for these Avengers to assemble, was one whose resonance was grounded in repetition. Audiences hear in the Captain's command every other time he has called for the Avengers to assemble; and in his exhausted expression they see every other time he has confidently said that he could "do this all day." This was our reward: this moment was the culmination of the themes and spirit of the franchise. These heroes endure, even when it seems like they have failed. The MCU itself has this same sense of endurance, and for many fans, their loyalty to this fandom has this endurance as well, despite the ways the fandom may flounder or fail. I still have

---

* Alex McLevy, "The 28-Hour Marvel Marathon Nearly Cost Our Writer His Sanity," *The AV Club*, May 3, 2015, https://www.avclub.com/the-28-hour-marvel-marathon-nearly-cost-our-writer-his-1798279197.

that, despite my wariness. I will still go to the opening night of a Marvel movie—not for every new Marvel movie, but enough of them.

Just as people ask, about historical events, "Where were you when it happened?" so do fans ask where they were when *Iron Man* came out, or when Captain America called, for the last time, for the Avengers to assemble. That story—the one of the fan—is the one that's truly limitless.

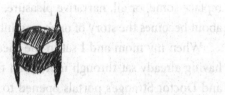

In the last few years, pop culture has evolved to grant fandom new power; fans have shown that they have a fresh influence on the media they consume. J. K. Rowling has been one of the largest cases in point in recent pop culture memory. In 2019 Rowling whipped the internet into a frenzy when she revealed that the characters Albus Dumbledore and Gellert Grindelwald had an "incredibly intense" and "passionate" relationship with a "sexual dimension." The declaration—which was, by the way, totally unsolicited—was bizarre, but only the latest of several years' worth of post-series changes that Rowling made to the Potterverse. Hermione is (possibly) Black; Nagini is an Asian woman; wizards don't have indoor plumbing; etc. Some of the changes were cringeworthy for the way they were such brazen, lazy attempts for Rowling to retroactively make her original book series more inclusive, and thus more marketable to fans like myself, who, though they dreamed of being part of the world of *Harry Potter*, had to reconcile with the fact that they weren't represented in this magical landscape. Other changes were odd and random, reading as weak attempts to grab attention for and sustain interest in the world of *Harry Potter*.

Rowling's Pottermore website has become a fountainhead for excess information about the wizarding world. Conveniently, much of that information has fallen into the category of diversity, as if Rowling thought she could add queer wizards and wizards of color and pretend they were actually there all along. Perhaps, like the horcruxes, we just didn't know they existed until the end.

The wave of jokes and memes that came at Rowling's expense after the Dumbledore-Grindelwald reveal, and several of the others, showed how dismissive fans had become of her updates, and this wasn't the first time fans poked back at the creator. Rowling has been notoriously vocal about her transphobic views, doubling down on them even after she's drawn the ire of many of her fans, many of whom are supportive of trans rights, and many of whom are trans themselves. Suddenly Rowling switched from being a childhood favorite to another (appropriately) canceled artist. With just a few comments, Rowling gave me and other Potterheads another reason to question our love for, and participation in, the fandom, given its problematic creator.

As Rowling has continued to build on her franchise, with the *Fantastic Beasts* films and the play *Harry Potter and the Cursed Child*, some fans have taken to being more discriminating in what they understand to be canon. For myself and many of my peers who grew up with *Harry Potter*, the canon means the original seven books, no more and no less. (And in my inner circle, there's also a firm dismissal of the Epilogue That Will Not Be Named.) Even despite my everlasting grief over the cruelest murders Rowling has inflicted on all my favorite characters of the series—Sirius Black, Remus Lupin, Albus Dumbledore, Fred Weasley (RIP to all)—I accept them as canon, but beyond that I have my doubts.

Rowling is not alone as a victim of fan backlash to changes in a universe's canon. In fact, in recent years, the very notion of canon— the official, undisputed, author-sanctioned account of every event that has occurred in a fictional universe and all the attributes of that universe and its inhabitants—has been transformed into something so pliable to the whims of creators that it's been made fragile, something meant to be broken and disregarded. Now more than ever before, fans have taken on the position of arbiters of their fandoms, calling out disingenuous revisions and editorial fouls and taking charge of their favorite fictional universes—as they very well should.

I was introduced to fan fiction late. In my freshman year of college, my roommate (who would later become my comic con companion, scrolling through fan fiction whenever she got bored as we queued up for panels) revealed just how much time she spent reading fan fiction. She always seemed so studious, sitting perfectly still, headphones on, eyes trained on her laptop screen as the rest of us chatted in between paragraphs of whatever papers we were working on. Lo and behold—half the time she wasn't working at all, but was reading the stories of random fans on the internet. Endlessly entertained by this revelation, I made running jokes about erotic fan fiction—asserting, of course, that she *had* to be reading about some sexy Harry Potter wand-play or XXX Klingon strap-on adventures, because what else was fan fiction for?

But my friend explained that there was so much fan fiction out there—for every fandom, with every ship, and in such varying qualities of writing. Because we were, after all, writers, there to study fiction and poetry. So fan fiction wasn't just a field of self-satisfying fantasy but a space where the original creator of a fandom had to step aside and let it grow into areas they hadn't explored or considered. Fan fiction could supply things that were missed and revive certain stories and characters and themes; at best, they could be a kind of collaboration—the creator supplies the work and the fan responds, providing corrections and improvements and alternative ways of seeing that the creator may have been blind to. It can be a way for fans to add in locales and characters that are familiar to them; the world becomes newly inclusive, whether in terms of race or sexuality or disability or any way a fan might identify. And lately, because of the ways social media has amplified our voices and given a worldwide community of people a platform on which to share ideas and debate, creators have been able to dialogue with their fans more easily and more quickly.

It wasn't too long ago that canon and fan fiction—always linked but always in clear opposition to each other—were much more clearly delineated. One belonged to the creator and the other to the fans. One static and authoritative, the other fuel for ever-changing and evolving conversation but with shared agreement that it was something separate. But in the last several years, there's been an uptick in the number of creators who, by continuously editing and expanding and retroactively changing their creations, have blurred those lines. Before, the canon was the canon and was respected as such. Now it's not that simple.

Certainly a large reason for creators' continued muddling in their worlds—like Rowling's—must be commercially motivated, but there may also be a more innocent desire to improve the text by fixing mistakes they made the first time, some of which may have been pointed out by fans.

Star Wars creator George Lucas has been dragged across the hot coals of fan anger so many times it's hard to keep track. When he introduced fans back into the world of *Star Wars* with the prequels, he aimed to expand the universe's mythology. But that resulted in him sloppily overinflating the story, the characters, and the logic of the universe. The Force and midi-chlorians, the circumstances around Vader's rise and Luke and Leia's birth—in revisiting his universe, Lucas repeatedly stumbled over his own feet, opening his writing up for critique by fans who noticed odd additions and inconsistencies.

When the prequels premiered, many fans wrote them off, claiming to be fans of only the original trilogy. The prequels weren't canon, they said. I watched the prequels as a preteen more excited about the universe than any breaches of consistency; still, I joined in with the fashionable bashing of the films but never personally doubted their authenticity. Even when I thought they were flawed, I still believed every part of the movies were of the universe Lucas designed.

But there are plenty of other examples of canon sequels or plot-lines that fans have ignored or totally rejected too: *X-Men: The Last Stand*, *Indiana Jones and the Kingdom of the Crystal Skull*, Willow's relationship with Kennedy in *Buffy the Vampire Slayer*, and the endlessly mystifying *Star Wars Holiday Special*.

Originally, fan fiction introduced a more democratic way for people to engage with their fandoms. Some creators' work, like *Harry Potter* and *Twilight*, became almost synonymous with fan fiction, as though the very worlds they created outgrew them. And that wasn't necessarily a bad thing, because there was a clear line between the original works and what came after.

Fans engage with fandoms as self-contained worlds, places where we can suspend our disbelief because we connect to the characters, setting, or story. When creators ungracefully step back into those worlds, leaving their footprints all over, their changes might not stick because they don't feel native to the works as we first knew them. Suddenly we become aware of the fiction as, well, fiction. In going back, the creator may put even more of a spotlight on their mistakes from the first time around, and, as in a game of Jenga, once you pull the wrong block, the whole tower starts falling down.

The situation is larger than writers who can't bear to step away from their laptops. Fandoms have grown—and with it, convention culture—and everywhere you can catch franchises, featuring sequels and spin-offs and crossovers. These fandoms don't just belong to their creators; the canon is more than what each creator produced. Fan universes expand so rapidly nowadays that the canon becomes large, unwieldy, constantly vulnerable to mistakes and edits. It makes sense that writers would want to participate in that process and go back in for another shot at their creations. But that also means that fans can pick and choose or outright reject those updates. We're in the age of fans: we make the culture.

IX.

Interdimensional Cable and Infinite Earths

Rethinking the multiverse and the real threats to our world

Hey, you've made it to the end now. There you are, wherever you're standing or sitting, reading the last chapter of this book.

At least that's what's happening in *this* universe.

In another, you may not have picked up this book at all. In yet another, you pick up the book but find it perhaps written in a language you can't read, as though you're in a dream. The possibilities are infinite, at least according to rules of the multiverse.

This is the best of all possible worlds: It's a notion that the naive Candide picks up from his mentor, Professor Pangloss, in Voltaire's famous satire. By the end of the book, Voltaire renders the phrase— which is repeated throughout, even with Murphy's Law well at work, stringing together misfortune after misfortune in the plot—facile.

But if we're to invest in the concept of the multiverse, or the many-worlds interpretation of quantum mechanics, we know this isn't the best of all possible worlds—not even close. Though, to be fair, I find myself particularly biased toward that belief right now, given the circumstances in which I'm writing this last chapter. I finished the outline for this book in an unremarkable winter during what seemed would be an unremarkable year. I'm finishing this book at the end of that same year, when I've spent the majority of the last several months staring at the inside of my apartment; when there were so many ambulances and not enough hospital beds; when the country erupted in protests because of the seemingly endless list of Black deaths; when a presidential election swallowed a whole week in a cloud of anxiety and fact-checking and vote-counting; and when we wore masks and stood six feet away from each other—even from our family and friends—and it was the most isolated many of us have felt in a long time. And yet the last year was a remarkable year of joys and successes for me personally—nominations, awards, and grants for my first book; a new job as a full-time arts critic at the *New York Times*; and, of course, this, my second book, and my first book of criticism, about all the things I love most about pop culture.

Lately I've begun thinking that perhaps I've watched too much *Doctor Who* in my time, because I think a lot about causality. Did any of the unfortunate events of the year directly or indirectly influence my own gains? How do I account for every new turn my life takes, every gain and every loss? I wrote my first book in response to my father's death; if my father were still alive, would that book still exist in some form? Would I have completed a book at all? Would I have still gone to grad school? How did that one point in my life, what the Doctor would call a fixed point in time—immovable, unchangeable—affect every other part of my life now?

These aren't idle quandaries; I find myself often wandering in Borges's Garden of Forking Paths, not only considering the ways I may have chosen wrong in my own life—say, my career or personal life, but also in a moral sense, ways my choices may have negatively affected other people—but also the ways my life could have been different, on a grander scale, for good or for bad. And I consider the ways our world could be different, and what sliver of that whole wide world we live in, with all its problems, I have improved or worsened in whatever minor ways, whether that means recycling and eating vegetarian or putting on a mask and staying in my room during a pandemic.

Because the multiverse, when we drill down to it, isn't always a conceptual playground where we might consider fantastical worlds where, say, heroes are swapped with villains (consider Plankton and Mr. Krabs switching roles in the *SpongeBob SquarePants* episode "The Algae's Always Greener") or where a character must face an alternate version of himself (as in *Loki* and the *Doctor Who* special "The Day of the Doctor") or where every person has an animal that embodies part of their soul, like Lyra Belacqua's companion Pantalaimon in Philip Pullman's *His Dark Materials* series. So often fandoms deliver plots involving the multiverse and different dimensions to illustrate the failings of our world right now—how things could be better, or how things could get worse—and reveal how culpable we are in the version of the world we find ourselves in today.

I initially found the idea of the multiverse frustrating. It came up quite frequently in the anime I watched as a kid, sometimes in the form of random filler episodes or original video animations (OVAs). At the end of the original *Fullmetal Alchemist*, which veered away from the manga and got mangled in its own odd, confusing plot, I was infuriated that we found ourselves in a totally different universe, an urban steampunk version of Europe, full of dirigibles. And in the shows *Tenchi Universe* and *Tenchi in Tokyo*, which I watched as a preteen as part of my weekday afternoon anime block, I was thrown off by the sudden, but playful, interdimensional alternatives to the main story and characters but learned to stick with it. (The one that changed my mind about the cleverness of this multiverse concept, which I initially found pointless and distracting, was Tenchi Universe's *Sailor Moon*–parody universe of *Magical Girl Pretty Sammy*.)

This is the risk with the multiverse, that it may read the same way an "it was all a dream" episode might, as an easy way for the writers to bring some fresh ideas to a series that is locked in the logic of its universe; introducing a dream sequence or an alternate universe allows the writers a loophole that they can use to write a totally new situation without being married to the repercussions. The series can ultimately maintain its status quo. Ideally, a show or movie that uses this transparent conceit will be familiar with the clichés and use the multiverse with good reason, to showcase some truths about the world left behind.

At one point in *Avengers: Infinity War*, Doctor Strange, one of the greatest masters of the multiverse in all of fandom (in the top tier with the Beyonder and Silver Surfer), gets into a kind of floating lotus pose and checks all the possible outcomes—14,000,605—of the Avengers' war against Thanos, concluding that only one showed them winning. The one-out-of-fourteen-million stakes define the tone of the film and that multi-film arc, providing us with the slightest sliver of hope in that single triumphant outcome. And yet it is up against such over-whelming odds of defeat—and so many permutations of defeat, the grimness of each we can only imagine. But even as *Infinity War* ends with half the universe—and many of our heroes—getting dusted, and *Endgame* picks up years later, with all those people still gone, the MCU can never resist the heroic ending. So that one version of events, in which Thanos is defeated, transpires, and Strange can open his portals onto the battlefield, summoning all the disappeared heroes back from the ether. (In the *Teen Titans* parody of this, *Teen Titans Go! vs. Teen Titans*, the heroes of *Teen Titans Go!* face off against their counterparts from the 2003 series, which I myself watched as a teen, and fight their big bad by similarly opening up portals to other dimensions, having the alternative versions of them join in the fight.) In this case, it is the best possible of all worlds, though we don't see those millions of alternatives; we're meant to think that this current universe, in which the Avengers lose and are mostly dusted, is the worst version, because what we've imagined for more than two hours is the possibility of Thanos's success and the horrors of a world half lost at the snap of a finger. But the fact that the tide turns in the end is presumably predicated on this giant loss; in the optimistic logic of the MCU, everything has happened for a reason—everything was part of a larger plan, even if Doctor Strange was the only one to see it. A universe with heroes is still a universe full of hope, even when everything goes wrong.

The adult animated series *Rick and Morty* takes a darker approach. Satirizing *Doctor Who* and *Back to the Future*, along with countless other fandoms, the show stars an emotionally abusive and morally bankrupt scientist, Rick, and his idiotic teen grandson, Morty, as they go on adventures in time and space, often wreaking havoc along the way. Six episodes into the series, Rick and Morty have an adventure that keeps getting worse until all humans are changed into feral masses of mutated flesh. Morty's relieved when Rick claims to still have a solution to this apocalypse he's brought on—only to find that Rick's damage was irreversible and his solution is to take the two of them to an alternate universe that most closely mirrors their own, and where their counterparts die. Arriving in the new universe and finding their own freshly dead corpses splattered in the garage, Rick and Morty bury their other selves and take their places, but Morty is traumatized by the experience, deciding that nothing in the universe matters. Rick destroyed their world and left it to rot, confident that there would be another universe that would be better and that they could just step into without missing a beat.

Rick and Morty has plenty of fun with the multiverse too, like in its interdimensional cable episodes, which depict the family flipping through infinite TV channels across all the dimensions. Odd, random, and meta, these interdimensional TV shows and commercials are also delightful—like my favorites, the action series *Ball Fondlers*, and the commercial for the restaurant Lil' Bits. However, the show mostly uses the concept of the multiverse to repeatedly examine the worst attributes of its characters.

In the episode "Close Rick-Counters of the Rick Kind," Rick is accosted by a group of Ricks from alternate dimensions who have banded together to form a trans-dimensional council. Rick is suspected to be responsible for the death of several other Ricks, leaving their Mortys homeless. Among the many Ricks we discover in the episode, of different races and species, and with different haircuts, most share the main Rick's abrasive personality and immorality. (One meek, kindhearted Rick, the odd one of the group, and the one with the lowest IQ, is cruelly mocked by the others.) Rick outsmarts his other selves and declares to Morty that he is perhaps the "Rickest" of all the Ricks, and Morty is likely the "Mortiest." In one of the final scenes of the episode, we find out that the murdering Rick was actually being controlled by someone else—an evil Morty. These developments are more than cute doses of intrigue in a comedy show; they bring up questions about what can be considered the essential character of a person, whether some parts of our personality are static or whether we are all molded by our circumstances. *Rick and Morty* assumes the former, which is a grim, fatalistic take—Rick will almost always be brilliant yet selfish and abusive, no matter the dimension, and Morty will almost always be meek and spineless. There aren't many hints of the best versions of themselves, only the worst, who destroy worlds and each other. Rick shows little compassion or empathy for those around him, and he always leaves worlds to die, even his own. He has the power to enact incredible changes in his universe—positive, lasting changes—and yet dismisses it to opt instead for things that satisfy his own curiosity and pleasure. Morty, who often tries to be Rick's conscience, questions his grandfather's abandonment of countless people and worlds as they travel through the multiverse, but the irony is that Morty doesn't have any solid footing on the moral high ground. In one episode, when granted a stone that will show him, in real time, all the various outcomes that will result from every decision he makes, Morty is so seduced by the stone and the idea of ending up with his crush on his dying day that he becomes an unfeeling killing machine, concerned only with getting closer to the possible reality he sees. He even turns down his crush in the present because he thinks it will change his path in the future.

When applied to our world, the moral of the multiverse becomes one regarding the dangers of such carelessly myopic vision—the idea that the world is disposable, or worth caring about only to the extent that it can be reaped for our personal benefit. When I think of other universes, I think of ones without climate change and without our most regressive politics, but to think that I am not also accountable for the world would be a mistake.

For all the negativity that *Rick and Morty* sees in its multiverse of characters, there is the same degree of hope in that of *Spider-Man: Into the Spider-Verse*. Miles Morales, the new Spider-Man in the main universe of the film, aims to stop the Kingpin—whom he witnesses killing the original Spider-Man—from opening a portal to other dimensions, which would destroy the city in the process. As a result of the Kingpin's experiment, other incarnations of Spider-Man drop in from their respective universes: Peter B. Parker's Spider-Man, Spider-Gwen, Spider-Ham, Peni Parker, and Spider-Man Noir. With the help of the Spider-Men (and girls, and pigs) from other dimensions, Miles is able to step into his role as the hero of the story. And it isn't just him—Peter B. Parker is shown as the sad understudy to the original, a version of Peter Parker who is beaten down by the world. He's older and alone, no longer with Mary Jane, and jaded—not to mention a mess. And yet he, like Miles and the rest of the Spider-Versions, have within them the capacity to embody everything Spider-Man is and represents. Even in worlds that are falling apart, in each one there is a hero; even if there is no Spider-Man or other caped crusader, there are people ready to rise up and make a change. This is what we're granted, our birthright: in each of us, multitudes, as a poet once said of himself. Within us lives every possibility, every choice, every characteristic, every experience. In a year of a pandemic, we may choose to go to a friend's house or stay at home. We may choose to wear a mask or forego it. In a year of protest, we may choose to lie low and support the system or make signs and cheer and chant in the streets. In a year—no, in a lifetime—of our world going wrong in ways we could not have even fathomed, there are other possibilities, ways for us to change and thus help the world change. This isn't the best of all possible worlds, but it absolutely could be.

By the end of *Spider-Man: Into the Spider-Verse*, an awkward, confused teen has saved the day. It's not so strange when you consider how often this happens in fandoms. As a kid, as I watched my favorite anime, like *Sailor Moon* and *Gundam Wing*, I dreamt of being part of these worlds, where middle schoolers and high schoolers marched into these fantastical battles and saved everyone. Somehow they balanced school (well, not so much Usagi, who, despite being the powerful moon princess, was a terrible student) and romance—sometimes even part-time jobs—with secret lives venturing into space, fighting villains, or working to topple whole regimes. Many of my favorite shows, past and present, feature such wunderkind protagonists: *Cardcaptor Sakura*, *Bleach*, *Fullmetal Alchemist*, *Death Note*, *Code Geass*, *Attack on Titan*, *Yu Yu Hakusho*, *My Hero Academia*, *Mob Psycho 100* . . . the list is endless.

It's not limited to anime, of course. I recall the thrill I felt reading *Ender's Game*, considering the genius Ender, who becomes a commander in a war that he believes is just a video game, an advanced simulation, at first. And movies like *The Goonies* and *The Monster Squad* have such a sustained cult following in part because of their juvenile charms, the precocious children who stumble their way through an adventure and ultimately triumph over evil.

Watching a ragtag group of kids save the day never seems to get old. I found this most recently in the Netflix series *Stranger Things*, which bets its success on this very idea. The Duffer brothers, the creative team behind the show, blatantly lifted inspiration from a whole subset of popular films that feature children as saviors. But despite the fun and pluckiness of *Stranger Things* and its peers in this genre, these shows reveal how the kids-save-the-day model represents a romantic but ultimately uneven idealism that has echoes in our current political moment. Guns in schools, climate change, terrorism—will the kids save us from those monsters?

In *Stranger Things*, the small town of Hawkins, Indiana, has been the site of secret government experiments. There's a bit of the multiverse here, too, as the experiments create a rift in this dimension that opens to another, a toxic bizarro-world version of Hawkins inhabited by malevolent creatures. A psychic girl named Eleven teams up with a nerdy band of preteen boys to take down the beasts and close the rift to the other world. The show's D & D–style monsters throughout the seasons are always symptoms of larger antagonistic forces: shady governments and adults with nefarious intentions. A Scooby Doo–esque group of tween friends and a few older teenage allies lead the charge in saving the day. Though a small team of adults sweep in for the assist, most of the heavy lifting falls on the kids, and they step up to the challenge, as they always do.

In the third season, one of the tweens' younger sisters gets roped into the monster madness and proves to be an indispensable asset because of her smarts and small size, but she requires a bit more convincing to participate in a break-in to what an adult later describes as a totally impenetrable underground facility. It's "Operation Child Endangerment," she quips, as she crawls into an air duct.[*] But none of the other kids seem to question their roles in the action, and none of them rely too heavily on the aid of adults. They insist that they have to soldier on by themselves.

---

[*] The Duffer brothers, "Chapter 4: The Sauna Test," *Stranger Things 3*, July 4, 2019.

The image of the group of kids boldly riding their bikes in the direction of, or away from, danger has become a cultural touchstone, thanks to, most famously, *E.T. the Extra-Terrestrial*. *Stranger Things* intentionally draws from this same imagery. And there are also those treasure hunters of *The Goonies*, monster fighters of *The Monster Squad*, the London alien-fighters in writer-director Joe Cornish's *Attack the Block* and his 2019 follow-up *The Kid Who Would Be King*, among many others. The 2019 Netflix movie *Rim of the World*, a less elegant and less fun sibling of *Stranger Things*, also features a group of young outsiders who take it upon themselves to defeat a beastly threat. One of the kids, in a moment of frustration, after nearly being killed by a seemingly indestructible alien, inquires, "Why is it up to *us* to save humanity?"* It's a valid question. In the course of the film, the kids must decide a jailed man's fate and deliver a key that will stop an alien invasion. When they attempt to pass their burden on to adults, the adults inevitably fail them.

These stories about the courage of children and teens suggest that bravery and heroism are innate qualities of youth. But in that assumption also lies its counterpart: that youths are simply more capable than adults, and that some vital majority of adults are, at best, unable to rise to the occasion of grave danger and, at worst, the cause of those very catastrophes. Often adults are drawn satirically, as fools and cowards who abandon the kids, or as immoral. Otherwise they may die or are just MIA, somewhere where they cannot help. In *Stranger Things*, the adults are oblivious or corrupt, with few exceptions. The ones who are most helpful to the kids are themselves divorced from the rest of adult society in some way or another: the neurotic Joyce; the brutish, alcohol-dependent Hopper; the abrasive conspiracy theorist Murray.

Such stories are neat fairy tales that we can place within the context of a larger political theme: the last few years have seen the rise of

---

* McG, *Rim of the World*, Netflix, 2019.

youth activists in the spotlight. After the Parkland shooting, March for Our Lives redefined the look of youth protest. Teens like Greta Thunberg and those involved in the Sunrise Movement have been actively fighting to raise awareness of climate change, as they are the generation that will suffer most from the legislative decisions older generations are making—or failing to make—now. And before them, there was also Malala, who in 2014 became the youngest person to receive the Nobel Peace Prize, at the age of seventeen. With these teens came ready-made media narratives of heroic action and justice, framing the activists as extraordinary for taking the baton and running with it into what we can only hope will be a new future. But one can assume that, for those teens, it's not so much about bravura and valor as it is about acting in line with their true feelings, facing down an issue that has turned into a moral imperative. Beneath the idyllic notion of a world in which kids, too, have the agency, power, and drive to incite change, there's the reality of the fouled inheritance that is dropped into their laps. In so many of these kids-save-the-day stories, kids are not simply fighting supernatural beasts or ghoulish villains, but the mess created and then passed down by adults and institutions.

Stranger Things, however, differentiates itself in delivering monsters that are terrestrial rather than extraterrestrial, chthonic creatures that resemble or are composed of dirt, mud, insects, amphibians, and flowers. The alternative world where these creatures reside, the Upside Down, simply looks like a ravaged, polluted version of Earth; the damage is just under the surface, ready to be let loose, so the Upside Down can become the new reality. One can easily see how the story serves as a metaphor for climate change in our current world. And then there's the added bit of intrigue that comes from the Russians, who are attempting to reopen an interdimensional gate between worlds—and are invited into town by a crooked, self-interested politician. (Sound familiar? A bit like collusion, no?) The Russians' motives for reopening the rift aren't clear, but the show gestures toward the

Cold War. The kids' easy infiltration of the Russian base and their breaking of the Russians' secret code, however, renders the Russians, and the prospect of war, foolish. What is a Cold War, the show seems to say, to a group of brassy, wiseass kids?

In *Stranger Things*, the day—and the world—is saved, but not without cost. At some point, the main creature, who they call the Mind Flayer, speaks to Eleven, saying that it was let into their world—it was a parasite welcomed in by those careless and foolish enough to do so. As the series wears on, the kids have a rougher go of fighting evil. At the end of season three, Eleven is drained of her powers as a result. And our heroes are increasingly distracted by the normal changes that come with growing up—drama and romance. Their role as defenders of the world conflicts with their ability to live unremarkable teenage lives. Teens who live normal lives, apparently, cannot be the heroes of the story.

Are these stories, where kids win, ultimately positive or negative? I'd say *Stranger Things* exists in a fundamentally cynical world. Its villains and threats are redundant because, despite the kids' efforts to save the world, adults keep making the same mistakes that put it at risk again. In a *New Yorker* article, Bill McKibben wrote about students who have been protesting to call attention to climate change, saying, "There's something fundamentally undignified about leaving our troubles to school kids to resolve. It's time for the elders to act like elders."*

Whether or not the multiverse really exists (and why not? I say. Surely stranger things—pun definitely intended—have happened?), we just have our world right now to contend with, and we are accountable for it. I say this well aware of the links I'm making between pop fiction and the very real catastrophes we're facing right now. Be-

---

* Bill McKibben, "It's Not Entirely Up to School Students to Save the World," *New Yorker*, May 24, 2019, https://www.newyorker.com/news/daily-comment/its-not-entirely-up-to-school-students-to-save-the-world.

cause these are the worlds I knew as a kid, my own private multiverse pocketed in my reality, and they influenced how I grew up. They made me see the world in new ways. Fandom colored my view of my city, informed my ideas about gender stereotypes and performance, and welcomed me into my Blackness in a way that not many other areas or individuals in my life have. Fandom has helped me reckon with my anxiety disorder, define my beliefs, and join a community of people who share the same passions. More than entertainment, fandom has led me back to myself, allowing me insight into not just my own life but the world at large.

These worlds only belong to children, we've been told for so long, with the implicit understanding that imagination, hope, and dreams may only survive in the innocence of childhood, before the real world drives silly notions like flying heroes and wizards and time-traveling aliens out of our minds. And yet, if the multiverse can teach us anything, it's that reality is what we make it: the possibilities are endless. Just because we tell ourselves these fictions and perhaps even believe them as children doesn't mean they don't contain truth. Just because these fictions may occasionally disappoint us as critics and fans doesn't mean they don't have value.

Why else would so many stories we love feature kids saving the day? Because we need imagination and hope and dreams. We need the openness and ingenuity and courageousness of childhood.

That means holding on to the things we love, whether that's *Buffy the Vampire Slayer* or *The Empire Strikes Back*. We're the dreamers and enthusiasts, the ones who aren't afraid to step on-board when a TARDIS or *Millennium Falcon* arrives on our doorstep. We're not symptoms of the culture or exceptions to it, but the leaders, deciding what is worth our attention—not just what wins the box office but what retains "cult" status, passed on through the generations.

This is the beauty of culture and the wonder of being a nerd, from my spot in front of my parents' TV watching Saturday morning cartoons, to where I am now, writing next to a poster of Adam West and Burt Ward's Batman and Robin scaling a wall as Sammy Davis Jr. pokes his head out to watch—and then finally to you, my reader and companion for these nine chapters and three decades of my life full of heroes, magic, and fandom, wherever you are, whether near on Earth or even, perhaps, in a galaxy far, far away.

Acknowledgments

Thanks to my editors at the *New York Times*, the *New Yorker*, the *Week*, *Slate*, *Mashable*, and *Polygon* for editing and publishing the early versions of essays that have been expanded and updated for inclusion in this book.

Thanks to my book editor, Melanie Iglesias Pérez, for her edits, insight, and impressive reserves of pop culture knowledge, and to the rest of the Simon & Schuster team.

Thanks to my agent, Julia Eagleton, for helping me conceptualize this project and finding it a home.

Thanks to Rebecca, for being my first reader, but also my friend and fellow cosplayer and convention companion for over a decade.

Thanks to the creators who made the fandoms I loved as a kid, are making the fandoms I love now, and will make the fandoms I'll love in the future.

Thanks to every community of fans I've encountered, for all the enthusiasm and passion and love you've poured into these movies, books, games, TV shows, and comics we all love.

And thanks to my parents for raising a nerd.

About the Author

Maya Phillips is a critic at large at the *New York Times* and the author of the poetry collection *Erou*. She received her BFA in writing, literature, and publishing with a concentration in poetry from Emerson College and her MFA in poetry from Warren Wilson's MFA Program for Writers. Maya's alter egos are Natsu Dragneel, the Eleventh Doctor, and Dustin Henderson from *Stranger Things*. She lives in Brooklyn. Visit MayaBPhillips.com and follow her on Twitter @MayaBPhillips.